IMMERSIVE ENVIRONMENTS SERIES

Virtual Worlds, also known as Multi-User Virtual Environments (MUVEs), have demonstrated remarkable growth during the first decade of the 21st century, largely due to the increased capability of computing technology and telecom networks. This development has effectively opened up a new field for exploration.

Activity in these immersive environments attracts professionals from a wide range of backgrounds, drawn by the richly varied opportunities for practice and research, often resulting in the formation of creative, multidisciplinary teams. Innovations entail both the application of tried and tested methods for research and evaluation and the tailoring of new approaches. It is important that studies advancing our understanding of this rapidly developing field are collated and disseminated in a timely fashion.

In this series we present current knowledge and discussion that explores how people interact with virtual worlds at all levels, what these environments have to offer us, and what their future might hold. The Immersive Environments Series will encompass theoretical perspectives, practical and technical approaches and social issues, including determinants of efficacy, usability and acceptability.

We welcome proposals for monographs, edited volumes, Briefs and other suggested publications.

For further volumes:
http://www.springer.com/series/10095

William Sims Bainbridge

The Virtual Future

Springer

William Sims Bainbridge
Virginia
U.S.A

ISSN 2192-631X
ISBN 978-0-85729-903-1   e-ISBN 978-0-85729-904-8
DOI 10.1007/978-0-85729-904-8
Springer London Dordrecht Heidelberg New York

British Library Cataloguing in Publication Data
A catalogue record for this book is available from the British Library

Library of Congress Control Number: 2011935370

Printed on acid-free paper

Springer is part of Springer Science+Business Media (www.springer.com)

Preface

I have always been fascinated by the ways in which intelligent people have speculated about the human future, both because I wanted to benefit from their wisdom to make a better life for myself, and because their often radical visions provided contrast from which to critique the world we currently inhabit. This book examines some of the newest visions, experienced through one of the newest technologies: virtual worlds that represent alternative futures in which one may explore alternatives, gain skills, and play games.

Science and technology have always loomed large in my imagination of the future, not only because I was born at the beginning of the "wizard war" – which is commonly called the Second World War and introduced long-range rockets, nuclear weapons, and even electronic computers – but also because my own family always possessed this orientation. My father's parents signaled their fascination with the future by intentionally conducting the ritual of their marriage proposal over long-distance telephone in 1911. In 1944 when I was a very small child, my mother's father took me to the mansion of his friend Alfred Lee Loomis, a multi-millionaire and physicist who played a leading role in the Manhattan project that developed the atomic bomb, and Loomis gave me a private tour of his personal nuclear laboratory. The first computer I owned was a Geniac, in 1956. Yes, it was a 20-dollar toy consisting of masonite disks, wires, and an assortment of nuts and bolts. It had zero bytes of random-access memory, and the output was flashlight bulbs. But it could play tic-tac-toe and solve the problem of getting missionaries and cannibals across a river in a small boat without eating each other. It was a very educational toy, because the user had to re-wire it for each new problem.

In the 1960s I applied wiring skills to electronic music, soldering together various oscillators and other devices, as well as writing compositions that combined accidents with mathematics. By the 1970s, I had gained degrees in sociology, and some of my methods used computer analysis that required serious programming. Managing the sociology funding effort at the National Science Foundation in the 1990s, I represented the social sciences on many interdisciplinary initiatives, including High-Performance Computing and Communications, Information Technology Research, the Digital Library Initiative, and the National Nanotechnology Initiative.

Then in 2000, I joined the computer science directorate of NSF, where I currently help run the Human-Centered Computing Program in the Division of Information and Intelligent Systems (IIS).

The research and writing for this book were done on my own time and computer, and was certainly not funded by any agency of the US government. Here, I do not speak for NSF, but I can say that the more I have worked professionally with computers and Internet-based communications, the more confident I am that a remarkable future lies ahead. Already, we have been holding many of our scientific review panels on "IISLand," our division's island in the non-game virtual world, *Second Life*, each time saving the taxpayer about $10,000 because the panelists did not need to be flown across the continent and housed in a hotel. Many of the grants we support are developing new avatar technologies, new forms of computer-supported cooperative teamwork, and indeed even new kinds of computer games. In May 2008 I organized the first large-scale scientific conference held in a game-world, encouraged by journalist John Bohannan and publicized by *Science*. In each of the three largest sessions, well over a hundred game researchers and students – living all the way from Australia, through the United States, Canada, and Western Europe, to Russia – were represented by avatars in *World of Warcraft*. The proceedings from this conference were published in 2010 by Springer, as *Online Worlds: Convergence of the Real and the Virtual*.

A guiding theme of this book is that future-oriented virtual worlds, while marketed as mere games, really represent a new form of art studio, social-science laboratory, and utopian community. Each of the nine chapters that comprise the core of this book describes and analyzes one remarkable vision of the future offered by a game-world: *The Matrix Online, Tabula Rasa, Anarchy Online, Entropia Universe, Star Trek Online, EVE Online, Star Wars Galaxies, World of Warcraft: Burning Crusade,* and *The Chronicles of Riddick*. I experienced each of them deeply myself, for example investing about 350 hours exploring each of the first two, and varying amounts of time on the others, depending on their complexity and the research goals, ranging from about 40 hours for the pair of Riddick games to a documented 2,400 hours in *World of Warcraft*. Each futuristic gameworld has its own focus on particular technologies, its own mixture of optimism and pessimism about the human future, and its own distinctive resonance with one or another branch of social-scientific theory.

I would be very surprised if the real future turned out exactly like one of these virtual worlds. All, with the possible exception of *The Matrix Online*, include impossibilities. But in so doing they stretch our sense of what might be possible. If my father's father were still alive today, I think he would love *Anarchy Online*, because he was a surgeon and it depicts amazing medical innovations. If my mother's father were alive, he might love *Tabula Rasa*, because he was an attorney interested in ancient cultures, and this gameworld taught players the laws of a bygone civilization. I wonder which one will be the reader's favorite. For a social scientist, comparison is the key to wisdom, so I love them all!

Contents

Chapter 1
The City and the Stars

Exploring a wild terrain, a team of friends braves grave dangers. Then, the saga dissolves, revealing that they have been playing a virtual reality game. So begins *The City and the Stars*, a 1953 science fiction novel by Arthur C. Clarke [1]. This story presages today's virtual worlds or massively multiplayer online role-playing games, and it raises the fundamental question about them. We should not merely ask whether they are a kind of reality, perhaps more pale than the material world, but real nonetheless. Rather, we should ask whether they give us important insights about the primary reality we will inhabit in the future. Will humans voyage across immensity to the stars, colonizing world after world, or remain imprisoned on a single planet?

Two of my own personal experiences point to this great question, although in both I was a mere observer of great events in which other people played the heroic and tragic roles. Thirty-three minutes after midnight, December 7, 1972, I stood on a Florida beach as the sky turned orange, reflecting the light of the last Apollo launch to the moon. At 8:39 Pacific time, January 28, 1986, I sat in the press room at Jet Propulsion Laboratory, where I had gone to study the scientists during Voyager II encounter with the planet Uranus, and watched NASA's direct video feed from Florida, as the Challenger exploded. We have not returned to the moon, nor gone on to Mars, nor have we found peace and prosperity for all peoples on Earth.

However, we have seen progress. Internet was born during the Apollo years, and now embraces our entire planet. The very first real computer game, *Spacewar!*, was created in 1962, the year John Glenn orbited the Earth in Friendship 7. In retrospect there is ample room to debate which event was more significant for human history. Perhaps our future lies in the rich realm of information, rather than the vacuum of outer space. Like much science fiction literature and many movies, computer games have often conceptualized the future in terms of space travel, but perhaps our real future will have far more to do with computers than with rockets.

W.S. Bainbridge, *The Virtual Future*, Springer Series in Immersive Environments, DOI 10.1007/978-0-85729-904-8_1, © Springer-Verlag London Limited 2011

Science versus Fiction

Hundreds of millions of years from now, in the long twilight of Earth, a city named Diaspar stands alone, surrounded by desert. Although once humanity had traveled to the stars, now not a single inhabitant of the city could bear the thought of leaving its walls, except one, a young man named Alvin, who is Clarke's fictional protagonist. Diaspar is an eternal city, and its people are eternal as well. Superficially they are like humans of the twenty-first century, except that they produce no children. In a 1,000 year lifetime, they enjoy adventure games in computer-generated virtual reality, create works of art that are destined to be erased, and gradually grow weary. Then they enter the Hall of Creation to be archived as patterns of electrical charges inside the Central Computer. After a few thousand years, they will be reconstituted again, to experience another life in Diaspar before once again entering the archive.

Each year, about 10,000 people are restored to life, always a somewhat different combination of individuals but existing within a fixed population size and following set laws of behavior. During a Diasparan's first 20 years, the individual does not possess any memories of previous lives. Then the memories return, and he or she lives out a life that is practically a replay of the previous one, content within the artificial womb of the city:

> They had forgotten much, but they did not know it. They were as perfectly fitted to their environment as it was to them – for both had been designed together. What was beyond the walls of the city was no concern of theirs; it was something that had been shut out of their minds. Diaspar was all that existed, all that they needed, all that they could imagine. It mattered nothing to them that Man had once possessed the stars [2].

Alone among citizens of Diaspar, Alvin has never lived before. Alone, he desires to explore the desert and perhaps even the stars beyond its sands. To everyone except him, "'outside' was a nightmare that they could not face. They would never talk about it if it could be avoided; it was something unclean and evil" [3]. The novel is the story of Alvin's quest for answers to the questions the other citizens never ask.

Our own world is a Diaspar. We play at spaceflight, but astronauts today never get more than a few hundred miles above the ground. After the Apollo flights to the moon and the Skylab "space station" that was abandoned in 1974, hopes for human spaceflight shifted to the shuttle. It proved far too costly and far too unreliable. A series of American administrations waffled, building the International Space Station without a clear scientific purpose, starting the Constellation program to return to the moon with neither clear goals nor sufficient funding to achieve them, then backing away from any definite plans. Space historian John Logsdon has described the many unsuccessful attempts to develop a successor to the space shuttle as a "failure of national leadership" in which sufficient funding for great accomplishments was never politically feasible [4]. In consequence, humanity's great dream has become a great illusion.

In the issue of *Time* magazine marking the tenth anniversary of the first moon landing, Clarke explained how humanity took its first short steps beyond the Earth: "As William Sims Bainbridge pointed out in his 1976 book *The Spaceflight*

Revolution: A Sociological Study, space travel is a technological mutation that should not really have arrived until the twenty-first century. But thanks to the ambition and genius of Wernher von Braun and Sergei Korolyov, and their influence upon individuals as disparate as Kennedy and Khrushchev, the moon – like the South Pole – was reached half a century ahead of time" [5].

However, this is not exactly what my research found [6]. Von Braun, who led the German V-2 rocket program, and Korolyov, who led the early Russian space program, exploited the leaders of their nations, manipulating their perceptions of rocketry to make them build space vehicles as solutions to the military and political challenges they faced. Thus, in the 1940s and 1950s, large liquid-fueled rockets were not an inevitable technological development that would have occurred "naturally" without the scheming of these dreamers. Here I agree with Clarke. Where I disagree is in the assumption that human beings would ever go into space without the improbable action of very special social forces.

In his classic 1951 non-fiction book, *The Exploration of Space*, Clarke predicted the first moon flight in the twenty-first century [7]. But it has never been clear where the money would come from if the aims of spaceflight were purely scientific, or what the profit might be for commercial organizations to invest in it. The first very limited phase of spaceflight was successful because von Braun and the other leaders of a radical astronautics social movement were able to make progress by a military detour, selling their spaceships as weapons. Today, a wholly new motivation is required if human beings are ever going to reach the planets. More than that, to reach the stars, we may need a wholly new conception of our very nature, to see ourselves as dynamic patterns of information, like the avatars that represent us in virtual worlds.

I have stood on many planets: Foreas, Arieki, Azeroth, Draenor, Tatooine, Naboo, Rubi-Ka, Calypso, Aguerra, and Qo'noS. I have also voyaged between solar systems with names like Amarr, Pator, and Luminaire. Yes, these were all virtual worlds, experienced through the computer on my desk in Arlington, Virginia, a suburb of *The City* – Washington DC. Computer science, in league with all the other sciences, is progressively redefining what it means to be real, and what it means to travel to the stars. Virtual worlds help us imagine what the society of the future may be like – a *City in the Stars*.

Massively multiplayer online games enact a vast number of dramas simultaneously, like carnivals of science-fiction speculation, as thousands of players undertake fantasy quests and engage in realistic economic exchanges. Internet-based virtual worlds are among the newest global communication media, and immersive gameworlds are the newest artform. Yet the genre has deep roots in literary fantasy and science fiction, and has existed for more than a decade. Therefore, gameworlds have matured sufficiently that design principles for viable virtual worlds are well established, and they can serve as laboratories where players experience alternative futures. Notably, just in the past 5 years extensive scholarly and social-scientific studies of online gameworlds have begun to be published in some numbers [8].

Each main chapter of this book begins by describing a particular future-oriented online gameworld and the challenges faced by its inhabitants, then examines its scientific and philosophical basis, the division of labor in terms both of technology and of social structure, and considers how the technologies depicted go beyond today's methods toward one or another kind of techno-social transcendence.

In other publications, such as my book on *World of Warcraft*, I have focused more on the role-playing through which users express themselves in the avatars or characters they control [9]. Here, the emphasis is on the futuristic science, technology, and technologically-shaped societies, stressing what they say about the prospects for the future of our own, "real world." My chief research methodology was exploring the worlds through a collection of avatars, taking tens of thousands of *screenshot* photographs to document the words of the non-player characters who assigned missions, the architecture and machinery of the environments, and the experiences of struggling through difficulties to the mission goals.

The Matrix Online and *Tabula Rasa* exactly replicate Clarke's dilemma: The first confines humanity within a single city, whereas the second scatters players across three solar systems. The fact that both these highly ideological gameworlds have been closed down suggests that players do not want such intense doses of intellectual medicine, yet for scholars both are exceedingly worthy of study. *Anarchy Online* and *Entropia Universe* are two European gameworlds that somewhat realistically depict the colonization of a distant planet in the distant future, and both have survived for many years. *Star Trek Online* is the newest of the worlds described here, offering a rich and familiar vision of the year 2409, in which humans have progressed both technologically and morally. *Star Wars Galaxies* and *World of Warcraft: Burning Crusade* depict conflict in galaxies far, far away, from a more richly fanciful perspective. *EVE Online* and *The Chronicles of Riddick* emphasize violence, the former generating high-solidarity social groups to manage security, and the latter responding to insecurity through nearly complete social isolation. The concluding chapter considers the range of futures in space, and the range of future human cultures, depicted in these gameworlds, concluding with a vision of what a future virtual world based on the immensely popular movie *Avatar* might be like.

Scenarios and Simulations

We may well ask: What is the engine of history? The nineteenth-century poet, O'Shaughnessy, asserted that "music makers," and "dreamers of dreams" like himself shape the course of human events:

> We, in the ages lying
> In the buried past of the earth,
> Built Nineveh with our sighing,
> And Babel itself with our mirth;
> And o'erthrew them with prophesying
> To the old of the new world's worth;
> For each age is a dream that is dying,
> Or one that is coming to birth [10].

Other writers have disagreed, contending that history is determined by impersonal, mechanistic processes. In 1922, sociologist William F. Ogburn offered a "technological determinist" theory of social and economic progress [11]. According to Ogburn, social change begins when an important new invention is made. He downplayed the role of the inventor, however, saying that any given invention is bound to appear as soon as the general level of technology is sufficiently high. New ideas spread from one place to another and from one technical application to another, through an automatic process of information diffusion. Knowledge accumulates, and new combinations of existing ideas create still more inventions. Throughout the middle of the twentieth century, many other social scientists endorsed this view that technology is the engine of history, sometimes even suggesting that this engine steers itself [12].

By the end of the twentieth century, however, it had become obvious to everyone that technological determinism was far too simplistic. New technologies are not self-launching, but often require a social movement or charismatic entrepreneurs to get them off the ground [6]. Even then, social factors can slow or halt a new technology, for example in the case of nuclear power. Some recent futurologists still give technology the primary role in social change, but they recognize that public opinion and government policies strongly shape the impact that a new technology will have [13].

In the 1960s, a "futurology" rage gripped American intellectuals, many of whom wished to serve as advisors charting the course of the Kennedy-Johnson administration's "New Frontier" or "Great Society" and the continuing competition with the Soviet Union in the "Cold War." The RAND corporation sponsored studies that sought to combine the views of many experts into unified forecasts concerning a wide range of possible technological and social developments [14]. Among the most interesting sequels were two visionary books, *The Year 2000*, by Herman Kahn and Anthony J. Wiener, and *Towards the Year 2000* edited by Daniel Bell [15]. Based on the work of think tanks and university scholars, these books not only attempted to extrapolate trends but also to sketch scenarios describing futures that might result if different decisions were made by societal leaders.

Since then, many serious writers have used the *scenario method* to explore the human meanings of possible futures. For example, Robert Constanza sketched four visions of the year 2100, depending upon whether technology will make it possible to overcome limitations in natural resources: [16]

1. *Star Trek*: public policies are optimistic, assuming that technology will overcome limitations, and in fact technology does achieve this, leading to expansion into the solar system.
2. *Mad Max*: public policies are optimistic, assuming that technology will overcome limitations, but technology fails to achieve this, so civilization crashes.
3. *Big Government*: public policies are pessimistic, assuming there are strict limits to economic growth, but in fact technology could have overcome these limits, so progress is unnecessarily suppressed.
4. *Ecotopia*: public policies are pessimistic, assuming there are strict limits to economic growth, and this assumption is correct, so civilization achieves a necessary harmony with the environment.

Rather more ambitious were the three scenarios sketched for the year 3000 by the Millennium Project of the American Council for the United Nations University [17]:

1. Human civilization still exists in the year 3000, in a form similar to the year 2000, but with numerous specific changes.
2. The human species has become extinct by the year 3000, but robots and other machines originally built by humans have evolved into the dominant form of intelligence.
3. Human civilization has given birth to several different kinds of intelligence: one similar to traditional Homo sapiens, others that have merged humans with computers, and others that are artificial life forms.

Such scenarios are thought provoking and based on careful analysis, but they are limited by the scholarly schools of thought to which their authors belong. Probably, professional expertise is valuable for projecting what some particular aspect of the world will be like a decade or two in the future, and for analyzing the near-term interaction of a few well-defined factors. But to look a century ahead, it may be more important to have a very wide range of ideas, contributed by many different kinds of people.

Thus, a vast library of publications has documented environmental issues piecemeal, but they do not provide a global prediction about how the future will resolve them. Increased sensitivity to environmental issues, and the development of computers, led scientists in the late 1960s to develop dynamic formal models that calculated the interactions among many variables simultaneously. For example, at MIT, Jay W. Forrester, developed *computer simulations* of the interplay of such factors as capital investment in industry, industrial use of non-renewable resources, and environmental pollution [18].

These scholarly developments became widely known in the early 1970s after the publication of *The Limits to Growth*, also known as "The Club of Rome Report." This book offered computer simulations of the global economy, population, and environment, covering the two centuries from 1900 to 2100, thus predicting the situation in the year 2100: "If the present growth trends in world population, industrialization, pollution, food production, and resource depletion continue unchanged, the limits to growth on this planet will be reached sometimes within the next 100 years. The most probable result will be a rather sudden and uncontrollable decline in both population and industrial capacity" [19]. That is, *The Limits to Growth* predicted a world-wide catastrophe, as depletion of resources led to economic collapse and sudden starvation of hundreds of millions of people.

Nearly 30 years later, in a scientific volume on the societal implications of nanotechnology, edited by Mihail Roco and myself, economist Lester Lave pronounced a harsh verdict on *The Limits to Growth*. He said the authors "erred by not accounting for the effects of technological change, with its inherent ability to substitute abundant materials for scarce ones. They also erred by not accounting for the feedback in a market economy. Scarcity causes increasing prices, which signal investors to find substitutes, prospectors to find other supplies, and consumers to use less or find substitutes" [20].

The aim here will not be to project which one future humanity will actually experience, but to consider alternative scenarios embodied in online gameworlds that raise a number of interesting possibilities. The designers of these worlds are tremendously creative people, who have drawn upon a rich culture that combines social theory with computer science. The players of these games have influenced their development, thus acting informally like research subjects calibrating the games' principles in terms of real human behavior.

We begin our voyage into the virtual future with two computer games that are not massively multiplayer but fall in the first-person shooter solo game and one-to-three person strategy game categories. *BioShock* illustrates the kind of future in Clarke's city, and *StarCraft* represents his stars scenario.

BioShock

This critically acclaimed 2007 game begins as the commercial airplane on which the player is riding crashes into the ocean. Swimming through a gap in the ring of fire surrounding the sinking craft, the player finds a small island and enters an elevator-like bathysphere that takes him to an undersea city, named Rapture, where an industrialist has built a utopian society, that happens, at that very time, to be disintegrating into chaos and bloody conflict. The year is 1960.

That sounds like the past, but really it is the future. As noted above, the 1960s were the decade of the future, and in many respects human history boomeranged through that period, moving backward ever since. In the United States, the 1960s were the golden age of the Civil Rights Movement, the anti-war movement, and widespread communal experiments. In 1961, the first human being orbited the Earth in a spacecraft, and in 1969 humans landed on the Moon. The psychedelic drug subculture celebrated better living through chemistry, and the rock music fad sang the body electric. This is not to say it was a good decade, as the assassinations of two Kennedys, the trauma of Vietnam, and street riots in many countries illustrate. For me, it was the decade when I discovered sociology, after encountering the social movement led by novelist Ayn Rand and named Objectivism.

Decades later this was the intellectual inspiration for the city of Rapture in *BioShock*. The fictional founder of Rapture was named Ryan, and the four letters in this name can be arranged "Ayn R." One time I visited the headquarters of the Objectivists, ironically (given the ambiguous status symbolism) in the basement of the Empire State Building. There I met Ayn Rand's chief real-world disciple, Nathaniel Branden. Originally named Blumenthal, he apparently took the name Branden because its letters can be rearranged ben-Rand, or son of Rand. Aside from one Objectivist wedding that I attended, the main activity of the local group was listening to recorded lectures presenting Rand's ideology, including some given by philosopher Leonard Peikoff, who founded the Ayn Rand Institute which continues the movement today, and economist Alan Greenspan who later served as Chairman of the Federal Reserve.

Objectivism is simultaneously anti-religious and anti-collectivist. Ayn Rand was born in Russia, under a more ordinary name, a dozen years before the revolution, during which her family suffered but survived. In early adulthood she migrated to the United States, apparently without difficulty. Her first novel, *We the Living*, was partly autobiographical, although her heroine dies in the attempt to escape the Soviet tyranny [21]. *The Virtue of Selfishness* is a collection of her essays, and the title suggests her ethical philosophy although it is often misunderstood [22]. Rand did not advocate meanness or the exploitation of other people. Rather she argued that each individual should have responsibility for seeking his or her own destiny, guided by rational self interest that was not incompatible with respect for other people's equal right to be individuals. Her two most successful works were *The Fountainhead* and *Atlas Shrugged*, novels that presented an heroic picture of individual artists, engineers, and scientists, and warned that they must not be dragged down by incompetent people such as politicians [23].

In the introductory scenes of *BioShock*, and in the game's instruction manual, Ryan expressed his own variant of Randism:

Is a man not entitled to the sweat of his own brow?
No, says the man in Washington. It belongs to the poor.
No, says the man in the Vatican. It belongs to God.
No, says the man in Moscow. It belongs to everyone.
I rejected those answers. Instead, I chose something different. I chose the impossible.
I chose Rapture.

In Rapture, Ryan turned to biotechnology to strengthen the superiority of his ideal individual, even as he rejected the notion that humans have moral obligations toward each other. One thing led to another, and soon his genetic engineering technology was based on implanting plasmids based on a substance called "Adam" that could be extracted from human bodies. Thus, in a "dog-eat-dog" interpretation of Objectivism, *BioShock* simulates a community in which some individuals steal the life substances of others to strengthen their own individual capabilities. The large-scale result is the collapse of the community, even as Ryan sends his agents around collecting the Adam from the growing piles of dead bodies. Figure 1.1 shows how the collection was done.

The ominous figure in the center of the picture is a *big daddy* body guard, standing over a corpse whose Adam is being recycled by a *little sister*. Genetically altered little girls have been programmed to extract the valuable substance, and how the player treats them is among the central moral dilemmas of the game. In the lower left corner of the picture, the hand of the player is about to fire an electro bolt at the big daddy, and in a few moments will have destroyed it. Then the little sister cowers in terror, while the player decides whether to kill her and take all her Adam, or free her from her captivity and take only a small portion of it. Modern followers of Ayn Rand have argued that *BioShock* distorts her message [24]. Yet it forcefully expresses a central question for our future: If technology is used to enhance the power of some people, in an extremely individualist and competitive society, will it thereby cause grievous harm to other people?

Fig. 1.1 A little sister and her big daddy in *BioShock*

StarCraft

This award-winning 1998 strategy game from the makers of *World of Warcraft*, expanded in 2010 with the first installment of *StarCraft II*, imagines a distant future in which humanity has spread across many solar systems, gone through a series of interstellar wars, and has come to be dominated by a military dictatorship called the Confederacy [25]. Uprisings frequently occur, and the Confederacy suppresses one on the planet Korhal IV by using a massive nuclear bombardment to kill all the millions of people living there. This provides a focus for an opposition movement, calling itself the Sons of Korhal, led by Arcturus Mengsk. The vile leaders of the Confederacy discovered another even more potent weapon, in the form of an alien hive species called the Zerg. To explore the potential of this biological weapon, they enticed the Zerg to the planets Mar Sara and Chau Sara. This drew in a second alien species, the Protoss, who were at war with the Zerg, leading to the complete destruction of these two human-inhabited planets as well.

In a strategy game, like *StarCraft*, each player operates a swarm of agents, like the pawns and other pieces in chess, but moving many of them simultaneously in realtime. Figure 1.2 shows a group of human soldiers being attacked by a much smaller group of Zerg, in an early training session for *StarCraft II*. This is a solo experience, but is also possible to play online with each player running one of the competing species. The circles around the human solders indicate that I have selected them, and I clicked my mouse on a point on the bridge telling my soldiers to go there. Each individual solder is run by a simple artificial intelligence routine

Fig. 1.2 Humans defending a bridge against Zerg in *StarCraft II*

that will allow it to find its way around barriers, including the swarm of other soldiers. Although I can give very detailed commands to different soldiers, here once the two groups get close they will automatically begin fighting.

The game is built around a rather deep story line that has been fleshed out in novels by multiple authors. A central theme is the various ways in which people exploit each other for selfish gain, in the context of military competition that demands obedience to a false ideology of self-sacrifice for the collective good. The novels describe how Confederate soldiers undergo neural resocialization to make them willing pawns, following any orders given them [26]. The only reasons I should regret the loss of a single solider in *StarCraft* are because the loss weakens my army, and it costs me time producing more soldiers in a training barracks. The Confederacy seeks to exploit me and my men in the game, because the locale is the planet Mar Sara, where the Confederacy is evaluating whether the Zerg can be used as a weapon. It does not want us to succeed in protecting the colony against the Zerg, but merely to put up enough of a fight to provide data for this military research [27].

The novel *I, Mengsk*, by Graham McNeill, charts the rise to power of Arcturus Mengsk, who defeats the Confederacy, exploiting public outrage over the Korhal massacre [28]. He was really motivated by his own narcissism and perhaps guilt he felt over his conflict with his father, which became unendurable when his father was assassinated by the Confederacy. Installing himself as the dictator of all humanity, he represents the player operating human forces in *StarCraft*. Mengsk constantly uses rhetoric of the greater good of humanity to motivate subordinates to do exactly what he wants of them, then abandons them mercilessly as soon as they are no longer valuable to him. The prime example is Sarah Kerrigan, a telepath who was engineered from childhood to be an assassin for the Confederacy, controlled by a brain implant and the eradication of her memories [29]. Because she was one of the killers of his father, Mengsk captures her. Rather than executing her as he does the other assassins, he tricks her into doing missions for him, then abandons her to the Zerg whom he assumes will kill her instantly. Scenes at the beginning of *StarCraft II* show Jim Rayor with a picture of Kerrigan, whom he loves, and an image of Mengsk, whom he hates, implicitly raising the question of whether the feelings of a single human individual could possibly matter in such a cruel future.

In *Queen of Blades* by Aaron Rosenberg, Kerrigan becomes our window into the Zerg, because rather than killing her, they attempt to co-opt her telepathic powers for their own purposes [30]. Individual Zerg, like all the playing pieces in *StarCraft*, lack self-consciousness. They are directed by the Overmind, who represents a player operating the Zerg and uses swarming attacks with high numbers of casualties. The verb *to zerg* in online game language means to launch a mass wave attack on the enemy with no concern for the loss of individual soldiers. Kerrigan initially functions like one of the intermediate Zerg commanders called *cerebrates*, but quickly asserts her individuality by seeking revenge against everyone including her own Swarm.

In several of the novels we learn that Zerg and Protoss were both created long ago by the same advanced species, the Xel'Naga, who have vanished from the universe. The two species represent alternative scenarios of what intelligence might become as the result of advanced technology, the Zerg defined by plague-like biology, and the Protoss by pure scientific intellect with the power to destroy worlds [31]. Our best picture of the Protoss is found in Christie Golden's novel, *Firstborn* [32]. An archaeologist named Jake Ramsey solves an ancient puzzle that causes his mind to be occupied by a Protoss Preserver. In a creeping psychic symbiosis, he gains the Protoss racial memory of how their species struggled to control the technological and mental power they quickly gained, thousands of years earlier when they ceased being a simple tribal society. The fundamental principle of Protoss civilization is a discipline called the Khala, which controls power by merging individual identities into a unity, although a group of renegades called the Dark Templar believe the Khala should be revised to permit even greater miracles.

Virtual Gameworlds

Despite their intellectual richness, *BioShock* and *StarCraft* are limited as visions of the future, because in different ways the players cannot live inside their worlds. A player of *BioShock* has very few options, and eventually learns his true identity – he is indeed male – which means he is not free to construct his own identity. A player of *StarCraft* exists above the fray and lacks an avatar that might represent him or her inside the game.

This is not true for the vast gameworlds to be described in the following chapters, because players can experience them from within in accordance with their own unique personalities. We begin by visiting a simulated city, not unlike the one invented by Clarke, in *The Matrix Online*, then move outward into space. Along the way, we will consider the real possibilities for humanity, and perhaps the impossibilities, suggested by these virtual futures.

References

1. Clarke, A.C.: The City and the Stars. Harcourt, Brace and Company, New York (1953)
2. Clarke, A.C.: The City and the Stars, p. 4. Harcourt, Brace and Company, New York (1953)
3. Clarke, A.C.: The City and the Stars, p. 8. Harcourt, Brace and Company, New York (1953)
4. Logsdon, J.M.: A failure of national leadership. In: Dick, S.J., Launius, R. (eds.) Critical Issues in the History of Spaceflight, pp. 269–300. National Aeronautics and Space Administration, Washington, DC (2006)
5. Clarke, A.C.: The best is yet to come. Time Magazine, p. 27, 16 July 1979
6. Bainbridge, W.S.: The Spaceflight Revolution. Wiley Interscience, New York (1976)
7. Clarke, A.C.: The Exploration of Space. Harper, New York (1951)
8. Bainbridge, W.S.: Online Multiplayer Games. Morgan and Claypool, San Rafael (2010); (ed.) Online Worlds. Springer, Guildford (2009)
9. Bainbridge, W.S.: The Warcraft Civilization. MIT Press, Cambridge (2010)
10. O'Shaughnessy, A.W.E.: Ode. In: Quiller-Couch, A. (ed.) The Oxford Book of English Verse, p. 1008. Clarendon Press, Oxford (1919)
11. Ogburn, W.F.: Social Change. Huebsch, New York (1922)
12. White, L.A.: The Evolution of Culture. McGraw-Hill, New York (1959); White, L.: Medieval Technology and Social Change. Oxford University Press, London (1962); Gilfillan, S.C.: The Sociology of Invention. MIT Press, Cambridge, MA (1963)
13. Coates, J.F., Mahaffie, J.B., Hines, A.: 2025: Scenarios of US and Global Society Reshaped by Science and Technology. Oakhill Press, Greensboro (1997)
14. Helmer, O., Brown, B., Gordon, T.: Social Technology. Basic Books, New York (1966)
15. Kahn, H., Wiener, A.J.: The Year 2000. Macmillan, New York (1967); Gilfillan, S.C.: The Sociology of Invention. MIT Press, Cambridge, MA (1963)
16. Constanza, R.: Four visions of the century ahead. In: Cornish, E. (ed.) Exploring Your Future, pp. 19–24. World Future Society, Bethesda (2000)
17. Glenn, J.C.: Millennium project's draft scenarios for the next 1000 years. Futures **32**, 603–612 (2000)
18. Forrester, J.W.: World Dynamics. Wright-Allen Press, Cambridge (1971)
19. Meadows, D.H., Meadows, D.L., Randers, J., Behrens, W.W. III: The Limits to Growth, 2nd edn, p. 24. Universe Books, New York (1974)
20. Lave, L.B.: Lifecycle/sustainability implications of nanotechnology. In: Roco, M.C., Bainbridgep, W.S. (eds.) Societal Implications of Nanoscience and Nanotechnology, p. 206. Kluwer, Dordrecht (2001); compare Nebba, G.: Twenty twenty-five. Futures. **33**, 43–45 (2001); Bell, W.: Futures studies comes of age: twenty-five years after the limits to growth. Futures **33**, 63–76 (2001)
21. Rand, A.: We the Living. Macmillan, New York (1936)
22. Rand, A.: The Virtue of Selfishness. New American Library, New York (1964)
23. Rand, A.: The Fountainhead. Bobbs-Merrill, Indianapolis (1943); Atlas Shrugged. Random House, New York (1957)
24. http://kotaku.com/354717/no-gods-or-kings-objectivism-in-BioShock
25. Farkas, B.: StarCraft: Prima's Official Strategy Guide. Prima, Rocklin (1998); Filion, D., McNaughton, R.: Effects and Techniques. In: ACM SIGGRAPH 2008 Classes, pp. 133–164. ACM, New York (2008); Barba, R., Marcus, P.: StarCraft: Wings of Liberty. DK/BradyGames, Indianapolis (2010)

26. Hickman, T.: Speed of Darkness. Pocket Books, New York (2002)
27. Grubb, J.: Liberty's Crusade. Pocket Books, New York (2001)
28. McNeill, G.: I, Mengsk. Pocket Books, New York (2009)
29. Neilson, M.: Uprising in StarCraft Archive, pp. 597–722. Pocket Books, New York (2000)
30. Rosenberg, A.: Queen of Blades. Pocket Books, New York (2006)
31. Mesta, G.: Shadow of the Xel'Naga. Pocket Books, New York (2001)
32. Golden, C.: Firstborn. Pocket Books, New York (2007)

Chapter 2
The Matrix Online

Of all the gameworlds, *The Matrix Online* (MxO) most explicitly concerns the relationships between the virtual and the real, and the future and the present. It was based on three popular science-fiction movies – *The Matrix* (1999), *The Matrix Reloaded* (2003), and *The Matrix Revolutions* (2003) – that were so pretentious in asserting their artistic and philosophical quality that they were subsequently published as a set of ten DVDs including extensive commentary and videos of their own filming. The entire Matrix mythos depicts the way the present might be conceptualized by the future, and in so doing perfectly realizes Arthur C. Clarke's vision of the future City. Dystopian rather than utopian, *The Matrix Online* predicts a grim destiny for the human species with only a dubious prospect for salvation. Crucially, while the movies rely upon high-tech special effects, and the game exists only through fast computers connected to the Internet, they prophesy that computer technology will doom human freedom.

The first opportunity to experience the Matrix personally came in 2003 with the release of a solo-player videogame, *Enter the Matrix*. However, players found it gloomy, grim, monotonous, and confining. *The Matrix: Path of Neo*, was better received when it was released in 2005, but it merely duplicated the story of the first movie, and gave players little opportunity to explore the Matrix freely. As an experience, watching a movie is both passive and constrained. A traditional videogame is active but constrained, because the player traditionally is forced to follow a linear path predetermined by the game designers. Released early in 2005, *The Matrix Online* offered greater scope for personally-decided exploration plus opportunities for social interaction, from completing missions in teams to dancing together at one of the city's many nightclubs, or even worshiping in a church together. The environment is huge and architecturally realistic, including parks and monuments as well as a vast number and wide diversity of buildings in various styles and conditions. However, players are still not free to escape the city, except when they log off the game. Quite apart from whether *The Matrix Online* realistically predicts the future humans will experience, it raises the troubling question whether anybody would really want to live under such conditions.

W.S. Bainbridge, *The Virtual Future*, Springer Series in Immersive Environments, 15
DOI 10.1007/978-0-85729-904-8_2, © Springer-Verlag London Limited 2011

Mega City

All the action of *The Matrix Online* apparently takes place in a major city dated about the year 1999, but actually a computer simulation running on large machines two centuries later. I wanted my character to learn how to create virtual objects and abilities within this vast virtual world, so I called him Cosmic Engineer. When he entered Mega City, he was offered the choice of two pills, a red one or a blue one. As in the original 1999 movie *The Matrix*, taking the red pill gave him awareness that the city was unreal, and thus the prerequisite knowledge for gaining powers that would seem magical to anyone who did not understand the truth. Aside from other *redpill* players, the city's virtual population is divided into three categories: *bluepills* who represent people who lack awareness that their world is a simulation, renegade artificial intelligence programs called *exiles* who pretend to be people, and *agents* of the computer system called the Machines that created the city to deceive and control human beings.

The city is divided into four main districts, each of which contains several neighborhoods, representing four levels of danger and difficulty: Richland (15 neighborhoods), Barrens (9), International (11), and Downtown (17). Cosmic Engineer entered the city in Richland, slums over which the computer system has lost control, and thus where agents cannot threaten. As he earned experience, rising slowly from level 1 toward the maximum level 50, he gained the ability to battle the ever more formidable gangs that roam the streets and infest the buildings. However, he was never able to defeat agents, who were at level 100, and the best he eventually could do was learn to avoid them and run away from them. Figure 2.1 shows a typical street scene, in which Cosmic Engineer is firing his virtual sub-machinegun at a Nightmare program around level 35, as his *proxy program*, a secondary avatar, helps him from the background.

There are several ways to travel across the city, of which walking is the most fundamental but risks encounters with exiles and agents. Bridges provide connections between districts, but there is also a subway system, and elevated superhighways afford some protection from attack. Within buildings, stairs and elevators allow travel between floors. As in the movies, it is possible for advanced characters to leap great distances, but this *hyper-jump* ability must be gained over time. Also as in the movies, public phone booths can be used as teleportation points called *hardlines*, analogous to Internet connections given that travel is not very different from clicking on a hyperlink. However, one cannot teleport to a hardline unless one has first walked there, and Cosmic Engineer was proud that he was able to add the last hardline to his collection when he was only level 25. Outside Richland, agents can attack without warning, but the chance they will do so is reduced by hacking a security node in the particular neighborhood, which requires obtaining a key card from gang leaders in a lower-level neighborhood, and somehow getting to the node which may be guarded or difficult to find.

Text chat may be used to communicate with other players, but there also is a system that communicates with the avatar's operator, a non-player character who guides the player remotely through the missions. Especially important are

Fig. 2.1 A typical street scene, battling a nightmare, in *The Matrix Online*

text-based communications with representatives of the three factions: (1) Zion, which is the revolutionary movement of the redpill humans, (2) the Machines who seek to regain control over the city, and (3) a group of exile artificial intelligence programs led by the Merovingian. Cosmic Engineer joined Zion, and his contact was a programmed woman named Tyndall whom he never actually met within the city. He also obtained a total of 240 missions from independent exiles found in most neighborhoods that sometimes provide insights into the mythos comparable to those obtained from critical missions for the factions.

When the beta version of *The Matrix Online* launched in 2004, *Wired* magazine's reviewer reported, "…the game's setting is tediously repetitive. The endless parade of grungy city streets and leather-clad hooligans gets very boring very quickly" [1]. Arguably, all parts of the city are boring, but only Richland and Barrens are really grungy. However, on close inspection the filth makes a philosophical point. The streets are strewn with garbage, and occasional pieces of trash paper blow across the streets. From a distance, one of them looks like a religious tract, because the printing on it forms a cross. From nearby, it can be read: "The system is a lie."

Thus, the dismal nature of the slum neighborhoods is part of an allegory critical of real-world social arrangements, designed to teach the player philosophical and political lessons. Education, as many educational game designers have learned to their distress, can be unpleasant rather than fun. The original 2 hour movie was remarkably popular, despite its intellectual depth, but after dozens and even hundreds of hours doing repetitive missions inside the virtual city it became extremely boring.

Most of the philosophical messages are communicated in early missions, many below experience level 10 and about all by level 25. I continued past that point in order to develop Cosmic Engineer's coding skills and to do missions for the local exiles. At level 35 he was able to program everything I thought was at all interesting, and on level 38 he had completed the missions for all but three of the exiles.

Given that I was doing research I probably progressed more slowly than the average experienced player, for example taking 6,458 screenshot pictures to document everything. Teaming up with other players would have speeded things up, but few were online this late in the gameworld's history, and they would have been frustrated by all the extra time I invested in collecting data. At the end, I saw it was taking 10 hours to ascend each experience level, doing very repetitive assassination missions that gained no information, and the three full work weeks required to reach the top level of 50 seemed better invested in one of the other worlds described in this book. While I could be accused of laziness, my fatigue and ultimate resignation provided a pessimistic insight: Perhaps the real human future will not really be worth living, either.

The Matrix can be taken as a fable of modern, alienated humanity, in which capitalist corporations promote unhealthy consumerism and discourage creative thought, or it can be seen more profoundly as an existential critique of the inescapable human condition. In one sense or another, traditional religions treated the world as an illusion, postulating a fundamental supernatural reality, but in a post-Christian culture we cannot expect God to define reality for us. However, about half way to maximum experience level 50, a message from Zion's Commander Lock praised Cosmic Engineer for being "someone whose priorities and judgment are grounded in the real world, and not some far-fetched philosophy."

Yet, *The Matrix Online* suggests that philosophical enlightenment can liberate people from oppression, and the world is not what it seems. The Prima MxO guidebook states this insight clearly in its description of the player's starter district:

> Though official maps label this area as Richland, most people simply refer to it as the Slums. Set against the south shore of the river that bisects the City, the Slums are rife with criminal activity, urban decay and random violence. However, this is a lesson in the deceptive nature of the Matrix. Though the area is among the poorest and least desirable to the populace of the City, it is a desirable holding for those who understand the nature of the Matrix. Indeed, many powerful Exiles compete for control of its resources [2].

When Cosmic Engineer used one of the common desktop computers in one of the hundreds of offices around the city, they sometimes displayed advertisements from Metacortex, the Microsoft-like information technology monopoly depicted in early scenes of the original 1999 movie. This reflects the fact that the years prior to 1999 were marked by severe competition between alternative operating systems, browsers, and hardware standards, leading to dominance by a particular computing culture promoted by particular companies. These messages suggest how the machines began their historic rise to power over humans. Explicitly called *factoids*, they are obviously meant to be parodies of the rhetoric used by a powerful corporation to consolidate its position:

> Metacortex needs your help in the fight against poor quality software. Buy only Metacortex approved products. A good consumer is a loyal consumer.

Metacortex Blue is the newest operating system due to be released from Metacortex. This state of the art OS will change your life. Buy it – because you need it.

The Metacortex Pioneer browser version 6.0 set records as the most downloaded software package in history. So many people use it, why shouldn't you?

Metacortex is working hard to bring all forms of media directly to your home. Soon all of your favorite television shows, music, and movies will be brought to you by Metacortex.

Metacortex works hard to ensure that you receive only the top quality digital recordings of the latest music and movies. Help us improve by reporting piracy.

Metacortex has donated computer systems to schools throughout the world. Metacortex – It's what you know.

Metacortex is involved in several government programs to index and catalog the history of all citizens in order to provide greater security for you and your family.

This last slogan suggests how it was that Metacortex got the data necessary to create the city. Similarly, progress for the player can be conceptualized as gaining data, in the form of icons that confer skills, progress in levels of access and the power to combat enemies, and money that is conceptualized as information units and abbreviated $i. Action is primarily motivated by the various ways a player can earn experience, which is essential for gaining access to all areas of the city quite apart from any sense of "winning" a potentially endless game. Some experience is gained simply by killing enemies, by crafting abilities or items, by practicing a data mining specialty, or by gaining safe access to new neighborhoods of the city. The primary method is accepting missions from one or more of the three main factions. Some of these are somewhat rare "critical missions" which advance story lines, but a player can also undertake an infinite series of "standard missions": assassination, courier, retrieval, rescue, escort, infiltration, and recruitment. Here, "retrieval" is a euphemism for burglary, and all the missions involve killing non-player characters (NPCs). Most require interacting with virtual computers.

For example, a typical assassination mission begins without information concerning the whereabouts of the victim. First, the player may need to fight his way past enemies to obtain a disc containing an access code either from the corpse of an enemy or from a small computer they are guarding. Then the disc must be placed in a computer at a different location, bypassing the security protections and making it either transfer the needed information to the avatar's controller at faction headquarters, or copy it onto a disk which the avatar must upload at a third location. Finally, the mission controller tells the avatar where to go in the city to complete the assassination.

One of Cosmic Engineer's earliest missions provides insights into how the communication system functioned as a battleground where numerous forces competed. Tyndall asked Cosmic Engineer to make an exchange between Zion and the Merovingian faction that would benefit both, giving the code for a computer virus in return for some valuable data. On the way to the designated location, he received a garbled message from his operator saying that someone was trying to block their communications.

After battling past guards, Cosmic Engineer met a Zion NPC named Franklinken, who explained their opponent was a computer program named Lyle Goodgame. Cosmic Engineer next found Goodgame, who was dressed in a white technician's coat but struggled fiercely as he went down to defeat under the barrage of software routines Cosmic Engineer hurled at him. After contact was reestablished, Tyndall and the operator guided him to a filthy upper-floor bedroom where a character named Buffer took the virus disk and told him to take the data from the laptop computer sitting on the bureau. Back on the street, he battled past members of the Crossbones gang, to reach the nearest hardline where he could upload the data, thereby earning both 36,000 experience points and Tyndall's warm congratulations.

Scientific and Philosophical Basis

The original *Matrix* movie explicitly quotes from Jean Baudrillard's book, *Simulacra and Simulation*, using phrases like "the desert of the real" which appears on the book's first page. The book begins with a bogus quotation from Ecclesiastes: "The simulacrum is never what hides the truth – it is truth that hides the fact that there is none. The simulacrum is true." The point is that everything is bogus, and under the corrosive influence of interpretations, existence has degenerated: "Today abstraction is no longer that of the map, the double, the mirror, or the concept. Simulation is no longer that of a territory, a referential being, or a substance. It is the generation by models of a real without origin or reality: a hyperreal. The territory no longer precedes the map, nor does it survive it" [3]. Baudrillard draws his metaphor from a one-paragraph literary work by Jorge Luis Borges, "On Exactitude in Science," but he could just as easily have begun with Alfred Korzybski, inventor of a pseudoscience called General Semantics, who wrote, "The map is not the territory" [4]. But there no longer is any territory, and all we have is a map of a map of a map…

Although Baudrillard believes that advancing technology contributes to human estrangement from reality, his book is not about computer simulation. Rather, it seems to decry human culture in general and express a postmodern view that progress has always been an illusion. I say *seems*, because the book is – pardon the expression – very French. Fulfilling the stereotype that French intellectuals are poets rather than scholars or scientists, the book lacks footnotes, bibliography, and data. I find it *amusant* that a chief opponent in the second and third Matrix movies, who claims to know everything, is a French-speaking computer program who praises the French language and is named Merovingian after a dynasty of French kings who ruled during the Dark Ages.

The typical interpretation of intellectuals who have written about the *Matrix* mythos is that it raises questions about the nature of reality and human knowledge, and thus perhaps relates most directly to the topics of ontology and epistemology in academic philosophy, but also perhaps to the philosophy of ethics. Matt Lawrence has written an engaging book from this perspective, *Like a Splinter in Your Mind*, taking the title from a passage in the first movie [5]. When Morpheus first meets Neo, and just before he offers the red pill of enlightenment, they discuss Neo's aversion to being controlled by the system. Morpheus observes that Neo has long felt there was something fundamentally wrong with the world. "You don't know what it is, but it's there, like a splinter in your mind, driving you mad." Lawrence plays the role of Socrates with his reader, using a discussion of *The Matrix* to get the reader to think more deeply and independently about a number of the issues covered by philosophy courses. This is a fine function for a professor of philosophy to perform, but it falls short of exhausting the meaning of the mythos.

More radical views were offered by leaders of the Transhumanist Movement, that promotes technologies its members hope will transform human nature utterly. Economist Robin Hanson has argued that if people find living in the Matrix to be rewarding, then it is real and really valuable to them, so it would be reasonable for them to decide to dwell within it. He argues that most people in this world are already slaves, and they can become free only by making fundamental decisions about who or what they will become, rather than merely playing pre-scripted roles in the existing social and economic system [6]. Philosopher Nick Bostrom argues there is no way in which we can conclusively determine whether the world we experience is not itself a computer simulation, and his chief alternative theory is that intelligent species may destroy themselves before they become capable of building a simulation that fools our senses into making us think it is real [7].

In the movies, a constant question is whether Neo is The One who will save humanity, perhaps not merely from the machines but also from its existential dilemmas. This is a fundamentally religious function. Michael Brannigan and James Ford have both analyzed the mythos from a Buddhist perspective, and the first movie does contain elements reminiscent specifically of Zen Buddhism, at least as it has been interpreted by westerners [8]. Neo learns from a small child to bend a spoon, not with his fingers or a Yuri Geller magic trick, but by bending his own mind [9]. In his martial arts training, and in learning to leap great distances through the virtual air, Neo follows in the arrow-shots of Eugen Herrigel's book *Zen in the Art of Archery* [10]. Gregory Bassham and Paul Fontana have both identified Christian themes, in which Neo takes the role of a self-sacrificing messiah just as Jesus did, but Bassham also analyzed the problem of pluralism [11]. How can there be a single truth, while leaving people free to believe incompatible ideas?

Martin Danahay and David Rieder offer a very different interpretation, writing "*The Matrix* does an especially good job of dramatizing the exploitation of the average American worker in late twentieth- and early twenty-first century America from a Marxist perspective. The film is full of allusions to numerous social and economic themes that can be traced back to Karl Marx" [12]. True, but the radical political heritage of the mythos is much broader than Marx the individual man; it is an entire century of European critical thought [13]. I believe it was Friedrich Engels, Marx's associate, who first articulated the concept *false consciousness*, the idea that people have been deceived by the system into accepting a false ideology divorced from reality:

> Ideology is a process accomplished by the so-called thinker consciously, indeed, but with a false consciousness. The real motives impelling him remain unknown to him, otherwise it would not be an ideological process at all. Hence he imagines false or apparent motives. Because it is a process of thought he derives both its form and its content from pure thought, either his own or that of his predecessors. He works with mere thought material which he

accepts without examination as the product of thought, he does not investigate further for a more remote process independent of thought; indeed its origin seems obvious to him, because as all action is produced through the medium of thought it also appears to him to be ultimately based upon thought [14].

Engels wrote these words in 1893, yet Friedrich Nietzsche had expressed a similar view already in *Also Sprach Zarathustra* in 1885 and *On the Genealogy of Morals* in 1887 [15]. The chief difference is that Marx and Engels focused on how the capitalist ruling class imposes false consciousness on the working class, in order to get them to accept their subservient status as just and necessary rather than rejecting control as unfair exploitation. Nietzsche believed, in contrast, that all societies imposed false consciousness upon their people, socialist ones as well as Christian or capitalist ones. In his optimistic moments, Nietzsche believed it is possible to become free of all ideologies, but this seems to require severing all ties with other people, and as in Nietzsche's own tragic case leads to insanity. Decades later, Sigmund Freud, who believed people tend not to be aware of their own subconscious desires and psychological conflicts, argued that civilization inevitably imposes painful inhibitions on the natural impulses of human beings, and we may well debate whether this surrender of liberty to achieve progress is worthwhile [16].

Take the argument from the perspective of the machines. Progress for humanity may be possible, but only if we embrace computer technology, and become embraced by it. Cybernetics offers entirely new theoretical paradigms for analyzing social phenomena, such as conceptualizing organizations as information-processing systems or modeling social interaction by artificial intelligence [17]. The collection and organization of data about "the information society" may come to be dominated by information scientists or computer scientists, rather than sociologists and anthropologists [18]. One likely area is in the understanding of complex adaptive systems. Using advanced computer modeling, the science of self-organizing chaos could predict multiple-outcome events like sociological trends and historical transformations. Accurate prediction of environmental change could be possible with mathematical models that couple atmosphere, ocean, land, and ecosystems. Powerful computer models might accurately predict how society needs to change in order to have sustainable development [19].

Throughout the home there will be special-purpose artificial-intelligence reference aids instantly providing information and advice, possibly without the need of a general-purpose computer. Every electric appliance will rely on a computer to operate it. Many homes will have smart sensors to detect who is in each room and adjust temperature, music, and other aspects of the environment to that individual's preferences [20]. The computer revolution will continue far into the twenty-first century [21]. The computer mouse and keyboard will become obsolete, because there will be quicker and more convenient ways to interact with the computer. Voice activated technology will eliminate computer keyboards. Computer interfaces will range from unobtrusive display glasses to direct stimulation of the brain.

One hope is that technological transformation will naturally move the world's economies away from the heavily polluting activities that characterize industrial society. If the world truly becomes an information society, then much production and consumption will be carried out with little use of material resources and little environmental pollution [22]. If rich societies continue to rely heavily on industrial production, and if they do not develop very effective technologies for controlling pollution, and if global politics is unable to limit growth, and if natural processes are unable to handle increasing pollution, then the Earth will become a hotter and on average less hospitable planet than it is today. Perhaps we need to take our blue pills and migrate into the Matrix.

The Matrix Online hints at some of these issues, but they are not central to much of the action. Players start in the slum areas, and struggle upward toward the elite business district, perhaps enacting a revolution of the proletariat. The top-level agents of the machines wear business suits, while players have the choice of wearing working-class clothing looted from defeated enemies or pop fashions made stylish by commercial advertising. However, players are forced to work exceedingly hard by whatever faction they associate with, Zion as much as the Machines or the Merovingian. It is never clear how the players can become liberated from their toil. The original movie ends with Neo's monologue, which exists in two forms. The monologue in the original script was ambiguous:

> I believe that the Matrix can remain our cage or it can become our chrysalis… to be free, you cannot change your cage. You have to change yourself. When I used to look out at this world, all I could see was its edges, its boundaries, its rules and controls, its leaders and laws. But now, I see another world. A different world where all things are possible. A world of hope. Of peace. I can't tell you how to get there, but I know if you can free your mind, you'll find the way [23].

As released to theaters, the movie version of Neo's final monologue is more radical and directed to the system that resists change rather than to people who are its prisoners. Neo says he does not know the future, but he knows that a revolution has begun. If successful, it will create "a world without rules and controls, a world without borders or boundaries, a world where anything is possible." Those words certainly do not describe *The Matrix Online*, where everything is under control of the system, and only by learning how to exploit the rules can even a sliver of freedom be achieved.

Hacking and Coding

In the three movies, a Zion operative *jacks* into the Matrix through a direct computer interface inserted at the base of the brain. Although direct brain-computer interfaces are an active area of research today, we are decades away from being to duplicate this in the real world [24]. Logging into MxO is like going back in time, to an earlier era of computing, because the user must enter username and password on command lines [25]. Throughout the offices and other rooms in the city's buildings are found many computers: desktops, laptops, and mainframes. The desktops have mice, but the displays on their screens show entirely green text ending with a flashing green rectangle representing the cursor. Many messages from these computers, all in green text, end with ">_" which was a common pre-Windows cursor where the user could type a command.

Entirely green text-based displays incorporating a command line interface were standard in the real world of the early 1980s, but personal computers displayed full color by the time mice were common a decade later. The mouse and windows interface that was nearly universal by 1999 was pioneered by the Alto computer in 1973, and incorporated in the commercially successful Macintosh already in 1984 [26]. Although the first Macs employed a monochrome display, it was black on white rather than green on black. Anachronisms are rampant in popular depictions of earlier historical periods, such as the stirrups used by cavalrymen in movies of ancient Greece and Rome, given that the stirrup actually did not enter Europe until long after Rome fell [27]. The chief guidebook to *The Matrix Online* explains repeatedly that the history in the matrix was fabricated by the machines and contains many brash lies as well as subtle errors [28].

Following are two examples of command line file searches from missions to assassinate characters named Arlon and The Exterminator. The first comes from a desktop computer, and the second from a mainframe. "(Y/N)" asks the user to answer the question by typing Y for yes or N for no. In the second example, "grep" is the Unix command to find a text sting.

```
>find -d -p -b Arlon
Searching 10851 files for Arlon.
Searching complete. 5 files found.
Download results? (Y/N)
> Y
Download complete!

> grep -f Lee The Exterminator
Searching all files for Lee the Exterminator
Displaying results for search...
Transfer search results? (Y/N)
Transfer complete!
```

Some of the computers are connected to local area networks and to Internet, but by wires rather than wireless as is become more and more the case in the real world. Much of the communication of information from one to another takes place by physically carrying a disk. Sometimes the network is specifically described as the telephone system, reminiscent of the use of stand-alone modems in the 1980s and 1990s. The simulated 1999 technology has serious vulnerabilities, as well as being primitive from the standpoint of human-computer interaction.

For redpill avatars, exiles, and all the miscellaneous NPCs except the bluepills, human-computer interaction is totally different from the 1999 system. Data disks are obsolete, outside the specific missions that require transporting them, and communications are wireless. Keyboards are obsolete, too, but when a coder programs something, he moves his hands as if typing in the empty air. When a hacker unleashes a virus against an opponent, he often moves as if throwing a ball of fire or casting a magic spell. The enemies possess similar abilities, so if both parties to a melee are hackers, the air is filled with bright, colored lights. However fanciful such displays may seem, they actually have a basis in the research on augmented reality, wearable computers, and data gloves that has been done over the past decade.

Virtual worlds are a diluted version of virtual reality, computer systems in which the user is entirely immersed in an artificial environment. Augmented reality is more modest, overlaying a small or partly transparent computer display on the real environment, following one or another of several different methods. Data gloves are indeed glove-like devices the user can employ to control virtual interfaces by moving either the whole hand or just a single finger [29]. Considerable research and development has been invested in them, but it is unclear what their future potential really is. Quite apart from the effort involved in moving hands, there is the question whether sensor-laden gloves will be necessary given the rapid development of computer vision techniques that can recognize gestures by ungloved hands. Cosmic Engineer has virtual data gloves in the Matrix, but they do not seem necessary for the tasks he undertakes.

Perhaps more interesting are the visual display devices Cosmic Engineer wears, which are directly modeled on EyeTap, MicroOptical head-up display, and comparable devices that actually exist today but have not yet caught on in the marketplace [30]. The upper image in Fig. 2.2 shows Cosmic Engineer wearing a fictional Lansford Mark II program launcher, and the lower one shows him in a Reeves Enhanced program launcher. The Lansford places a half mirror in front of one eye so that it can overlay data on the scene, whereas the Reeves appears to obscure vision, perhaps because it incorporates a camera like today's actual EyeTap device. Images from the Reeves are not in fact incorporated in the action, and the camera I tried out when I recently visited the MIT Media Lab was an inconspicuous pea-sized component easily supported on the bridge of an ordinary pair of eyeglasses. So if such interfaces are really used widely in future, they are likely to be less obtrusive than these two program launchers.

Note that these fictional devices are called *program launchers*, rather than *wearable computers*. They are connected to the ubiquitous wireless network, and whether the computing is done locally or remotely is a matter of design choice. Certainly, each is large enough to contain an entire computer at the level of current computer chip development, let alone what may be possible in 2199. Thus, in several respects the advanced technology depicted inside the Matrix is about as anachronistic as the 1999 command-line technology, representing 2005 technology that is already being superseded.

In doing his programming work, Cosmic Engineer would stand on a rooftop in the Tabor Park section of the slums, where there is a microwave dish that communicates via broadband with the main computer system, rendering coding and crafting more reliable. Nearby there is a hardline where he can upload anything he makes to his personal inventory. The high point of this work was when he assembled the computer programming code to allow him to create a Remote Proxy 5.0, the best quality secondary avatar that a coder could use to fight alongside him during his missions. There were two main prerequisites for creating and using this proxy: to reach level 35 in general ability, and to possess the Transmit Code ability associated with being a Proxy Master and which itself could be coded at level 33 and Proxy Technician status. Coding actually increases general experience, and in this action he earned 7,650

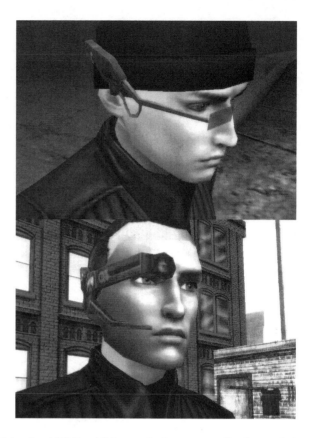

Fig. 2.2 Two "program launcher" wearable computer interfaces

experience points toward gaining level 36. In addition, to do the proxy coding he needed to have $i49,612 of Information currency and the necessary code fragments to assemble. The money was no problem, and after expending the $i49,612, he still had $i5,608,167.

The seven code fragments were another matter, sometimes costly to obtain and embedded in a distinctive programming language. The first one was the coder ability function subroutine, and the second was the ability class routine. Cosmic Engineer had bought the ability class routine from a non-player vendor in the Kedemoth neighborhood of the slums, named Len, for $i1,000. Four others were ordinary variable fragments that may be looted from dead enemies, burglarized from their offices, or assembled out of smaller byte-like fragments that have been acquired in these same nefarious ways. The last was a coder patch, obtained by killing members of the Sleeper exile gang in the Vauxton neighborhood in the advanced Downtown district.

Exiles and Personalities

Considered as a vision of the possible human future, *The Matrix Online* suggests that technological and social progress will cease and people centuries from now will pretty much live as we do today. In this respect its vision is identical to that of

Clarke's *City and the Stars*. One obvious difference is that the people in Clarke's novel seem to have chosen their fate, whereas the socio-technical stasis in *The Matrix Online* was imposed by the machines. Another is that it is technically possible to leave Clarke's city, but there is no place to go other than Mega City in *The Matrix Online*. One can transcend its reality only by shutting off the program, and perhaps walking outdoors to enjoy the sunlight.

When I entered the Matrix in 2008, its social life was already far into decline, more than 3 years after its original launch. I occasionally encountered other players on the street, although never upstairs in the office buildings because taking an elevator separated my avatar from the others. There were always a few hanging out at Mara Central near the Congregational Church, because there were many vendors at that location and no dangers. Occasionally I would see a couple at Tabor Park because it was a good location for crafting, and one time a group of about 20 assembled there. One indication of how unpopular MxO had become was how little material was available to buy from other players in the online market system. Once, Cosmic Engineer was recruited to a group, but it evaporated immediately. The videos available on YouTube indicate that some groups of friends continued to enter the Matrix together, but the kind of vibrant social life I had seen in *World of Warcraft* and *Second Life* did not exist.

Perhaps appropriately, given the mythos, I found the exiles very interesting, and of course they were constantly available for Cosmic Engineer to interact with. At the bottom of their status ladders were the four dozen gangs that infested the spaces around the buildings and some of their rooftops. Killing their members afforded experience and loot but not much ethnographic information. However their general premise was sociologically plausible. As Frederic Thrasher observed in the 1927 classic, *The Gang*, when overall social order disintegrates, people will tend to establish their own local groups which the authorities will contemptuously consider *gangs*, unaware that on some level all societies are gangs [31].

Since most missions required traveling across the city and entering one or more buildings, there was a constant challenge to get past the lurking, hostile gang members. With luck, a route could be found, running down the center of the relatively safe streets or along the elevated highways, to a point near the desired door, which with luck was unguarded. If a gang blocked the way, Cosmic Engineer had two choices. First, he could kill them, being careful to pick them off one at a time but hurrying because more gang members would soon appear. Second, he could dash directly past them, realizing that in most cases they could not enter the building; a risky course, this was especially difficult with office buildings that had revolving doors, because they were hard to operate quickly. As he advanced in experience and learned how to operate his secondary avatar proxy, on occasion he could combine the methods by sending the proxy on a suicide mission to distract the gang, while he slipped into the door and prepared to create a new proxy.

Inside the buildings, some gang members and many employees of corporations or factions served to defend against interlopers like Cosmic Engineer, and to advance the story by things they said and did. Some of them are friendly and offer help, but sometimes in an ambiguous manner. When Cosmic Engineer was hunting for Lee The Exterminator, an NPC named Fox philosophized: "One who searches will never find. One who seeks will always find." When he was hunting for Franklinken, Chi advised him, "Just follow all signs that point to 'red.'" On a different mission, Arago observed: "Once red, twice blue. Rabbit you seek is behind you. If you turn now, they will speed away. If you strike with patience, they will end this day."

There are many nightclubs across the city, where avatars may dance with exiles without any worry of violence, and where some of the mission-giver exiles hang out. Two exiles in the international district, Operetta in Club Pandora and Lotus in the Jade Room, experience reality through music. Operetta asked Cosmic Engineer to retrieve a musical score composed by a rare bluepill who understands the unreality of the Matrix but chooses to stay within it for the benefit of her enraptured listeners. Lotus asked Cosmic Engineer to deliver a CD of her music to Milankovitch, who turned out to be in great distress but calmed when he played it for her. The next mission for Lotus was motivated by her anger that an Internet server was distributing pirated copies of her music. Once he had retrieved that copy, he brought it to Kat, Tube, and Wren, three friends of Lotus who asked him to play the healing music for them. As soon as the first notes came from the computer, they attacked Cosmic Engineer, and he discovered that the pirated copy had been altered with a subliminal message causing violent behavior among exiles. The piracy of the music had been a clever ruse by the Merovingian to attack Lotus.

French intellectual that he was, the Merovingian was probably aware of the theory by the German idealist philosopher, Arthur Schopenhauer, that the world is embodied music [32]. In the Matrix, this may be literally true, because a computer program is practically the same thing as a musical composition, enacting variations on a theme over time. Yttri, an exile in one of the lowest-level slum neighborhoods, draws analogies between music and computer programs, saying that a "coda may become a code" that alters the Matrix if played. Another analogy is that reality is a suite of computer programs written in the language of chemistry. Raini, dancing at the Jacob's Ladder nightclub, sends players in search of narcotic code that act like narcotic drugs on her, saying "If you aren't living on the edge, then you simply aren't living."

The most prominent group of exile leaders is the Spectrum family consisting of two parents, Mr. Black and Dame White, and eight children: Amber, Cerulean, Greene, Grisaille, Indigo, Mandarin, Rose, and Violet. Love is not the principle that unites them, as the Prima guide for the game explains:

> The two parents each covet the other's power, but never admit it. They work against each other covertly through their children. The siblings compete for the attention and favor of both parents, as well as playing their parents off against one another. The emotional turmoil of the conflict and the mental and physical exercise involved in waging it are the family's bread and butter [33].

The most intense sibling rivalry rages between Indigo and Grisaille (Gray), who are only half-brothers because Mr. Black fathered Grisaille without Dame White's cooperation. Indigo is the oldest and is favored by his mother, whereas Grisaille is favored by his father. As the Prima guide explains, "Gray considers the other siblings to be incompetents. They despise him for being Mr. Black's favorite when he's an outsider to their family. In truth Gray hates both Dame White and Mr. Black, and would eagerly see the entire twisted Spectrum destroyed, even if he had to sacrifice himself to do it [34].

Many of the mission-giver exiles represent a specialized role that humans are programmed to play in modern society. The Auditor is constantly worried about balancing his books, which presumably are in the form of computerized spreadsheets, and the recipes valuable to the Chef are computer program code. For the Sculptress, sculpture is the most meaningful thing in life, and for the Seamstress, tailoring is. The Chessman stands before an open-air chess table in Tabor Park, ready to challenge all comers, and naturally he has a ludic view of reality. In hiring Cosmic Engineer to kill an exile who had worked for him in the past, the Chessman commented, "Sometimes you have to sacrifice pawns in order to better your position on the board. Don't worry, I'm not referring to you." When assigning the next mission, he observed, "The French have a saying, 'You cannot play at chess if you are kind-hearted.' The same goes for the Matrix." In his view, a player must learn to be both unpredictable and dependable, study the opponent as much as the game positions, and know when to resign.

As players interact with the exiles, they may learn new philosophies of life, but their characters acquire statistics that shape their strengths and weaknesses in a more mechanical manner. Unlike many other gameworlds, a character is not locked into one talent tree or list of professions, because a variety of abilities can be acquired and temporarily downloaded from any hardline, in exchange for others placed into storage. However, a list of five *attributes* are developed in a manner where change is extremely costly, starting at the moment the player creates the character. High *perception* benefits martial arts, *vitality* increases the character's health points, and *focus* facilitates actions that require precision such as sneaking. *Reason* is valuable for intellectual tasks such as writing code, whereas *belief* represents a kind of confidence such as shown by Neo in the movies when he is finally able to fly.

While progressing up the levels of general experience, a player may build any of these five attributes, but at the very beginning the player must choose among ten different combinations of attribute points, each of which is presented as a personality type. For example, the *detached spectator* is described thus: "You watched the passage of the stars and planets over head. They came and went like the people in your life. Friends, parents, nothing ever affected you. Now you know why. Because none of it was real." This type is high in perception but low in focus. Each of the ten personality types expresses the unreality of the Matrix in a distinctive manner. Inquisitive genius, which is high in reason but low and belief, described the decision to escape the Matrix this way: "You worked out the math, studied the formulas. Something just didn't add up. The universe was missing something. And now it's missing you." It opposite, lunatic fringe, is low in reason but high in belief: "The snakes, man, the snakes! They just kept hissing! Why didn't anyone else hear them! But you showed them. You got out! There aren't any snakes on the outside. Not as many at least" [35]. However, unlike the players, these characters cannot leave the Matrix, but are forced to struggle within it, where personality types are merely different sets of point scores conferring advantage or disadvantage under a set of conditions set by the virtual world and its rules.

The Matrix Online incorporated some elements from the second and third films, notably having a faction led by the exile called the Merovingian, but its fundamental concept did not go beyond the original film because players could not attack the machines directly nor visit the underground Zion city. A key philosophical debate in the pair of 2003 films was whether a free and liberated human society would merely be another form of control. The people in Zion depend completely upon their own machines, as we depend on technology for our own survival, and their political system is marked by hierarchies in which an individual can gain some semblance of free will only by cooperating with some others who hold high positions.

If human society is also simply another kind of machine, then machines can be humans. In all three films we see this in Agent Smith who battles again Neo and the Zion freedom fighters precisely in order to gain his own freedom. The passionate affair between Neo and Trinity, and their bonds of loyalty with Morpheus, suggest that only humans can feel love. But in *Matrix Revolutions*, Neo encounters three exiles in a subway station who refute this deduction: a father, mother, and their little girl. The little girl is a program without a function, so she has been scheduled for deletion. But her parents love her, so they have made a bargain with the Merovingian to let her escape to live with a benevolent program named the Oracle, in return for their own loyal hard work inside the system. As a prediction of the human future, therefore, the entire Matrix mythos suggests we may never become really free, but we may also never entirely lose our humanity.

Conclusion

In 2009, after 5 years of operation, *The Matrix Online* prepared to shut down. On June 20, a newcomer to the official game forums posted this plaintive message: "i wanna play matrix online but i can't find it in stores or online where to buy it. does anyone know where i can get it/?"

Exsuscito, who had posted 5,052 messages since joining the forums on November 18, 2005, replied, "Unfortunately, as of July 31st we are being shutdown, so as much as it pains me to say, there's really no point playing. If only you and 499,999 of your closest friends came sooner." In a sense, the future had been cancelled due to lack of interest.

Two of the game developers, whose avatar names were Walrus and Dracomet, invited players to a final celebration with music and a satisfying climax, consisting of the deaths of all the redpill avatars: "Come party with us in game on Friday, July 31st from 12 Noon Pacific Daylight Time till Dracomet crushes everyone's RSI just before Midnight" [36]. On August 26, 2009, this post-mortem was posted on Wikipedia:

> A grand finale was planned where all online players were to be crushed, but due to a server glitch, most players were disconnected before the final blow came. What had been envisioned as a last hurrah transpired as a gruesome slide show. High pings and low framerates caused by the developers giving out advanced powers (with graphically demanding effects) and abilities to all players, coupled with the flooded chat interface, meant many players were unable to experience the final event as intended [37].

On an independent MxO forum, Daving confirmed: "I got crashed out 5 hours early and couldn't jack back in. Got the same message and eventual black screen as those that got meatballed, but didn't get meatballed. Like the game shut down 5 hours early for me." Players quickly put up a website called *mxoemu* encouraging each other to create a software emulator so that the virtual world could continue, but their comments suggested that they really lacked the skills and resources to succeed [38]. Of course this is a nice metaphor for the possible real future of the human species: We may lack the technical skills, material responses, and social organizations needed to prevent our own world from ending. On mxoemu's forum, seven players expressed their feelings:

> I am sad that the end of my little "escape from reality" is ending.
> Since shutdown, things just aren't the same for me. Big hole in my life for some reason.
> I miss MxO more than anything.
> Good luck, looking forward to seeing what you guys can come up with!
> Unfortunately I probably don't have any skills that would help out at this stage, but the best of luck to everyone!
> I hope that this project has a future.
> Long live the Matrix!

References

1. Lore Sjöberg: Matrix online: gaming repackaged. Wired. http://www.wired.com/gaming/gamingreviews/news/2005/04/67088. Accessed 4 Apr 2005
2. McCubbin, C.: The Matrix Online: Prima Official Game Guide, p. 126. Prima Games, Roseville (2005)
3. Baudrillard, J.: Simulacra and Simulation, pp. 1164. University of Michigan Press, Ann Arbor (1994)
4. Korzybski, A.: Science and Sanity: An Introduction to Non-Aristotelian Systems and General Semantics. International Non-Aristotelian Library, Lancaster (1941)
5. Lawrence, M.: Like a Splinter in Your Mind: The Philosophy Behind the Matrix Trilogy. Blackwell, Malden (2004)
6. Hanson, R.: Was cypher right? Why we stay in our matrix. In: Yeffeth, G. (ed.) Taking the Red Pill: Science, Philosophy, and Religion in The Matrix, pp. 23–32. BenBella, Dallas (2003)
7. Bostrom, N.: Are we living in the matrix? The simulation argument. In: Yeffeth, G. (ed.) Taking the Red Pill: Science, Philosophy, and Religion in The Matrix, pp. 233–241. BenBella, Dallas (2003)
8. Reps, P. (ed.): Zen Flesh, Zen Bones. C. E. Tuttle, Rutland (1957); Watts, A.: The Way of Zen. Pantheon, New York (1957)
9. Brannigan, M.: There is no spoon: a buddhist mirror. In: Irwin, W. (ed.) The Matrix and Philosophy: Welcome to the Desert of the Real, pp. 101–110. Open Court, Chicago (2002); Ford, J.L. Buddhism, mythology and the matrix. In: Yeffeth, G (ed.) Taking the Red Pill: Science, Philosophy, and Religion in The Matrix, pp. 125–144. Benbella, Dallas (2003)
10. Herrigel, E.: Zen in the Art of Archery. Pantheon, New York (1953)
11. Bassham, G.: The religion of the matrix and the problems of pluralism. In Irwin, W (ed.) The Matrix and Philosophy: Welcome to the Desert of the Real, pp. 111–125. Open Court, Chicago (2002); Fontana, P.: Finding god in the matrix. In: Yeffeth, G (ed.) Taking the Red Pill: Science, Philosophy, and Religion in The Matrix, pp. 159–184. BenBella, Dallas (2003)

12. Danahay, M.A., Rieder, D.: The matrix, Marx and the coppertop's life. In: Irwin, W (ed.) The Matrix and Philosophy: Welcome to the Desert of the Real. p. 216. Open Court, Chicago (2002)

13. Mannheim, K.: Ideology and Utopia: An Introduction to the Sociology of Knowledge. Harcourt, Brace, New York (1936); Berger P.L., Luckmann, T.: The Social Construction of Reality: A Treatise in the Sociology of Knowledge. Doubleday, Garden City (1996)

14. Letter from Engels to Franz Mehring. http://www.marxists.org/archive/marx/works/1893/letters/93_07_14.htm (1893)

15. Nietzsche, F.W.: Also Sprach Zarathustra. Kroner, Stuttgart (1885); On the Genealogy of Morals. Vintage Books, New York (1887 [1967])

16. Freud, S.: Civilization and Its Discontents. Hogarth, London (1930)

17. Carley, K.: A theory of group stability. Am. Soc. Rev. **56**, 331–354 (1991); Bainbridge, W.S., Brent, E.E., Carley, K., Heise, D.R., Macy, M.W., Markovsky, B., Skvoretz, J.: Artificial social intelligence. Annu. Rev. Soc. **20**, 407–436 (1991); Prietula, M.J., Carley, K.M., Gasser, L (eds.) Simulating Organizations MIT Press, Cambridge (1998)

18. Soergel, D.: Organizing Information: Principles of Data Base and Retrieval Systems. Academic Press, San Diego (1985); Lesk, M.: Practical Digital Libraries. Morgan Kaufmann, San Francisco (1997)

19. However, policy makers may not be able to decide how credible such models are: Saunders-Newton, D., Scott, H.: 'But the computer said!' credible uses of computational modeling in public sector decision making. Soc. Sci. Comput. Rev. **19**, 47–65 (2001)

20. This idea was popularized by Microsoft founder, Bill Gates: The Road Ahead, pp. 251–252. Penguin, New York (1996)

21. Cornish, E.: On the World Future Society bookstore page, http://www.wfs.org/wfsblurbs.htm, The Cyber Future: 93 Ways Our Lives Will Change by the Year 2025. World Future Society, Bethesda (1999); Computer science and telecommunications board. In: Fostering Research on the Economic and Social Impacts of Information Technology. National Academy Press, Washington, DC (1998)

22. Jokinen, P., Malaska, P., Kaivo-oja, J.: The environment in an 'Information society.' Futures **30**, 485–498 (1998); compare Bernardini, O., Galli, R.: Dematerialization: long-term trends in the intensity of use of material and energy. Futures **25**, 431–448 (1993)

23. Wachowski, L., Wachowski, A.: The Matrix (script); http://www.dailyscript.com/scripts/the_matrix.pdf (1998)

24. Berger, T.W., Chapin, J.K., Gerhardt, G.A., McFarland, D.J., Principe, J.C., Soussou, W.V., Taylor, D.M., Tresco, P.A.: Brain-Computer Interfaces: An International Assessment of Research and Development Trends. Springer, Berlin (2008)

25. Grudin, J.: History of HCI. In: Bainbridge, W.S. (ed.) Berkshire Encyclopedia of Human-Computer Interaction, pp. 316–326. Berkshire, Great Barrington (2004); Wellman, B.: A personal story: highlights from my forty years of HCI. In: Bainbridge, W.S. (ed.) Berkshire Encyclopedia of Human-Computer Interaction, pp. 317–318. Berkshire, Great Barrington (2004)

26. Bainbridge, W.S.: Alto. In: Bainbridge, W.S. (ed.) Berkshire Encyclopedia of Human-Computer Interaction, pp. 12–13. Berkshire, Great Barrington (2004)

27. White, L.: Medieval Technology and Social Change. Clarendon Press, Oxford (1962)

28. McCubbin, C. (ed.): The Matrix Online: Prima Official Game Guide. Prima Games, Roseville (2005)

29. Park, I.-K., Kim, J.-H., Hong, K.-S.: An implementation of an FPGA-based embedded gesture recognizer using a data glove, In: Proceedings of the 2nd International Conference on Ubiquitous Information Management and Communication, pp. 496–500. Association for Computing Machinery, New York (2008); Witt, H., Lawo, M., Drugge, M.: Visual feedback and different frames of reference: the impact on gesture interaction techniques for wearable computing. In: Proceedings of the 10th International Conference on Human Computer

Interaction with Mobile Devices and Services, pp. 293–300. Association for Computing Machinery, New York (2008)

30. Mann, S.: Continuous lifelong capture of personal experience with eyeTap. In: Proceedings of the 1st ACM Workshop on Continuous Archival and Retrieval of Personal Experiences, pp. 1–21. Association for Computing Machinery, New York (2004); Mann, S., Fung, J., Aimone, C., Sehgal, A., Chen, D.: Designing eyeTap digital eyeglasses for continuous lifelong capture and sharing of personal experiences. In: Proceedings of ALT.CHI 2005. ACM, New York (2005); Lyons, K., Starner, T.: Augmenting cognition with wearable computers, CHI 2005; http://www.cc.gatech.edu/~thad/p/032_50_misc/augmenting-cognition-with%20wearable-computer-HCII05.pdf

31. Thrasher, F.: The Gang. University of Chicago Press), Chicago (1927)

32. Schopenhauer, A.: The World as Will and Idea. Trübner, London (1883-1886); Gale, H.: Schopenhauer's metaphysics of music. New Englander Yale Rev. **48**(218), 362–368 (1888); Ferrara, L.: Schopenhauer on music as the embodiment of will. In: Jacquette, D., Kemal, S., Gaskell, I. (eds.) Schopenhauer, Philosophy, and the Arts, pp. 183–199. Cambridge University Press, New York (1996)

33. McCubbin, C. (ed.): The Matrix Online: Prima Official Game Guide, p. 176. Prima Games, Roseville (2005)

34. McCubbin, C. (ed.): The Matrix Online: Prima Official Game Guide, p. 149. Prima Games, Roseville (2005)

35. http://www.gamefaqs.com/computer/doswin/file/931849/35989; http://www.thematrix.rumbaar.net/index.php?action=RSI_Guide;sa=rsi

36. http://thematrixonline.station.sony.com/players/news_archive.vm?id=1043&month=072009

37. http://en.wikipedia.org/wiki/Matrix_Online

38. mxoemu.info

Chapter 3
Tabula Rasa

Intensely ideological, but also rather fun, *Tabula Rasa* was a glorious failure. Its demise warns that the real human future may fail as well. The name refers to the "clean slate" with which many early psychologists believed an infant enters the real world, and with which an avatar enters this outer space gameworld. Step by step, the avatar adds fundamental concepts to a *tabula* or tablet, which confer ever greater powers through gradual enlightenment. *Tabula Rasa* therefore offers fresh thinking about the future and in a sense requires a person to abandon preconceptions and strongly held values. Perhaps that is why it failed: Most people avoid any challenge to the basis on which they live their lives, and few game players are emotionally or intellectually prepared to clean their slates. *Tabula Rasa* advocated nothing less than escaping the world we currently inhabit.

Space travel is the chief way of escaping Earth yet remaining in the real world, as Clarke's *City and the Stars* reminded us. Gamelike virtual worlds can be accused of being one of the most seductive ways of leaving the real world altogether. Thus the interplay between realities and unrealities is germane to *Tabula Rasa*, although the game presents its planets as fully real and minimizes explicitly magical elements. The central theme is the motivations that might inspire people to undertake the costly, dangerous, and possibly unrewarding flight into the cosmos. Thinking back over the four decades since the Apollo moon expeditions, it seems that humanity has not in fact found sufficient motivations for spaceflight. *Tabula Rasa*, thus, has some elements of a revival meeting, designed to rededicate players to achieving transcendence among the stars.

Exploring Two Worlds

William Bridgebain arrived on the planet Foreas on US Independence Day, 2008. He was a refugee from Earth, which had been invaded by the extraterrestrial Bane army, and a recruit to the Allied Free Sentients, an alliance of intelligent humans and humanoids that sought to liberate their worlds from this galactic scourge.

W.S. Bainbridge, *The Virtual Future*, Springer Series in Immersive Environments,
DOI 10.1007/978-0-85729-904-8_3, © Springer-Verlag London Limited 2011

A copy of the *AFS Field Manual* was pressed into his hands, and he was quickly instructed in the use of weapons, armor, and other technology adapted to this alien world, then sent on brief training missions. Some of the devices were quite humble, such as the ordinary-looking toilets that avoided the need for toilet paper by vigorously flushing upwards. Other devices were exotic in the extreme, such as the teleport waypoints used for quick medium-distance travel within a geographic zone, the dropships for long-distance travel on a planet, or the rare wormhole stations for interplanetary travel.

An early mission took him deep into Luna Caverns, in the Wilderness region of the Concordia continent, the first of many caves he would explore on the world. There he encountered his first Logos Shrine, where he acquired the Power pictogram which he placed in the tabula he carried in his backpack. A sepulchral voice told him that an advanced species called the Eloh had left shines like this across several solar systems, each Logos expressing a hidden truth they had discovered about nature, and bestowing a fresh ability to anyone who could master it. Bridgebain was gratified to learn that he was one of the *receptives*, who possessed the requisite innate spiritual or intellectual capacity. The *AFS Field Manual* explained, "Troops receptive to the Logos language can learn new symbols by visiting ancient Logos Shrines in remote locations on Foreas and other worlds. A soldier must master one or more specific Logos symbols in order to use Logos abilities. The Eloh left puzzles in certain areas, which cannot be passed without understanding Logos." When he activated the shrine, a mysterious geometrical symbol rotated before his eyes, and in the darkness of the cave he thought he saw a shadowy form. Was that the ghost of an Eloh, or a hologram?

An alien voice explained, "Many years ago, our kind visited many worlds – among them, your own Earth – seeking to share our knowledge of the power of Logos." At that moment, the Logos element representing power appeared in Bridgebain's previously empty tabula. Searching the databases available to him online, he learned that the *power* Logos gave him the ability to use lightning as a weapon, and could in future help him gain bio-augmentation abilities as well.

That week he gained Logos abilities in three other Wilderness caverns: *area*, *enhance*, and *target*. At widely dispersed open-air shrines he also found: *attack*, *damage*, *enemy*, *mind*, *projectile*, *self*, and *time*. Another Logos, *here*, was locked behind a gate he could not open until he had acquired both *mind* and *power*. This was an important Logos, because it was needed to create bots and clones. Other elements were contained in instances, sub-areas he explored completely alone, although many other AFS warriors did so in groups. In the Caves of Donn he collected: *feeling*, *heal* and *trap*. In Crater Lake Research Facility, he gained: *around*, *chaos*, and *movement*. The extremely important *future* Logos was also locked away in Wilderness, inside the Chamber of Eternity within an archaeological instance of Eloh ruins called Guardian Prominence. He could not gain it until months later, when his powers had reached level 40 and he could brave its dangers.

Searching for Logos elements, and carrying out military missions to the frontline and two hotly disputed outposts, gave Bridgebain an appreciation for the really rather beautiful Foreas countryside, green with vegetation and sculpted with diverse terrain. Among his favorite places on the planet was Pinhole Falls. Water rushed into a medium-sized pond, where he loved to swim, despite the danger that one of the Bane's minions might shoot at him from the bank. The water did not exit the pond by cascading over the edge of the cliff, but through a natural drain at the bottom. Although somewhat dangerous, letting the falling water flush him through the pinhole was an exciting experience he repeated many times. He tried not to think of the obvious toilet analogy.

In Wilderness, Bridgebain quickly made friends with humanity's Forean allies, tall humanoids with leathery reptilian skin, soulful eyes, and a spiritual demeanor. Council Elder Solis helped him understand more about the fundamental nature of reality, "You know of the Benefactors, the race also called Eloh? It was they who discovered the power of Logos. Their sacred artifacts are scattered on planets across the galaxy, including this one. I understand that your people found some on your homeworld as well, and used them to create the wormhole that brought you to Foreas." Thus, the Logos, which are mere ideas, have the power to control matter. But when he visited many Forean villages, he found that they understood more technology than they used, and sought to live in harmony with nature rather than to dominate it.

In the southwest corner of Wilderness, he encountered the Cormans, pacifist refugees from Earth who had left their planet even before the invasion, conducting research along Ranja Gorge. Ordinary AFS soldiers tended to despise the Cormans as "treehuggers," yet the military also protected them and drew on their greater knowledge of the planet. As Sergeant Conway once commented, "They may be damned hippies, but they don't deserve to die out here." Bridgebain also saw Cormans at Cumbria Research Facility in the Palisades region of Concordia, and a rebel offshoot group called the Retreads in the Marshes and Pools regions of the other Forean continent, Valverde. The Retreads had rejected pacifism in favor of waging their own guerilla war against the Bane, but like the orthodox Cormans they refused to join any alliance. Corman architecture was distinctive, despite their terrestrial origins, often in the form of glass-walled geodesic domes.

Despite many skirmishes against the Bane, Bridgebain never really got a good sense of what their core society was like. He understood that the Bane were led by Neph, a faction of Eloh that had long ago turned toward evil. Undoubtedly, the names Eloh and Neph are drawn from the Bible, where Elohim refers to God or gods, and Nephilim are somewhat ambiguous beings who may be fallen angels, Titans, or other wicked entities opposed to the Elohim. What Bridgebain did encounter were the minions of the Bane. Most notable were the Thrax who served as infantry initiates, common soldiers, grenadiers, and technicians. The humans tended to think of Thrax as insects, calling them cockroaches or "Crusty." However, their form was that of sturdy humanoids with the same number of limbs as humans. The Bane used technology to transform captured Foreans into *machina* who would serve in their ranks, and they brought to Foreas wasp-like animals called *fithiks* to harass their enemies. Especially lethal were two kinds of huge machines, 20 ft-tall *stalkers* that strode across the battlefield, and *predator* aircraft that attacked from above.

Blending into the natural environment, but also potentially dangerous, were six kinds of indigenous Forean animals. Bridgebain first encountered pig-like *boargar* who could be tough but would not attack unless aroused. Eyeless, they navigated by

Fig. 3.1 A wormhole for travel between Foreas and Arieki

means of a natural sonar like that of bats, emitted from an organ between their horns, so they were especially sensitive to sonic weapons. In contrast, *tree lurkers* were aggressive but vulnerable to fire, while slow-moving *treebacks* were so huge that vegetation grew on them. *Miasmas* looked like flying squids, dwelled in caves where it was impossible to avoid them, and were best handled with incendiary weapons. *Warnets* were wasplike, spawned in hives, and used electric discharges to shock their victims. *Filchers* were scavenger birds, not really dangerous but often stealing valuable loot from the battlefield.

Most of all, Bridgebain loved the land. Ranja Gorge was beautiful but completely overshadowed by the magnificent chasm that cut the Plateau region of Valverde, running east and west. Crossing its center was the beautiful Trinity Bridge, built according to Eloh designs and containing many secrets. The Descent region of Valverde is dominated by Dante's Pit, an absolutely immense sinkhole reminiscent of Tycho crater on Earth's moon. Among other notable environmental features were the volcano in Howling Maw, the eponymous marshes of Marshes, and the nearly ubiquitous caverns, some of which connected the zones.

Half way through his service with the AFS, Bridgebain was temporarily posted to the other planet, Arieki. Travel between planets was accomplished through wormhole portals, which were much rarer than local teleport sites and even than dropship landing platforms. Figure 3.1 shows the wormhole at Foreas Base in the low-level Divide region. Presumably, the funnel-shaped force field at the top center of the installation warps space, under control of the equipment in the structure, and transmits a person across vast distances to another similar installation that acts as the receiver.

To use the wormhole, a person needs only to mount the stairs and stand under the force field, at which point a menu of available destinations appears.

If Foreas was green, then Arieki was red, and most of its seven regions glowed from the molten lava flowing in what passed for rivers on this arid world. I say seven regions, although the maps provided with *Tabula Rasa* show six. The seventh region, Abyss, was apparently discovered after the others. Situated on the continent Torden, it is a practically subterranean realm connected to the Abyssal Zone on the south edge of Torden's Plains region. With the exception of Ashen Desert on the Ligo continent, lava flows obstruct free movement across all the zones, and the Bane are extremely well entrenched at many bases.

At Irendas Colony in the Plains region, Bridgebain met another race of intelligence extraterrestrials, the Brann, who were now nominal allies of humanity but did not seem to be of nearly so much value as the Foreans. Criminals and the descendents of convicts, at first they seemed merely like annoying beggars. Then he reached the Crucible region on Ligo, and was ordered by AFS Captain DeLisi to spy on the Brann at Staal. As DeLisi explained, "Staal Detention Center was one of the biggest Brann prisons on Arieki. After the Bane invaded, the prisoners rioted and overwhelmed the Warden Bots. Now the Brann are using it as their city. Intel says there are four crime syndicates calling the shots at Staal. They run guns and sell black market goods, but they're also damn good fighters and they don't have any love for the Bane."

Bridgebain completed missions for all four Brann syndicates, and formed his own impression of them. They seemed more enthusiastic about technology than the Foreans, and often used it in attempts to improve themselves. A Brann scientist named Eugin told Bridgebain, "We cannot be setting limits to the potential of our races. All that is best in us can be made better. On my homeworld, our government believed that no environment could be too good for our people, but as scientist of genetics, I say that our people can never be too good for their environment." Ordinary Brann tend to be in the salvage business, making commercial use of wrecked and abandoned machines. This is a more humble form of technology-based redemption than the science-based redemption offered by the Eloh.

Another species on Arieki may have been intelligent natives of the planet, the gigantic, arachnoids called Atta. Living in hives and dominated by queens, it was easy to imagine they were stupid animals, like gigantic ants. Yet when fighting they threw rocks with great accuracy, and they had constructed networks of ramps and bridges, rather like Earth's superhighway overpasses, around their city-sized hives. The official AFS guide says the intelligence of Atta is disputed, but the now-unavailable *Tabula Rasa* website reported, "Exobiologists have discerned that the Atta are probably solely responsible for maintaining Arieki's ecosystems and maintaining the habitability of the planet." Their main colonies were Kardash in Plains, Ojasa in Incline, and Rivasa in Thunderhead, but they also had four smaller outposts in Ashen Desert. Apparently indigenous to Arieki, and equally distributed across both continents, they did not seem to be involved in the great cosmic war against the Bane, and would have been the dominant species on the planet had not the Brann, Bane and Humans arrived.

Arieki had its own menagerie of creatures, four of which were constant annoyances. According to the *Tabula Rasa* website, *barb ticks* and *beam mantas* have a symbiotic relationship. The ticks are "small, colony-based creatures [that] live on and beneath the blasted sands of Arieki. They grind food for nutrition and sustenance, and the high mineral content of Arieki's soil collects in their bodies over time, allowing the Barb Tick to spit out these chunks at high velocity." Beam mantas fly slowly in the air over the ticks, providing protective cover while consuming food which the ticks have broken into pieces small enough for the mantas to eat. "Beam Mantas gather electrical energy with their long, slender tails and store this energy in muscle tissue arranged across their back. When the Beam Manta attacks, it bridges a connection between its forward appendages, allowing it to direct a strong electrical pulse at its target." *Geyser hoppers* feed on bacteria associated with the planet's sulfur geysers, producing oxygen on which the ecosystem depends, and *magmonix* are huge and slow moving defenders of the territory around geologically active areas. Notice that these four species have evolved co-dependently, and the Atta also were shaped by evolution to cooperate in maintaining life on an otherwise inhospitable world.

Had the war not ended unexpectedly, wormholes to a third planet, Mycon, might have been opened. But the "real world" intruded upon Foreas and Arieki when the NCsoft corporation decided to shut *Tabula Rasa* down, and on December 9, 2008, urged its subscribers to move over to a new fantasy virtual world it was preparing to launch, *Aion*. For its final months, until its closure at the end of February 2009, *Tabula Rasa* became cost-free for established players, and their enthusiasm was sustained by the addition of one final instance. Bridgebain received his last Logos element, *Earth*, back in the Wilderness zone of Foreas, inside Enigma Caverns, past a gate that could be unlocked only by a level 50 receptive who possessed these three Logos elements: *defend, planet, yours*.

The Earth symbol is a diagram of the inner solar system, with the sun at center, and the Earth in the third orbit. There are, of course, may ways to conceptualize Earth, but calling it a planet and describing it in terms of its orbit place it in an astronomical context. One could argue that the Earth is not a planet at all, but a biosphere unlike any other place in the solar system. Planets, historically, are wandering stars given astrological significance, that in the centuries after Galileo came to be seen as physical worlds comparable to Earth, but initially without full awareness that they are crucially different in that they cannot naturally sustain life. Realization that the concept of *planet* is dubious came when astronomers debated removing Pluto from the list of planets, rather than adding some dozens of other moon-sized non-satellites to the roster of planets, from Ceres to Sedna. The word *planet*, therefore, is an anachronism, originating in ancient astrology and only temporarily having real scientific meaning during the period of perhaps four centuries. However, conceptualizing Earth in astronomical terms as a planet sets the stage for leaving Earth to inhabit other worlds.

The Earth Logos allowed Bridgebain to enter a previously hidden wormhole in Wilderness and return to his home planet. Thoroughly disoriented, he emerged in the 23rd Street subway station in New York City, on the south edge of Madison

Square Park. Occupied by Bane stalkers, predators, and Thrax soldiers, the park had been blasted into a wasteland of devastation. An AFS captain named Pauly instructed Bridgebain to report to General Murphy at an outpost on Lexington Avenue, but that would mean crossing the park through the enemy forces. Pauly admitted, "Getting there isn't going to be easy. Unless you've got a proven squad together, I'd strongly suggest you turn around right now and get your **** back through that Wormhole." Unfortunately, Bridgebain was alone, and several attempts to sneak past the Bane failed. He returned to Foreas and spent his remaining days deciphering ancient Eloh inscriptions.

We cannot be sure what happen afterward to humanity, but we have some hint when these events all occurred. The flash screen that appeared upon entering *Tabula Rasa* showed a view of the city of New York, devastated and marked by several teleport waypoints, implying a lengthy struggle would be required to save Earth from the Bane. In the distance, where the Twin Towers of the World Trade Center had stood, rose a new building, which, as I write these words, does not yet exist.

Scientific and Philosophical Basis

First and foremost, *Tabula Rasa* was an expression of the spaceflight social move-ment that seeks to propel humanity out into the universe. The key person in the development of this game was Richard Garriott, son of Skylab astronaut, Owen Garriott. As of June 2009, his Wikipedia article began:

> Richard Allen Garriott (born July 4, 1961), also known as Lord British in *Ultima* and General British in *Tabula Rasa*, is a significant figure in the video game industry. He was originally a game designer and programmer, but now engages in various aspects of com-puter game development. On October 12, 2008, Garriott launched aboard Soyuz TMA-13 to the International Space Station as a self-funded tourist, returning safely 12 days later aboard Soyuz TMA-12 [1].

Soon after launch, during a broadcast back to Earth, Garriott held up a piece of paper on which he had written some Logos pictographs. The first one was the Earth pictograph, and I immediately understood what they said: "Earth is the cradle of humanity, but a person cannot stay in a cradle forever." This is one of many versions of the English translation of a famous proverb by the Russian spaceflight pioneer, Konstantin Tsiolkovsky. Googling "earth cradle humanity Tsiolkovsky" gives 40,700 hits, some sign of the influence of these words. Tsiolkovsky was one of three intellectuals in the early twentieth century who identified the correct principles for initial spaceflight, based on multi-stage liquid-fuel rockets. The other two were the American, Robert Goddard, and the German, Hermann Oberth. Out of their writ-ings, and the practical technical and organization work of many men they inspired, grew the spaceflight social movement [2].

It began almost simultaneously in four great nations: Germany, the Soviet Union, Britain, and the United States. First, individual theorists like Tsiolkovsky, Goddard, and Oberth developed the principles of space travel. This was the phase of maturation of a social movement I call *parallel behavior* – individuals doing essentially the same thing but without any communication among them. Then a cascade of books, articles, and lectures established networks of communication and a shared space culture. This was the phase of *collective behavior* – individuals influencing one another but without formal planning and organization. Soon the moderate level of organization that defines a *social movement* was achieved in the founding of amateur space travel clubs in Germany (1927), the United States (1930), the Soviet Union (1931), and Great Britain (1933). Once the great government rocket programs had been established, first the V-2 project in Germany, then the intercontinental ballistic missile programs of the USSR and US, primitive spaceflight was assured but the movement had been transformed into a *societal institution*. Now it is a minor appendage of the military-industrial complex, and it has lost the capacity to innovate.

In the 1960s, an ideology consolidated and was shared widely throughout society, asserting what humanity should accomplish through spaceflight in the following decades. Questionnaire research I carried out in the wake of the Challenger shuttle disaster in 1986 indicated that a great diversity of specific goals could be grouped into a small number of major themes [3]. In 2009 I assessed the progress that had been achieved by then in each theme [4]. Among the more technically oriented goals, some have largely been achieved already and can be enhanced without new rocket technology: communications satellites, earth observation, navigation systems like GPS, and fundamental research in physics, astronomy, and general science. Today, exploitation of low earth orbit space does have commercial applications and contributes to employment in technical fields, but there are questions about whether it will be economically feasible to exploit extraterrestrial resources, for example by beaming solar power down to earth from satellites, mining the moon and asteroids, or manufacturing high-tech materials in weightless conditions. Full-fledged colonization of the Moon or Mars seems very far off, and today there exists neither the will nor the way to accomplish this tremendously challenging goal. With the possible exception of space tourism, there seems to be little activity today exploring new commercial applications.

Similarly, most military applications of space appear to have stabilized – using satellites for reconnaissance, navigation, and communications – leaving still unresolved the question of whether a defense against intercontinental ballistic missiles will be technically possible. Short of the invasion of Earth by aliens which *Tabula Rasa* imagined, there may be no need to develop the weapons or the launch vehicles required for war in outer space.

However, many traditional justifications for space exploration were emotional and idealistic, rather than scientific, economic, or military. On the basis of the questionnaire research, here are ten subcategories of idealistic motivations, each illustrated by two typical statements:

> Human spirit. "Space exploration is a human struggle, expressing the unconquerable human spirit." "Space offers new challenges, and civilization would stagnate without challenges."
> Personal inspiration. "The space program encourages people to make achievements and solve problems." "The space program inspires young people to study the sciences."

Noble endeavor. "Spaceflight is a noble endeavor, expressing the hopes and aspirations of humankind." "The space program allows people to think beyond the triviality of Earthbound conflicts and concerns."

Curiosity. "Investigation of outer space satisfies human curiosity." "Humans have an innate need to search and discover."

Exploration. "We should explore the unknown." "We should boldly go where no man or woman has gone before."

Frontier. "We must broaden our horizons." "Space is the new frontier."

Adventure. "Space exploration fulfills the human need for adventure." "Space stimulates the creative, human imagination."

Aesthetics. "The beauty of space creates a sense of wonder." "New experiences and perspectives gained in space inspire art, music, and literature."

Insight. "We could gain greater understanding of the world we live in." "We could gain knowledge about ourselves."

Responsibility. "Space travel makes us realize that Earth is a fragile, unique, unified world that deserves more respect and better care." "In space, we see how small our world is and thus learn humility."

Arguably, experiencing the challenge of gamelike virtual worlds could accomplish many of the same things. I have certainly seen young people turn toward computer science and cognitive science after playing computer games, and I am convinced these environments trigger valid insights about the real world and about human beings. Their aesthetic qualities are undeniable. It is more debatable whether battling the Bane across Foreas and Arieki is a noble endeavor, involving real exploration and adventure, but subjectively that may be at least somewhat true. One certainly expands one's horizons interacting with diverse other people, because the gamelike worlds described in this book all attract international participants. *Tabula Rasa*, for example, functioned simultaneously in English, French, German, and Korean. Despite sometimes being called *aliens*, foreigners do not meet the traditional definition of extraterrestrial life, but one of the other items from the 1986 research asserted: "We could learn much from contact and communication with intelligent, extraterrestrial beings."

Some ancient religions located the gods in the heavens, and in the European Enlightenment speculation intensified about the inhabitants of other worlds [5]. This took two tracks, one mystical and the other more scientific. A major influence for the mystical track was Emanuel Swedenborg's remarkable 1758 book, *The Earths in Our Solar System, which are Called Planets and the Earths in the Starry Heavens, their Inhabitants and Spirits and Angels thence from Things Seen and Heard* [6]. Incorporating ideas from Theosophy and other quasi-religious movements, 200 years after Swedenborg a belief system has emerged in which ancient extraterrestrials were responsible for the birth of human civilization and might even be available today to guide us to higher levels. This hope is part of the New Age subculture, and people who favor it also tend to see merit in astrology, biorhythms, and extrasensory perception as well [7]. One influential "flying saucer cult," the Raëlians, even call the ascended space aliens *Elohim*, suggesting the biblical origins of *Tabula Rasa's* Eloh [8].

A century ago, some professional astronomers thought that Mars could harbor life, and its supposed (but illusory) canals really might be technological infrastructure built by Martians [9]. That theory was demoted to fantasy over the following decades, especially after space probes actually visited the red planet [10]. However, it soon became apparent that radio technology might be developed to the point at which interstellar communication would be possible, whether or not physical travel to the stars ever could be, and many reputable scientists wrote encouraging essays on this "far-out" topic [11]. After a few decades of false starts, astronomers began amassing solid evidence that planets exist outside our solar system, and by March 2010 the online Extrasolar Planets Encyclopedia listed fully 429 of them [12].

One critical fact to consider when examining the meaning of *Tabula Rasa* and the real prospects for interstellar flight is that we are not currently in contact with an extraterrestrial civilization. Even if only one star in a million produces intelligent life, a hundred thousand civilizations would appear in our galaxy. Simple calculations suggest that a single colonizing species could fill the galaxy in a few million years, far less than the time since civilization probably began to appear [13]. Thus, either these calculations are wrong or interstellar colonization must be exceedingly difficult and unlikely. Yet technology capable of achieving it can already be sketched – not using the mythical wormholes but 1,000 year-duration travel either in city-sized ships or in some form of cryonic, DNA, or computerized storage. Therefore, the apparent lack of colonization may be due to social rather than technological considerations.

As technology advances, we can better fulfill our needs by reengineering not only our environment but also our species itself. Birth control seems to solve population pressures better than does interplanetary colonization. A static, information-centered industrial base might be more satisfactory than the heroic mining of the asteroids. Direct intervention in human genetics and brain physiology might end crime and deviance, even to the point of reducing mankind to automatons. Bread can be manufactured from sewage, and circuses can be simulated with computer graphics. Once a species has the power to transform itself, it has no utilitarian need to explore and conquer the universe. The threat of self-annihilation, whether through nuclear war or some other miss-application of science, must be overcome. A species might establish an absolute cultural and political freeze in the service of its own preservation. Perhaps only highly unlikely and risky accidents, occurring just before a species arrives at such a stasis, can propel it out across the gulf of space to the stars [14].

If interstellar colonization, therefore, is ever to be possible, it must be begun very rapidly, within a few short decades of the development of nuclear physics and biological engineering. Ordinary socioeconomic forces will be insufficient to launch galactic exploration this rapidly, and only transcendent social movements could possibly channel enough of a society's resources into the project to succeed before either stasis or annihilation. Whatever else it may be, *Tabula Rasa* was an attempt by Richard Garriott to restart the spaceflight movement by inspiring players to imagine distant worlds and bring to real life the motivations to explore them [15].

In the mythos of *Tabula Rasa*, Garriott flew a second time into space, but his Vostok was thrown off course by an encounter with a Bane reconnaissance vessel, and hurled to the planet Foreas. Bridgebain was able to find the craft, long after

Garriott escaped from it. Represented by his avatar, General British, Garriott became the commander of the Allied Free Sentients. The first flight also connected the real and virtual worlds, because Garriott carried with him a memory unit containing data representing Bridgebain and all the other *Tabula Rasa* avatars.

This was part of a larger effort called Operation Immortality. As announced August 15, 2008 on websites that now have been taken down, this project "intended to collect and archive the very best of what humanity has accomplished, is creating a digital time capsule of the human race, including messages from people around the world and DNA samples from some of our brightest minds and most accomplished athletes." DNA samples were donated by a score of people, including comedian Stephen Colbert, physicist Stephen Hawking, singer Joe Ely, athlete Matt Morgan, *Playboy* magazine's cybergirl Jo Garcia, and Heather Ash who wrote scripts for the Stargate SG-1 sci-fi TV program.

Although I did not contribute my DNA, I did register for the other parts of the project, and on October 23 received this email: "Thank you for participating in Operation Immortality! Through your dedicated effort to save humanity we have secured the Bridgebain Tabula Rasa characters aboard the Immortality Drive, which is now safely stored on the International Space Station." I also took the opportunity to add what amounted to a Twitter tweet to the database taken to the space station, using an easily decoded compression algorithm to fit my 200 responses to the questions about the value of space exploration from some personality capture software I had programmed [16].

One intended function of Garriott's space voyage was to boost the fortunes of *Tabula Rasa* through positive publicity for the vision that motivated it. This tactic was not apparently successful, and the subscriber base remained low compared with *World of Warcraft* or even NCsoft's flagship virtual worlds *Lineage* and *City of Heroes*. A series of ambiguous messages informed the public that Garriott and NCsoft had parted company, and the fate of *Tabula Rasa* was sealed. *Tabula Rasa* was not a commercial success, but Garriott is a legitimate member of the spaceflight movement, and the gameworld incorporated a remarkable collection of ideas that could promote the movement, if only the players would pay attention. Central to the ideology is the tabula of Logos elements.

The Logos Language

In addition to its advocacy of space exploration, *Tabula Rasa* is rich in science-related metaphors of transcendence. This is especially true in the Logos language. Although directly inspired by the Bliss system of pictograph communication [17], more abstractly it is based on the hypothesis of Platonic Idealism that physical reality is a reflection of a higher conceptual truth. Long before Plato developed this perspective, the ancient Greek philosopher Heraclitus employed the term *logos* to refer to the fundamental order of the universe, which he considered to be a set of concepts that could be discerned by an enlightened human mind. Classical Greek thinking in this area blended scientific with mystical motivations, but we can see the beginnings of modern science in the view of Pythagoreanism that the ideas on which the universe was based are largely mathematical in nature. Thus it is revealing that whenever a character in *Tabula Rasa* gains a new Logos, the rotating image that traditionally represents the concept *phi* appears.

Phi is a mathematical concept, also called the Golden Ratio, expressed as an irrational number, approximately 1.6180339887... but extending to an infinite number of decimal places. In some respects, therefore, it is comparable to the much better known irrational number, pi (3.14159265358979...). Phi can be generated mathematically in a number of ways, but among the most often cited is the ratio of two adjacent integers in a Fibonacci series, such as 1, 1, 2, 3, 5, 8, 13, 21... in which each later integer is the sum of its two predecessors. As the integers get larger, the ratio approaches ever closer to phi, but can only equal phi at infinity. Phi has been used extensively in both the arts and in mystical speculations for more than 2,000 years. For example, in the *StarCraft* mythos, the discovery of phi opened the door to profound mental abilities for the Protoss, marking the dawn of their high-technology civilization [18]. As a metaphor, the Golden Ratio suggests that the universe may contain hidden meaning that harmonizes with human hopes and perceptions.

Figure 3.2 shows eight separate Logos that are philosophically significant, plus three inscriptions that illustrate how they can be concatenated into sentences. While interpreting the philosophy behind these symbols, it is impossible to avoid a certain amount of speculation, but there are good reasons for suggesting much of what follows. The symbol *Logos* itself is a triskelion sign, employed as an emblem for *Tabula Rasa*, and identifying each friendly character in the game. Its first appearance may have been on the Triskelion Disk or Benefactor Stone that was released to promote the future game in 2004. Both sides of this disk had a large triskelion in the center, with a set of Logos symbols around the edge.

The second symbol is *phi*, in a traditional geometrical representation of a series of ever smaller squares arranged in a spiral pattern. Shortly before public release of *Tabula Rasa*, a long Logos inscription was distributed, including this sentence: "Phi combines all forces of the cosmos." Interestingly, the symbol for *cosmos* consists of three stars, and the Logos symbols for *star* and *spirit* are both almost identical to the symbol for *force*. The next two symbols in the left column of Fig. 3.2 represent the two factions of the most advanced galactic species: Eloh and Neph. Note that the Eloh symbol looks like an angel, and the Neph symbol could represent a fallen angel with horns rather than a halo. The pictograms for *good* and *evil* are similar, but depicting ordinary people without angelic wings. The next element in the left column expresses *function* in the form of two gears meshing, a very mechanical way of representing a mathematical relationship between two variables, but also hinting at the idea of intended purpose. The final symbol, for *immortality*, shows a traditional symbol for infinity over the symbol for life, which is two living cells undergoing division.

The first *Tabula Rasa* mission that requires a player to understand the meaning of Logos elements, Eloh Translations, combines the biosphere and astronomical

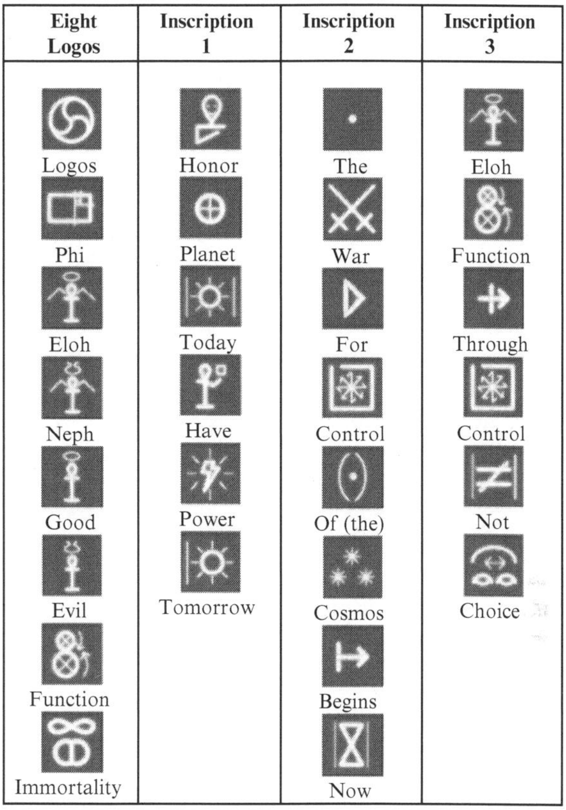

Fig. 3.2 Logos elements
and Eloh inscriptions

Eight Logos	Inscription 1	Inscription 2	Inscription 3
Logos	Honor	The	Eloh
Phi	Planet	War	Function
Eloh	Today	For	Through
Neph	Have	Control	Control
Good	Power	Of (the)	Not
Evil	Tomorrow	Cosmos	Choice
Function		Begins	
Immortality		Now	

conceptions of Earth. An NPC named Corporal Orton sends the player to an ancient ruin to decipher six symbols displayed in light on an obelisk, shown here in the second column of Fig. 3.2. Orton said, "I feel like it's something important or something [sic] like how to stop the Bane. Or maybe it's like a clue as to how to find some Eloh treasure." I already possessed half of the Logos, so I looked the others up in an online database called Logos Atlas [19]. Then, I merely needed to read the concepts off the obelisk from top to bottom to translate the six-word sentence: *Honor planet today, have power tomorrow.* Corporal Orton was very disappointed in the result, saying, "I thought for sure it would be something cool like how to blow up mountains or something. This makes no sense to me. So much for getting rich. At least I don't have to be thinking about that stupid thing again." Clearly, the message proclaimed that power comes not from destroying nature but from honoring it, and Orton was unable to comprehend this environmentalist principle because he was stupidly obsessed with violence and quick profit.

Orton reflects the narrow thinking of people who are not receptive to the enlightenment offered by the Logos. This is common among AFS personnel who are not avatars of players but non-player characters operated by simple programming routines or artificial intelligence. Perhaps their defect is that they lack souls. They tend to see science and technology as means by which to achieve military goals or comparable unenlightened purposes. For example, Engineer Salter says, "I'm a mechanical engineer. You know the difference between a mechanical engineer and a civil engineer? Mechanical engineers build weapons, civil engineers build targets."

The six symbols are pictographs, representing abstract concepts in the form of simple drawings. The pictograph for *honor*, for example, is the cartoon of a person's head and arms, with one hand over the heart. Similarly, *have* shows a person holding something, namely the thing that he has. *Power* is a small lightning bolt. The symbol for *planet* is very interesting from an environmentalist standpoint. It is the astrological and astronomical symbol for Earth. Thus, a batter translation than "planet" might be "the planet" or "home planet."

Today and *tomorrow* both show an image of the sun in the center. *Today* frames the sun between two vertical lines, and *tomorrow* has only one vertical line at the left. This reflects a conception of time moving from left to right, with today being inside the frame of our perception, and tomorrow just beyond it. We would predict that the logo for *yesterday* would show a sun with a single vertical line at the right. Unfortunately, *Tabula Rasa* does not apparently incorporate a symbol for *yesterday*, so we cannot confirm this guess. However, we do have confirmation that the Eloh, like our own civilization, conceptualized time as moving from left to right. The pictograph for *past* shows a dot to the left of an hourglass, whereas *future* is an hourglass with a dot on the right. *Time* is simply an hourglass with no dot, and *now* is an hourglass framed by lines on left and right, like *today*.

The second inscription in Fig. 3.2 is a slogan found in the *Tabula Rasa* publicity, and the third is the solution to a puzzle. At level 50, Bridgebain entered Sanctus Grotto to cross a heavily defended bridge and reach a Forean temple to gain the *function* Logos. On each side of the span were three mysterious Eloh objects marked by Logos symbols and beaming pillars of light skyward. Forean holograms would attack him, unless he activated the six objects in the right order. For a long time he thought the correct order was *Eloh function through choice not control*, wrongly imaging that the ancient Benefactors respected the free will of their disciples. But then he was forced to realize, however painfully, that freedom was not part of their system: *Eloh function through control not choice*. He should have remembered what an Eloh hologram named Jumna told him back at level 38: "The stones that form your path were set in place many millennia ago, friend. Let their strength be your strength as they guide you along."

Twenty of the Logos shrines are locked in caverns behind doors that can be unlocked only by someone who already possesses a specific set of other Logos elements. As we have already seen, *mind* and *power* are required to unlock *here*. Possessing *north*, *south*, *east*, and *west* gives one access to *few*, although what this means is not clear to me. Rather more intelligible are two military concepts. *Enhance*, *power*, *transform*, *attack*, and *enemy* unlock *victory*. *Increase*, *area*, *attack*, *damage*, and *here* unleash *war*. In order to obtain *bomb*, one must already have: *You hold the planet together*. Although this particular set is especially obscure, it may imply that the consciousness of a sensitive person holds the fabric of reality together, and the ultimate bomb is not nuclear or thermonuclear, but intellectual. At the extreme, if one were fully aware that the universe is entirely chaotic, then reality would explode into its constituent elements.

Two of the Logos elements are found in the same cavern, *clarity* and *death*. Apparently, they are connected in some deep manner, especially if clarity is interpreted as enlightenment. Life is a mystery, and full clarity can come only at death. Or, full clarity would bring life to a conclusion, because the dynamic interplay of passions and forces that generates life is incompatible with perfect clarity. The four Logos elements required to obtain both *clarity* and *death* are: *It is not time*. This suggests that a person in the midst of life, or in the middle of exploring the *Tabula Rasa* universe, cannot expect finality, whether in understanding or in living.

Some of the keys to unlock shrines are insights. The *growth* element can be obtained only by a leap of faith, from a cliff overlooking Torden Abyss. One must first have the *believe* and *jump* elements, then step into thin air at a certain point. Perhaps this also explains why the key to *lightness* is: *Many will not question the past*. If free will does not exist, then we have no need to feel shame or cast blame over past misdeeds. The key to *empower* echos the parable of the Forean bridge: *The choice not yours*. However, the key to *knowledge* is *transform man life*, implying that awareness not desire can change a person's fate. Later, one must unlock the shrine containing *question* with: *Knowledge will be yours*.

A different perspective on free will comes from the fact that the *man* element is unlocked by *life*, *power*, and *control*. And *permit* is gained, *If you give choice*. The *summon* element, needed for creating clone assistants and bringing back dead enemies as allies, requires five elements: *friend*, *star*, *life*, *enlighten*, and *here*. These all suggest that fate can be transcended, not by individual free will, but some kind of magical communication between beings. The paradox of personal property, that only society can define the laws of ownership, is suggested by the fact that the key to *everyone's* is: *Take that which is yours*. In the place of freedom, the Logos language seems to place *vortex*, the element unlocked by: *Eloh empower only the strong*. Strong, yet not willful, because the element *submit* is unlocked by: *Everyone plant seeds of evil; Logos is how transform*. The key to *evil* is: *Fear the Neph in you*. And the key to *love* is: *Good is asleep in Neph*. If the Neph is within ourselves, we may be cleansed through love. Within any evil person, love exists but slumbers. A logical conclusion is that we should love our enemies, and seek to awaken the love within them.

The Cultures of Spaceflight

In his exploration of the planets Foreas and Arieki, spaceman William Bridgebain encountered six groups that had voyaged across space, each for its own reason. The first, of course, was his own army of humans, and Fig. 3.3 shows him standing in one of the AFS bases, as three comrades run past, in front of one of the dropships used for medium-distance travel which is sending down the transporter beam by

Fig. 3.3 Bridgebain watching three comrades run past a dropship

which it picks up passengers. His army left Earth because it was exiled by the alien invasion, thus representing involuntary exploration of space.

The second group was the Cormans. In a geodesic dome at the Cumbria Research Facility, Derac Bensen Corman explained that the group was formed by an engineer and scientist named Alan Corman who established an institute to study alien artifacts found on Earth. When he learned the government was keeping secret a crashed spacecraft it had found in Nevada, he planned to steal it so the entire world could learn from it. Later, Kaven Corman revealed the ignoble part of the story, admitting that two government agents were killed in the encounter, and the stolen ship was pre-programmed to go to Foreas, rather than intentionally flown there by the Cormans. Thus a mixture of utopianism and opposition to the suppression of scientific truth motivated the Cormans, perhaps augmented by cultic zeal and pure luck. Thirty-five years later, there was no sign of Alan Corman, but guided by his own zeal and luck, Bridgebain found him living as a hermit, at a remote location on Fractured Butte in the Pools region of Valverde continent.

The third spacefaring group, Foreans, were not native to Foreas, but went willingly when the Eloh offered them this planet as a second chance to gain wisdom. Warden Kahlee of the forbidden Forean temples, reported shamefully, "Long ago, before the Eloh found us, we abused and ravaged our homeworld through war and competition. My ancestors were oblivious as countless beasts fell extinct around them." Inscribed on the Memory Tree in the very center of Wilderness are these words: "Our ancestors' ignorant choices destroyed our home world. The Eloh gave us this planet to release us from past failings. Now to defend this planet is our eternal duty. Our spirit is intertwined with this world." A Forean savant named Mentor

Ensine told Bridgebain, "To learn the gifts of Logos is to learn awareness and, thus, being." A Forean blessing says, "May the Benefactors guide you and watch over you." And one of their prayers to the spirits of the Benefactors says, "Let me learn the lessons you have hidden in every leaf and rock of this world."

On Arieki, Bridgebain met the last survivors of the Brann species of intelligent humanoids, the fourth group of interstellar travelers. Natives of the planet Erdas, they had developed a high civilization with a strong sense of justice. Unable to reform the small criminal element within their society, they were too humane to destroy them, so they turned to space technology for a solution. As the now defunct *Tabula Rasa* website explained, "In order to maintain the purity of their society, the Brann apprehended and relocated criminal offenders to off-world reeducation colonies on the neighboring planet of Arieki. These penal colonies were designed to force inmates to create self-sustaining societies on a planet where survival hinged on working for the common good." Sadly, the Bane destroyed Erdas with all its people. At the Old Brann Landing Zone, Jhulyus commented, "The Bane invasion is our way of paying for the sins of our past. Those of us who were brought here were criminals. Sometime we get what we deserve."

The fifth group is the Bane army whose goal in crossing space is conquest. They have many methods for enslaving the other intelligent species, including operating upon their bodies to insert control devices. However, one of the more subtle methods was placing a toxin in the water that drove Foreans mad with a form of false spirituality. Like zombies they lurked in the Shrine of the Penitent, chanting in unison: "This flesh is only a vessel. The pain is an illusion. My spirit is my strength. The shadows cannot touch me." A computer database at the Eastern AFS Listening Post in Valverde Pools describes the Thrax minions of the Bane as born killers. In passing, the database says that the species most similar to the Thrax are the humans.

The sixth group of space voyagers, actually the first historically, is the Eloh who crossed interstellar space in order to spread wisdom. A hologram in the Eloh Temporal Chambers, who teaches self-sacrifice and protection of the weak, proclaims they were the bringers of enlightenment. A hologram in Vogren's Tomb speaks several proverbs connected to the Logos elements of Trinity Bridge, including: "The essence of Logos is the simple. It is we who insist on making it complex." This hologram is actually not an Eloh but Vogren himself, a Forean who studied Eloh wisdom closely and may understand it better than anyone. In the Eloh Sanctuary, Bridgebain met an actual Eloh, named Gabriel like the archangel, who explained that Neph were once Eloh, and said, "We fight them with all our being because they would destroy and not create."

Conclusion

On March 20, 2010, the *New York Times* reported a new development in one of Richard Garriott's other space-oriented visionary projects: "Photographs by NASA's Lunar Reconnaissance Orbiter captured the tracks and final resting place of

Lunokhod 2, a Soviet lunar rover that landed in January 1973 and covered 23 miles in 5 months." In 1993, Garriott paid $68,500 to buy the rover from Sotheby's auction house, but he has never been able to take possession of it. In the new photograph, the rover appears only as a tiny dot, but its owner remains optimistic: "'The next thing is I hope to find my own way to the moon,' Mr. Garriott said" [20].

At the end of February, 2009, *Tabula Rasa* was destroyed, apparently having failed in its twin task of earning sufficient money from subscribers, and inspiring them to join the spaceflight movement. Left unexplained was how enthusiasts could actually voyage to other planets, short of stumbling across an abandoned Eloh vehicle. Although the Vostok spacecraft could take Richard Garriott to and from the International Space Station it is incapable of going any higher. The space travelers in *Tabula Rasa* had ready access to wormholes, although truth to tell real science offers no hope for this mode of travel, because the mythical wormholes are supposed to be a variety of black hole, and real black holes rip apart any matter that nears them. The dropships and zone-limited waypoints employ a milder but equally mysterious form of teleportation; some towers and bases used them prosaically as elevators, and it was even possible to purchase portable waypoints, one small kind for use by a single individual, and a larger one for teams. Thus *Tabula Rasa* did not offer a reliable blueprint for technology that could transport people to the stars.

However, the quests for the Logos shrines offer a metaphor that may take on new meanings as the centuries pass. *Tabula Rasa* asserts that the universe ultimately is meaningful, and that by increasing human scientific knowledge we gain enlightenment that is beneficial for life. Whether it really is necessary to voyage personally to other planets to achieve enlightenment is doubtful. However, surely some of the answers to our questions can be found only very far from home, so some people must travel there, or we must send smart machines to act as our avatars. Virtual worlds like *Tabula Rasa* can share the experience of cosmic discovery with the mass of humanity, although we may well wonder whether enough people are interested in this form of enlightenment to support them commercially.

References

1. http://en.wikipedia.org/wiki/Richard_Garriott
2. Bainbridge, W.S.: The Spaceflight Revolution. Wiley Interscience, New York (1976)
3. Bainbridge, W.S.: Goals in Space: American Values and the Future of Technology. State University of New York Press, Albany (1991)
4. Bainbridge, W.S.: Motivations for space exploration. Futures **41**, 514–522 (2009)
5. Dick, S.J.: Plurality of Worlds: The Origins of the Extraterrestrial Life Debate from Democritus to Kant. Cambridge University Press, New York (1982)
6. Swedenborg, E.: The Earths in Our Solar System. Massachusetts New Church Union, Boston (1910). http://books.google.com/books?id=GmcXAAAAYAAJ
7. Bainbridge, W.S.: Chariots of the gullible. In: Kendrick, Frazier (ed.) Paranormal Borderlands of Science, pp. 332–347. Prometheus, Buffalo (1981)
8. Palmer, S.J.: Aliens Adored. Rutgers University Press, New Brunswick (2004)
9. Lowell, P.: Mars as the Abode of Life. Macmillan, New York (1908)

10. Cooper, H.S.F.: The Search for Life on Mars. Holt, Rinehart and Winston, New York (1980)
11. Cameron, A.G.W. (ed.): Interstellar Communication. Benjamin, New York (1963); Sagan, C. (ed.): Communication with Extraterrestrial Intelligence. MIT Press, Cambridge (1973)
12. http://exoplanet.eu/
13. Jones, E.M.: Colonization of the Galaxy, Icarus **28**, 421–422 (1976); Hart, M.C.: An explanation for the absence of extraterrestrials on earth, Quart. J. R. Astr. Soc. **16**, 128–135 (1975); Clarke, J.N.: Extraterrestrial intelligence and galactic nuclear activity, Icarus **46**, 94–96 (1981)
14. Bainbridge, W.S.: Beyond bureaucratic policy: the spaceflight movement. In: Katz, J.E. (ed.) People in Space, pp. 153–163. Transaction, New Brunswick (1985)
15. http://www.richardinspace.com/
16. Bainbridge, W.S.: Massive questionnaires for personality capture. Soc. Sci. Comput. Rev. **21**(3), 267–280 (2003)
17. Wood, C., Storr, J., Reich, P.A.: Blissymbol Reference Guide. Blissymbolics Communication International, Toronto (1992)
18. Golden, C.: Firstborn. Pocket Books, New York (2007). p. 92, p. 232
19. www.logosatlas.com
20. Chang, K: After 17 years, a Glimpse of a Lunar Purchase. New York Times. http://www.nytimes.com/2010/03/31/science/space/31moon.html. Retrieved 20 Mar 2010

Chapter 4
Anarchy Online

In the distant future, a Solitus engineer named Nanobic explores Rubi-Ka, with his trusty robot companion, Tobor. Although covered largely with deserts, this planet does have some rivers and forests, which support a number of indigenous life forms, some of them hostile, and many dangerous if attacked. The landscape is also inhabited by many kind of fugitive mutant, the often horrifying results of genetic experimentation on human beings. Some sections of the planet have been terraformed to make them more like Earth, but most of it is a vast wasteland. Weapons and many other aspects of material culture are based on nanotechnology, and this is a true science fiction world that lacks any hint of magic or other supernatural forces.

Nanobic is my *Anarchy Online* avatar, so-named because he expresses my real-world involvement with the technological convergence movement that seeks to bring together nanotechnology, biotechnology, information technology, and new technologies based on cognitive science – the "NBIC" domains of science and engineering [1]. Thus a key framework for understanding both Rubi-Ka and the real human future is the nature of nanotechnology. It may turn out that "nano" is merely a politically advantageous buzzword for investing in conventional materials science and microbiology, achieving only limited and unexciting progress. Or, it may be that nano will radically increase our power over nature. The issue would then become how nanotechnology affects power relations between people.

The Planet Rubi-Ka

Anarchy Online (AO) is a pioneer among future-oriented role-playing virtual worlds, having been launched way back in 2001 by the Norwegian company, Funcom. This happens to be the same year that the National Science Foundation published the first major report on the societal implications of nanotechnology, of which I was co-editor [2]. Nano excitement was very much in the air, and it was entirely plausible that its long term consequences could be enormous. "Long-term" takes on a very precise meaning in the case of *Anarchy Online*, because the treaty that established

W.S. Bainbridge, *The Virtual Future*, Springer Series in Immersive Environments,
DOI 10.1007/978-0-85729-904-8_4, © Springer-Verlag London Limited 2011

the current political situation on Rubi-Ka was signed in the year 29,470. It divided the planet into two major spheres of influence, the Omni-Tek Corporation and the Clans, leaving a smaller territory Neutral [3]. My avatar, Nanobic, began as a Neutral but eventually pledged allegiance to the Omni-Tek Corporation.

For purposes of this chapter, I took Nanobic only up to level 36, and other researchers should explore *Anarchy Online's* full scope, encompassing four major expansions that extend the world and story well beyond the elementary stages described here. As with some other gameworlds discussed in this book, much of the early action centers on completing missions that only incidentally have anything to do with the overarching story on which the virtual world rests. They often involve killing someone who has been scheduled for execution by the government, typically a presumed criminal holed up in a hideout or a mad bomber who must be prevented from practicing his profession. Other missions require obtaining some valuable object from a similar location, or performing a task involving using an object at a particular location.

Some missions can be acquired from questgiver NPCs, but most of Nanobic's were obtained at dispensing machines to be found in cities and some lesser outposts. These stand in pairs, one for solo missions, and the other for groups. A primary slider in the machine's user interface sets the difficulty of the mission, from easy to hard. Six other sliders set the quality of the mission: good-bad, order-chaos, open-hidden, physical-mystical, head on-stealth, and earning credits versus experience points. However, when he was level 16, Nanobic found a nice area southeast of Newland City, where he and his trusty robot companion could kill animals and humanoid mutants, one after another, reaching level 19 far more quickly than available missions could have done – what is called *grinding* by gamers. It was especially informative to battle the mutants that were the results of genetic engineering experiments, in most cases unsuccessful ones. Apparently, specialized humanoids had been created, gone into production, then were discontinued or escaped. The surplus were left to wander the wastes of the planet, fair game for anyone who wanted to kill them. Depending upon their level, they were described as failed, rejected, discontinued, outcast or escapee.

One kind, called Claw-C22 looked like a human being but had a gigantic left hand, whereas the fingers on the right hand of a Tac-V85 are long and rubbery, resembling whips. Eye-Q93 was headless and had a huge right hand with an eyeball with which it would punch Nanobic. After killing one, he was able to examine the eye and discovered it contained a biotechnology laser weapon. Breed-B37 looked like a ordinary athletic human but possessed a silvery skin that presumably protected it against lasers. The Shade-Y42 type seems like a hybrid insect human, resembling a milder version of the extraterrestrial killer in the *Alien* movies. There were also many of the Rhinoman type, who battle by butting their heads into their enemies in a manner reminiscent of the rhinoceros, although lacking its distinct nose horn and sporting tusks on the lower jaw instead. These Rhinoman hybrids were not rejects, and groups of them inhabit wide areas north and east of Newland.

For grinding to work, the enemies must be of the right level to confer experience points without overpowering Nanobic, and the area must be one in which their hostile instincts are sufficiently suppressed so they will not attack without cause. AO uses the metaphor of a violence-suppression gas or field that can set the degree of aggression in an area, depending upon how dense it is. Notice that inhibition of aggression is conceptualized in terms of physical science, rather than legal prohibitions, another reflection of the strong physical science orientation of this world. Where the gas or field was relatively strong, Nanobic could trust he would not be attacked by all but a few especially hostile creatures – notably the nasty little roller rats – yet his own aggression against them was not inhibited.

My research goals required Nanobic to accept many missions from the dispensers, even though they tended not to be very informative about the culture. Many required him to walk a great distance, which took him past an occasional monster who could be safely and profitably killed, so the treks were not a total loss. At the destination, a typical mission required going into a *microinstance*, a small space separate from the wider world where all of the enemies were about the right level, often standing alone in separate rooms of a building, so a solo player could easily defeat them one at a time. On occasion, the enemies in microinstances did provide some information, as for example when Nanobic met a number of Aquaans around level 27, genetically engineered amphibian humanoids.

Although missions and grinding were not very valuable ethnographically, they indirectly led to things that were: examining the physical environment and gaining skills or objects. Missions forced Nanobic to travel over wide territories, thereby exploring them. Much time was invested running across wide wastelands, to get to the microinstance where the main work of a mission would be carried out. Rubi-Ka has a very large number of microinstances, all of which consist of mazes of rooms and corridors, either underground or inside a building. These are *persistent microinstances*, small subsets of the informatic geography that do not reset when a character leaves temporarily. Many of the rooms are occupied by enemies, as are some of the corridors. The rooms do not appear on the user interface map until they have been visited, and one cannot guess ahead of time which one holds the key to the mission. Figure 4.1 shows Nanobic and his robot companion, resting in one of these microinstance rooms, and contemplating some advanced technology, perhaps a holographic display of weather patterns on the planet.

The natural instinct when entering such a maze is to search the closest rooms first, but Nanobic developed a very different approach. First he would clear the main corridor of any enemies, then do the same for the rooms at the very ends. This would give him a long raceway along which he could run if he was having difficulty dealing with a powerful enemy or a pair of weaker enemies. While running around or back and forth, he and the enemies could exchange only occasional shots, so with the passage of time Nanobic could rebuild his health. If all else failed, he could run entirely out of the microinstance, rebuild health, and then reenter. Sometime he would run back and forth between two microinstances; if several enemies grouped near the entrance of one, leaving and returning later after entering the other would cause them to redistribute themselves in a more manageable arrangement. Thus, the ability to run fast and accurately through a maze was a definite advantage, as was the ability to run away from powerful enemies in open territory.

Fig. 4.1 Nanobic and Tobor inside a microinstance

Microinstances contain various boxes which can be opened, often to find valuable objects. After a couple of these objects turned out to be bombs that exploded in his hands, Nanobic timidly avoided this method of gaining goods. Instead, he took whatever he could when looting the corpses of enemies he had just killed. These resources could be sold or transformed into useful goods, and gradually an avatar would build up considerable wealth. At higher level, avatars could afford to rent their own apartments, fill them up with furniture and artworks, and even combine with friends to construct their own private city.

Scientific and Philosophical Basis

The novel *Prophet Without Honour* by Ragnar Tørnquist communicates the philosophy underlying *Anarchy Online*. It begins with two quotations about dreams. One was Edgar Allan Poe's famous words, "All that we see or seem, is but a dream within a dream" [4]. While acknowledging that a virtual world is a dream, Poe would say that the "real world" encompassing it is no less unreal. The other quotation came from Genesis 28:12, in the King James Version: "And he dreamed, and behold a ladder set up on the earth, and the top of it reached to heaven: and behold the angels of God ascending and descending on it." A virtual world can be a Jacob's ladder, to help humans achieve a higher level of being, first in their imaginations, and later, in reality.

The slogan of a recruitment poster for the monopolistic Omni-Tek corporation on Rubi-Ka says, "Don't dream it – be it." The question then becomes whether

Anarchy Online suggests a realistic means for achieving dreams of human transcendence, lifting us above this Earth, either to Heaven or to a habitable planet in the heavens. Or, perhaps the question becomes whether science and technology can help us become angels.

The *Anarchy Online* instruction manual explains that the fundamental technical basis in the world is nanotechnology: "All characters have access to nanotechnology through an invisible cloud of nano-bots surrounding them. Controlling these nano-bots requires skill and inner strength… Commanding the nano-bots is done through nano programs, which are uploaded to your program storage. Executing a program gives the nano-bots commands, which they carry out to produce the effect of the program, e.g. healing your body, increasing your aim, or damaging an enemy." "You need nano-energy to run programs; when you are out of nano-energy, you have to recharge before you can run any new programs" [5]. Nanobots are nanoscale robots. Tørnquist's novel defines a nanobot thus: "a machine so small it can go anywhere, so versatile that it can build and repair anything" [6]. Elsewhere Tørnquist explains nanobots are "capable of receiving programming, of self-replication, and of performing automated tasks in cooperation with other bots" [7].

As luck would have it, I played a central if not exactly influential role in the National Nanotechnology Initiative, helping to organize several major conferences of nanoscientists and nanoengineers, co-editing major reports both inside and outside government, and writing extensively on the social implications of nano [8]. Thus, my during my experience in *Anarchy Online*, I constantly pondered the relationship between real nano and fictional nano, with an unusual awareness that the two often combined in powerful ways in the history of the nanotechnology movement in the real world. The website of the National Nanotechnology Initiative defines the real nano:

> Nanotechnology is the understanding and control of matter at dimensions between approximately 1 and 100 nanometers, where unique phenomena enable novel applications. Encompassing nanoscale science, engineering, and technology, nanotechnology involves imaging, measuring, modeling, and manipulating matter at this length scale. A nanometer is one-billionth of a meter. A sheet of paper is about 100,000 nanometers thick; a single gold atom is about a third or a nanometer in diameter. Dimensions between approximately 1 and 100 nanometers are known as the nanoscale. Unusual physical, chemical, and biological properties can emerge in materials at the nanoscale. These properties may differ in important ways from the properties of bulk materials and single atoms or molecules [9].

In computer hardware technology, transistors and other microelectronic chip components are already smaller than 100 nm. In biology, researchers are learning about the nanoscale structures and processes inside living cells, gaining detailed knowledge about how the atoms of life fit and interact together. Autonomous nanobots that can carry out complex jobs remain a fantasy. Whether future centuries will be able to build nanobots is doubtful, and we are nowhere near being able to do so today. Yes, it is plausible to believe that we could engineer viruses to do useful jobs in medicine and biotechnology industries, and they operate at the nanoscale. However there is good reason to believe that nanobots based on non-biological principles are simply impossible.

Science fiction and a popular nanotech social movement have presented a very much rosier picture, based on superficial literary analogies and unrealistic assumptions. The key person in this phenomenon is K. Eric Drexler, who first came to notice as a prominent member of the L-5 Society, a group dedicated to building cities in outer space. In 1986, Drexler published a non-technical book, *Engines of Creation*, promoting his vision of nanotechnology, and then a second one, *Unbounding the Future*, in 1991 [10]. In his 1992 book, *Nanosystems*, he presented his ideas more technically, in a way that many non-technical readers wrongly assumed demonstrated their feasibility [11]. Drexler often refers to biological systems as proof that mechanisms can operate at the nanoscale, and to microelectronics as a second analogy to bolster plausibility. But his own idea is very different. He primarily conceptualizes nanoscale machines in terms of the principles of mechanical engineering, as assemblages of wheels, gears, and other clockwork mechanisms, under some kind of computer guidance.

This was very easy for non-technical people to visualize, and one additional idea seemed to add great power to nanotechnology. Drexler and the science fiction writers who took up his ideas said that nanoscale machines could self-assemble. They could be imagined either as armies of tiny robots, or as miniature factory assembly lines, that grab atoms from surrounding resources and fit them together to make anything we desire, including more copies of themselves. Unfortunately, real-world factors like van der Waals forces transform conditions on the nanoscale, compared with the much larger-scale objects that humans can see and manipulate with their hands. Conventional mechanical engineering cannot work on the nanoscale.

Richard Smalley, one of the scientists who contributed to the National Nanotechnology publications I co-edited, refuted Drexler. Smalley was a genuine expert, having shared in a 1985 Nobel Prize for discovering fullerenes, notably the molecule that arranged 60 carbon atoms in the form of a hollow sphere, whereas Drexler had little training and no research background in chemistry. Smalley calculated that even if nanobots were possible, they would operate so slowly as to be useless, and be exceedingly difficult to control and to supply with the resources they would need. Drexler had imagined assemblers similar in design to the arms of industrial robots, but Smalley pointed out that at the molecular scale their fingers would be both too fat and too sticky. The fingers are too fat because it takes many atoms to build a structure complex enough to function as a hand, but the individual atoms are too small. An analogy from mechanical engineering is if the pin-setting machines in bowling alleys had to be made entirely from bowling balls. The sticky finger problem arises from the fact that atoms are not hard spheres, like bowling balls, but are bundles of forces that interact with nearby atoms. Smalley wrote, "the atoms of the manipulator hands will adhere to the atom that is being moved. So it will often be impossible to release this miniscule building block in precisely the right spot" [12].

Smalley once commented to me that biological processes work only because they occur in an aqueous solution. Water is a compound of hydrogen and oxygen, and the third most common element in the body is carbon. But Drexler's nanobots are based on chemical elements of much greater atomic weight, which means chemically much less reactive. Take carbon, for example, with 6 protons and an atomic weight of about 12. (Atomic weight is based on a mixture of isotopes with different numbers of neutrons, so the weights are not exact integers.) The next element in carbon's column of the periodic table of the elements is silicon with 14 protons and an atomic weight of almost exactly 28. Science fiction writers have often imagined extraterrestrial life based on silicon rather than carbon, and the familiar toy "silly putty" and silicone rubber substitutes are silicon-based compounds that have some of the look and feel of organic substances. But silicones cannot compete with carbon-based compounds for the reactivity and complexity that make carbon the building-block of life. A century ago, biochemist Laurence Henderson observed that life would have been impossible in the universe had the properties of carbon been even slightly less conducive to it [13]. Thus the fact that living cells consist of assemblages of nanoscale machine-like structures does not at all imply that it would be possible to achieve the same thing with non-organic nanoscale machines built from other, heavier chemical elements.

Ultimately, therefore, Rubi-Ka is a fantasy world, comparable to those that do not employ metaphors from advanced technology. One of the decorative objects one could buy to put in one's apartment, a "Wonderful Marble Statue of the Goddess Buffy Summers," referred to the main character of the movie and television series, *Buffy the Vampire Slayer*. Its description noted, "Early during the twenty-first century there was a cult worshiping the Goddess of Buff. It is now believed that the Buff religion is one of the major contributors to the Buffs generated by nano technology. Some people believe that all nanobots contain the essence of Goddess Summers." The pun on *buffs* refers to the fact that temporary enhancements to a character's abilities, rather like magic empowerment spells, are commonly called *buffs*. Although expressed through television and print media rather than an online environment, Buffy has some of the qualities of a virtual world for fans, an imaginary world called the *Buffyverse* [14].

Anarchy Nanotechnology

The part of the universe we experience in *Anarchy Online* is central to nanoconvergence in the 295th century, and may exhibit it in more fully developed form than other places. Rubi-Ka is valuable for the *notum* that the planet possesses, a mineral that greatly improves the functioning of nanobots [15]. Ordinary manufacturing is not done in factories, but by a nanoassembler machine called a *builder*. Although it could potentially make anything, from food to weapons, it was not magic. "It could only create what it'd been programmed to create, and the complexity and authenticity of what it could create was dependant on how much energy it had at its disposal. The builder needed raw materials to work from – naturally occurring chemical elements, elementary particles... space dust?" [16].

Logically enough, the precondition for *Anarchy Online* technology is the skill set of the individual character. To begin with, the player must choose one of 14 different specializations: metaphysicist, adventurer, engineer, soldier, keeper, shade, fixer, agent, trader, doctor, enforcer, bureaucrat, martial artist, or nanotechnician. I selected *engineer* for Nanobic, because I wanted him to be able to craft and control robots, for research I was doing on secondary avatars. I could have selected *bureaucrat*, who also can control robots, but engineering seemed more central to the technology of robotics. Given my involvement in nanoconvergence, and Nanobic's very name, I might have selected *nanotechnician*, but all technology in this world is based on nano, and I wanted to emphasize convergence with other fields.

As Nanobic gradually climbed the ladder of experience levels, he gained improvement points that could be invested in abilities. *Anarchy Online* has one of the most complex systems of ability choice for a character, although *Entropia* and some of the other virtual worlds described in this book are close rivals in complexity. There are fully 10 general categories encompassing a total of 75 parameters: general abilities, body (physical abilities), melee (close distance fighting), miscellaneous weapons, ranged weapons (shooting at a distance), speed (such as top speed running or swimming), trade and repair, nano and aiding, spying, and navigation with includes the ability to read maps of various levels of difficulty. Naturally, Nanobic always upgraded his running speed, the abilities that strengthened his defensive shield and the pistols he used for weapons, plus the talents needed to maximize the effectiveness of Tobor.

When he reached level 30, Nanobic noticed belatedly that his otherwise trusty robot was no longer very helpful in fights, and determined to upgrade it. At a store he examined the various automaton programs that were for sale. His immediate favorite was a quality level 50 gladiator bot that cost 43,277 credits. He had enough money, 58,700 credits, which would leave him 15,000 for supplies, but being only at level 30, his abilities were too low to use this advanced bot. To learn and run the gladiator program, he would need to have reached ability level 246 in both matter creation and space time control, but he was only 148 in each. According to his improvement points display, matter creation "is used to make matter appear from energy, the basic functioning of the nano bots." Space time control "is the nano skill used to run nano programs affecting space and time." Although nanobots may draw some energy from the body of the person using them, the creators of *Anarchy Online* recognized this would not be enough [17], and they also suggested that nanobots for different purposes could be created from energy. Of course as the reverse process in nuclear weapons demonstrates, a very huge amount of energy would in fact make very little matter.

Nanobic had a few spare improvement points he could have invested in raising each of these two parameters, but his experience level would have prevented him from getting much above 160. After looking at other choices that were above his capability range, he settled on a rather inferior 4,721-credit semi-sentient automaton that had a quality level of only 17 and required only 89 points in the two crucial parameters. Much below what Nanobic thought he could handle, it was a big improvement over the feeble bot he had been using. For 13,275 credits, he also bought the quality level 30 program, "partial harmonic cocoon," to add to his protective shields. The sales literature said it "surrounds the target with a defensive barrier that deflects a portion of all damage being dealt by the attacker away from the target. Some of this damage is deflected back onto the attacker."

In theory, an automaton consists of the shell that is its visible body, a swarm of nanobots that perform its actions within this shell, and the program that guides them. To launch the semi-sentient automaton, Nanobic went through the following actions. First he clicked an icon on his pet toolbar to run the nanoprogram to create the shell, which appeared in his inventory backpack. He then right-clicked on the shell to launch it and fill it with nanobots. The bots cost him 172 units of nano energy, which he could easily replenish from a store he carried in his backpack. The semi-sentient automaton also required 6 nano controlling units or NCUs, compared with only 3 required by his old robot. These NCUs are like RAM memory space in a computer, limiting the number of programs of various sizes that can be run simultaneously. Nanobic's shields and weapon enhancements also took up NCUs, and during missions at this point in his progress, typically 19 or 20 of his 21 NCUs were monopolized by one program or another. For example, his partial harmonic cocoon took up 10 NCUs.

Automata are often killed during missions and must be restored in the same manner they are created. Occasionally, Nanobic could reuse the shell of his old automaton, but most of the time he had to create a new one. He liked to think of them as the same being, a kind of robot friend, restored to life, rather than a fresh creation. When one launched, its default name was Engineer Automaton II, but to give a sense of personality to it, he called his companion Tobor. This common robot name is the word "robot" spelled backward, and from my childhood I recall where it originated. On the television series, "Captain Video and His Video Rangers," in November 1953, a scientist put the finishing touch on a powerful robot he had made, by using a stencil to paint "Robot I" on it. But he held the stencil backward, so the result was "I Tobor."

To name the robot this time, Nanobic used a more modern method, writing a one-line macro program. In the ordinary text chat, he typed "macro Tobor/pet rename Tobor." This created a macro he could invoke in either of two ways. First, he had to select the robot by clicking on it, then he either entered "/Tobor" into the chat line or clicked a black square icon with "Tobor" written on it that he had placed on his pet toolbar. Using the same macro system, he prepared Tobor to speak words of encouragement: "Nanobic is my hero!" (macro Hero/pet chat "Nanobic is my hero!") and "Great job boss!" (macro Job/pet chat "Great job boss!"). A useful standard macro, "/pet report," made Tobor upload information about his status to the chat text. Here are four examples from one mission:

Tobor: Health: 58% Nano: 100% NCU: 9/23 Position: 14,234 Fighting: Soft Scoundrel
Tobor: Health: 54% Nano: 100% NCU: 9/23 Position: 55,238 Fighting: Soft Nanoaddict
Tobor: Health: 66% Nano: 100% NCU: 9/23 Position: 40,244 Fighting: Soft Torpedo
Tobor: Health: 100% Nano: 100% NCU: 9/23 Position: 6,236

The first three of the reports show Tobor in combat, and the fact that his health is lower than 100% shows he has taken some damage. In the last one, he has rested and his health has returned to 100%. During this mission, he did not use up any nano energy, so it was always 100%, and the "NCU: 9/23: refers to the fact that the shield Nanobic gave him took up 9 of Tobor's own nano controlling units. The position employs a simple X,Y coordinate system within the microinstance to say where Tobor is at the moment.

Note the three different enemies the pair fought and defeated during this episode: soft scoundrel, soft nanoaddict, and soft torpedo. These are job titles for NPCs, rather than individual names, and I believe the word "soft" refers to software. Europeans whose native language is not English often use the term *soft* to mean *software*. A significant fraction of NPC enemies encountered in other battles also possessed technological job titles. Some are clearly related to computers, including botrunner, rebooter, programthief, programsmuggler, gridcourier, and perhaps also assembler. Others denote different orientations toward technology in general: techhunter, techdabbler, and techrejector.

General stores include a bank machine, so Nanobic took every opportunity to store some of the loot he had acquiring recently. General stores and special implant stores both have facilities for installing nano technology implants. He contemplated buying high-level implants, but again his abilities were not yet sufficient to use them, so he installed a couple of low-level ones he happened to have acquired during his missions.

Implants are nanotechnology body parts that can replace ordinary organs and limbs, thereby enhancing the character's abilities in specific ways. They are one kind of thing that can be installed from the character's inventory backpack (perhaps after being stored in his bank account for a while). Two other equipable items – weapons and armor – are familiar from other gameworlds. When Nanobic happened to loot a nice pistol from one of his enemies, he would immediately check to see if it were better than one of the two pistols he was already using, one in each hand. If so, and if he had the necessary abilities and ammunition to use the pistol, he would simply drop the old one and pick up the new pistol in his hand. Similarly, he could don a new helmet in the field without special effort. This is not the case with implants.

In theory, installing an implant would require major surgery, but it can be performed swiftly and painlessly. Each general store has one or more surgery clinics, bureau-sized pieces of equipment which the player right-clicks to get permission to exchange implants for a period of 5 min. Specialized implant stores tend also to have a bloody surgical operating table, but thankfully it is not necessary to use it. On this particular occasion, having just reached level 30, Nanobic installed a section of spine called a *waist implant* that was quality level 27 and would boost his maximum health by 35 points. He also installed a pair of lungs called a *chest implant* that was quality level 23 and boosted his nano by 21 units. Implants confer a wide range of abilities, potentially adding to any of the attributes of the character. They also differ in terms of how many cluster components of what kinds have been installed inside them to augment their owner's powers.

Anarchy Society

With good reason, this virtual world is called *Anarchy*: A previously monolithic tyranny has broken down into competing factions, and its fragmentation has unleashed widespread lawlessness. The Omni-Tek corporation held a thousand-year lease on the planet Rubi-Ka, but the Clans rebelled against the company's oppressive ownership. The very name *Clans* suggests that they were *primitive rebels*, lacking a fully modern ideology of class conflict, comparable to the countless minor rebellions against world capitalist neocolonialism of the nineteenth through twenty-first centuries [18].

Omni-Tek was born millennia earlier, on January 27, 2007 to be exact, in San Francisco, with the merger of two companies to form Farmatek, a conglomerate that combined biotechnology with information technology [19]. Within a very few years, and with input from shadowy conspiracies that had already been at work for decades, Farmatek had expanded the bio-info convergence to include nano and produced nanobots capable of doing almost anything, including making a human immortal.

What happened next in the fictional history is apparently unknown to the people on Rubi-Ka, but quite astonishing. The leaders of Farmatek went literally underground, where they cultivated their immortality – calling themselves *Omegas* – while the humans remaining on the surface of Earth were largely exterminated. Secretly, Farmatek spread genetically engineered plagues that killed off most people and left the survivors in savagery. Although the philosophy behind this near-genocide is not explained at length in Tørnquist's novel, its logic is clear enough. Immortality is incompatible with ordinary demographics, because if people are born but do not die the planet could not support the increasing numbers. Rather than release immortality and wait for a demographic crash that might lead to total extinction of the species, Farmatek carried out severe preemptive pruning of humanity, in hopes that eventually travel to the stars would provide an escape from this demographic trap. At one point in his novel, Tørnquist quotes the classic science fiction writer, Robert A. Heinlein: "The Earth is just too small and fragile a basket for the human race to keep all its eggs in" [20]. Nanobic is a *Solitus*, a descendent of the remaining surface-dwelling humans.

Thousands of years later, the competition between Omni-Tek and the Clans reflects not only the eternal conflict between masters and slaves, but more fundamentally the issue of whether property is legitimately held by an abstract corporation under the rule of formal law or by a people through either ancient custom or living democracy. More abstractly, the conflict is between order and freedom, or between oppression and chaos as they would slander each other.

Slogans on wall signs throughout Rubi-Ka express the Omni-Tek ideology of order, stability, and obedience: "Omni-Tek... behave exemplary." "Unfocused minds fumble." "We bring order." "Be good! Now!" "No intoxication." "No running!" "No bleeding!" "We will keep you safe." "Omni-Tek is your friend." "Join our family, Omni-Tek," "Get well with Omni-Med."

Clan ideology, in contrast, stresses individualism and populism: "Clans: your future. You decide." "Rubi-Ka belongs to the people, not to the corporation."

"Omni-Tek is bland – join the Clans." A character speaks for the Clans in Tørnquist's novel, saying Rubi-Ka should be a "place of opportunity and progress. Omnis are reactionary, conservative. The clans are… more fun. They encourage individuality, reject conformity" [21].

The application form for joining Omni-Tek calls the Clans "rebel scum." The equivalent Clan form refers to their "struggle for independence" and calls Omni-Tek "oppressors." Forms for both factions warn it will be very difficult to change affiliations later and admonish: "Take your stand in the struggle and stay with it." Outside the towns, a more complete kind of anarchy prevails, as large numbers of wild animals and escaped human genetic experiments roam uncontrolled, posing dangers or opportunities to travelers.

When he reached level 30, Nanobic decided it was time to join one of the main factions, in order to gain more insight into the conflict between them. A number of Neutral quests had already taken him into Clan territory, and he believed he understood how many people might resent the degree of control Omni-Tek sought to impose on its citizens. Also, he figured it was possible that Omni-Tek might afford more training in the use of advanced technology. Therefore, he resolved to join the corporation, but beforehand he would do one last tour as a Neutral, including territories outside corporation control.

He employed the standard teleportation system called the *whom-pahs*. The *Anarchy Online* wiki explains, this is a "system of transportation used throughout Rubi-Ka. In essence, the whom-pah system breaks an individual down at the cellular level, transporting them instantly to another location on-planet, and rebuilding their body. Urban myths say the name is derived from the sound the whom-pah makes" [22]. There is a second more complex teleportation system called The Grid, giving more convenient access to several locations, but it requires the user to have achieved various levels of "computer literacy" to reach different destinations. In contrast, the whom-pah system is a little inconvenient but open to anybody.

The whom-pah system consists of three separate networks, Neutral (connecting 5 locations), Clan (8 locations), and Omni-Tek (9 locations), connected to each other only via the very limited ICC base operated by the Interstellar Confederation of Corporations that oversees the truce. Nanobic actually visited each of the 23 locations via the whom-pahs and inspected the environment at least briefly. When he visited both 2HO and 4 Holes in the Omni-Tek network, he was immediately attacked, and he exercised caution at all locations despite his supposedly protective Neutral status.

Exploring Tir, the Clan capital, was somewhat dangerous, because the guards were hostile to Neutrals and attacked Nanobic if he neared them, unlike the guards in other Clan towns who were indifferent to him. As Fig. 4.2 shows, the layout of this extensive city was complex, and the architecture was appealing if somewhat stern in mood. The buildings tended to be a combination of subdued sandy and gray colors, but lacking the orange tone of the surrounding desert. Smaller buildings were assemblages of blocks representing rooms and substructures, often topped with a darker gray dome. The low structure near the middle of Fig. 4.2 is the whom-pah teleport station.

Fig. 4.2 Tir, the commercial capital city of the Clans

While clean and in perfect repair, Tir was rather less attractive than other Clan towns, and it had a few disreputable qualities like those Nanobic observed later in the largest Omni-Tek city. Most notable was a nightclub with a pink neon sign showing two apparently naked women kickboxing, with the slogan, "Enjoy it while it lasts." Inside, Nanobic did indeed find two women boxing, but not kicking, in a shallow pool of water, clad in two-piece bathing suits and boots. One knocked the other unconscious, and Nanobic found he could not climb into the pool to help the poor woman, so he left in disgust.

A second major Clan city is Athen, divided into two parts, Old Athen and West Athen. Architecture varies, but one large section consists of tall, almost prismatic buildings, dark in color, surrounded by carefully tended lawns and trees. Bliss, a small fortress town, has trees and lawns as well and is built around a park with pond, but the buildings are very solid gray pillboxes, looking as if their rounded walls were intended to resist artillery bombardment. The Avalon district boasts an imposing castle named Camelot, which, like the surrounding walled town, is built from stone that varies in color from medium gray to brown.

The largest corporation city, Omni-1, is divided into two main areas somewhat distant from each other and connected via whom-pah, the Trade District and the Entertainment District. The apartment, office, and business buildings are massive, although slum districts composed of ramshackle shacks exist nearby. Among the recreational businesses is Baboons, a nightclub that has dancing NPCs. The nearby Rompa Bar is a restaurant, with artwork on the walls and many booths for patrons. Its bathrooms are positively primitive, not unlike those found on Earth today. The men's room has troughs for urinating in, and private stalls for doing more serious business. The ladies' room has a nice basin for washing hands, lacks the troughs, and possesses similar stalls. After so many thousands of years, one would have thought that some micro teleportation system would have been devised to dispose of human waste products in a more advanced manner, without the need of privacy or bathrooms. However, there is something reassuring about seeing that the inhabitants of Rubi-Ka are not very different from ourselves, after all.

As the Clans have their Athen, Omni-Tek has its Rome. Simple notions of classical civilization connect Athens to democracy, and Rome to imperial tyranny, which is mirrored in the comparison between Clans and Omni-Tek. One reading of classical history is that it was a race to see which city state or tribe could dominate the entire Mediterranean: Athens, Sparta, Thebes, Macedon, Carthage, or Rome. As the *Anarchy Online* wiki explains, "True to its name sake, Rome is a towering city with grand architecture the combines the noir aesthetic of Omni-Tek with a more gothic approach to towers; add in thousands of lights and the city is quite breath taking at night" [23].

Nanobic also visited the Galway Castle area, which seems more like a resort town of single-storey buildings with a two-storey villa than a traditional castle. Just south of a nature preserve, it boasts an heroic statue: Galway – "A born again Omni-Tek." Depicting a man who looks like a ranger or explorer, the statue projects a violet laser message writing on the sky, "Galway Omni-Tek."

Once Nanobic had joined Omni-Tek, he undertook several quests for the corporation, being treated to its propaganda. Here is an assassination quest notice: "I know, it never feels like every finished mission really furthers our cause. Believe me… this is not a pre-programmed propaganda machine telling you this… the clans do indeed tremble when they think of all the people doing their share in the good fight. We must all pull together to succeed! Quickly, friend, there is a mad bomber planning new attacks in Omni-1 Trade. He is in a building. Go there and kill him and Winstone Shone will respawn back in the asylum." The mission dispenser options were set for a "Good" quest, which probably explains why Shone was described as a mad bomber who will come back to life in the insane asylum which is his proper home, a situation that justifies the assassination to protect the public and get him the psychiatric treatment he needs.

Another corporation assignment recognizes the competing ideology of the warring faction: "To the clans you, my friend, are an oppressor. To the clans you, your friends, your family, are all slave-dealers and power mongers. How does that make you feel? Well, hold on to that feeling, let it carry you through doing your duty to your friends, your family and your employer." Yet another dismisses ideology in favor of loyalty: "When all the lies of the propaganda war are stripped away… what remains is those values we know in our hearts to be true: friends are friends, family is family! We, Omni-Tek ask you not to fight for lofty ideals or abstract values. We ask you to fight for what is closest to you… your family and friends. Believe in them, and believe in yourself!" A fourth assignment put the point more personally: "Do your duty, and you shall be remembered. Be selfish, and you shall be forgotten!"

At level 35, Nanobic traded in his feeble quality 17 android for a much better one at quality level 33, although he continued to call it Tobor. As the android represented nanoconvergence with information technology, convergence with biotechnology was represented by his new quality 33 bio-comminutor which could extract valuable blood plasma from samples of monster flesh. To operate this device, he had to increase his pharmaceuticals skill from 28 to 62. He happened to have a dozen monster parts of varying quality in his bank vault, and when he translated them into blood plasma he was pleased to discover he could sell them for 10,667 credits.

He decided to get an apartment in Rome, very near the whom-pah and Grid access. The apartment complex had a secondary virtual world, called *Holo World*, which was intended as a training simulation for novices. The monsters infesting it were far below Nanobic's level, so he merely enjoyed it as a recreational park. The nearby Grid was also a kind of secondary virtual world, represented a bluish space with pathways on several levels that allowed transport between locations in the main virtual world, rather like travel through a hypothetical hyperspace. The traveler is represented as an inverted pyramid, and when Nanobic traveled with Tobor, the robot was represented by a separate such icon. However he conceptualized himself, whether as a two-legged human or an inverted pyramid, Nanobic had found a stable identity as an employee of the Omni-Tek Corporation, on the planet Rubi-Ka. Given that AO does not require a paid subscription, he can live there forever and ever, or at least as long as *Anarchy Online* exists.

Central to the *Anarchy Online* ideology, and to other gameworlds, is avatar immortality. A character always revives after death, but it is possible to imagine *permadeath*, the kind from which there is no return [24]. One of Nanobic's most interesting missions was killing Cyrus Cervenak, who was murdering avatars. As the quest instructions explained, "The Permanent Killing Weapon is quite new and not functioning 100% yet. (Apparently, not all people are susceptible to it.) When the killer manages to encode the neural signal of the victim onto a Neural Disruption Weapon, and then strikes the killing blow with it, the 'essence' or 'soul' of the victim is lost to the world! The result is terrible: no resurrection in our wonderful resurrection machines, resulting in permanent DEATH! (As in the 'good' old way.) Please stop this lunatic before he can send more people away with no return ticket! Hurry, he is in Galway County for 48 h! May Omni-Tek rule forever!"

When Nanobic and Tobor killed Cervenak, they learned nothing further about the Permanent Killing Weapon, but the very concept raises two fundamental questions about the future of technology: First, for every good technology, will there also be an evil counter technology or an unintended consequence that leaves us no better than before? Second, how far toward godlike power can technology take us, even before we ask whether it will make us more like gods or like demons?

Tørnquist's novel, *Prophet Without Honour*, contains one of the great scenes of science fiction literature, the excruciatingly difficult series of steps a woman named Emilie must undertake in order to kill her immortal Omega husband, Dr. Jonas Stenberg. The eponymous prophet seems to be David, the son of Jonas with a Solitus slave girl named Katerina. The novel is a set of flashbacks and episodes involving different characters, framed by the slow interstellar travel of David as a grown, immortal man, headed from Earth to Rubi-Ka toward a destiny that is not described in this book. The title, of course, comes from Matthew 13.57: "Only in his home town and in his own house is a prophet without honour" [25].

Despite having perfected themselves physically, the Omegas had gradually lost the capacity to reproduce. Thus this pregnancy was a miracle, and one worth keeping secret. Emilie became obsessed with the pregnancy, as if the child were going to be her own, and an argument with Katrina led to the girl's accidental death. Jonas performed an emergency Caesarean, then prepared to give the child over to the Omega authorities. Crazed by her desire to have the child herself, Emilie decides to kill her husband and hide the body.

As Tørnquist explains, "To kill an Omega, you had to cause a huge amount of damage in a very short time so that the bots would not have time to make repairs before the brain was deprived of oxygen for too long, although with the revival techniques at their disposal, that might take hours. Or, in a much less messy (but potentially much crueler) approach, confining a person so completely for so long that the bots stopped functioning and the body was returned to its mortal, and vulnerable, state, at which point death would be inevitable" [26]. After cutting her husband to pieces, she dragged his body into the basement, used a spade to cut off his head, then covered him with quick-hardening cement. Before the nanobots could complete their repair, he was encased in concrete, and we do not know if he regained consciousness as he finally and permanently died. Shocking as it is, this episode is a nice metaphor for the problem not only of immortality, but of perfect stability more generally: Absolute security is not compatible with creativity, growth, and freedom.

Conclusion

Nanobic continues to explore Rubi-Ka, but the needs of this research project do not require him to go above the rather low level 36 he has currently reached. If he were to achieve the top level of 220, the following message would be distributed to everyone: "You feel the core of your being shift, as the source makes room for a divine presence. 'Nanobic' has reached enlightenment." That may never happen, but even his limited experience on Rubi-Ka has given us valuable insights on how nanotechnology could conceivably change some aspects of human life, and of how the constant tug-of-war between social order and individual liberty may play out over the coming millennia.

Some of the shops in Rubi-Ka's cities sell instruction manuals, and the description of *A Guide to Creating Useful Medical Libraries* offers insight into the limits of future engineering: "Jane Flowers once said: 'There is more available technology than there are creative people to make use of it.' Partly the reason for this is the heavy restrictions put on the use of much of this technology. The heavy lock and seals put on many technologically advanced items doesn't make it easier. Be aware that the methods described in this document might not be legal to use on your particular planet." The laws prohibiting non-biological nanobots were not, however, enacted by Omni-Tek or any other human authority, but by Nature herself.

Despite this technical limitation, *Anarchy Online* offers a fascinating picture of the human future, in which technologies we cannot yet imagine set a new stage for the eternal human struggle between control and freedom.

References

1. Roco, M.C., Bainbridge, W.S. (eds.): Converging Technologies for Improving Human Performance. Kluwer, Dordrecht (2003); Bainbridge, W.S., Roco, M.C. (eds.): Managing Nano-Bio-Info-Cogno Innovations: Converging Technologies in Society. Springer, Berlin (2006); Progress in Convergence: Technologies for Human Wellbeing. New York Academy of Sciences, New York (2006); Bainbridge, W.S.: Nanoconvergence. Prentice-Hall, Upper Saddle River (2007)
2. Roco, M.C., Bainbridge, W.S. (eds.): Societal Implications of Nanoscience and Nanotechnology. Kluwer, Dordrecht (2001)
3. http://www.anarchy-online.com/anarchy/frontend/files/CONTENT/download/documents/tir_accord.pdf
4. http://www.heise.de/ix/raven/Literature/Authors/poe/works/dream.within.a.dream.html
5. Anarchy Online: Getting Started on RubiKa. http://www.anarchy-online.com/anarchy/frontend/files/CONTENT/gameguide.pdf; pp. 43, 28
6. Tørnquist, R.: Prophet Without Honour. Online novel at http://www.anarchy-online.com/anarchy/frontend/files/CONTENT/download/documents/prophet_without_honour.pdf, p. 33 (2001)
7. Tørnquist, R.: Prophet Without Honour. Online novel at http://www.anarchy-online.com/anarchy/frontend/files/CONTENT/download/documents/prophet_without_honour.pdf, p. 68 (2001)
8. Roco, M.C., Bainbridge, W.S. (eds.): Societal Implications of Nanoscience and Nanotechnology. Kluwer, Dordrecht (2001); Nanotechnology: Societal Implications – Maximizing Benefit for Humanity. Springer, Berlin (2006); Nanotechnology: Societal Implications – Individual Perspectives. Springer, Berlin(2006)
9. http://www.nano.gov/html/facts/whatIsNano.html
10. Drexler, K.E.: Engines of Creation. Anchor Doubleday, Garden City (1986); Drexler, K.E., Peterson, C.: Unbounding the Future: The Nanotechnology Revolution. William Morrow, New York (1991)
11. Drexler, K.E.: Nanosystems: Molecular Machinery, Manufacturing, and Computation. Wiley-Interscience, New York (1992)
12. Smalley, R.E.: Of chemistry, love and nanobots. Sci. Am. **285**(3), 74–75 (2001)
13. Henderson, L.J.: The Fitness of the Environment: An Inquiry into the Biological Significance of the Properties of Matter. Macmillan Company, New York (1913)
14. http://en.wikipedia.org/wiki/Category:Buffyverse
15. Tørnquist, R.: Prophet Without Honour. Online novel at http://www.anarchy-online.com/anarchy/frontend/files/CONTENT/download/documents/prophet_without_honour.pdf, p. 10 (2001)
16. Tørnquist, R.: Prophet Without Honour. Online novel at http://www.anarchy-online.com/anarchy/frontend/files/CONTENT/download/documents/prophet_without_honour.pdf, p. 13 (2001)
17. Tørnquist, R.: Prophet Without Honour. Online novel at http://www.anarchy-online.com/anarchy/frontend/files/CONTENT/download/documents/prophet_without_honour.pdf, p. 302 (2001)
18. Hobsbawm, E.J.: Primitive Rebels: Studies in Archaic Forms of Social Movements in the 19th and 20th Centuries. Manchester University press, Manchester (1959); Wolf, E.R.: Peasant

Wars of the Twentieth Century. Harper and Row, New York (1969); Chirot, D.: Social Change in the Twentieth Century. Harcourt Brace Jovanovich, New York (1977)

19. Tørnquist, R.: Prophet Without Honour. Online novel at http://www.anarchy-online.com/anarchy/frontend/files/CONTENT/download/documents/prophet_without_honour.pdf, p. 31 (2001)

20. Tørnquist, R.: Prophet Without Honour. Online novel at http://www.anarchy-online.com/anarchy/frontend/files/CONTENT/download/documents/prophet_without_honour.pdf, p. 290 (2001) this widely quoted, characteristic statement by Heinlein lacks a precise citation, but it is often claimed he said these words in an undated speech, rather than writing the words in one of his stories.

21. Tørnquist, R.: Prophet Without Honour. Online novel at http://www.anarchy-online.com/anarchy/frontend/files/CONTENT/download/documents/prophet_without_honour.pdf, p. 308 (2001)

22. http://anarchyonline.wikia.com/wiki/Whompah

23. http://anarchyonline.wikia.com/wiki/Rome

24. Klastrup, L.: Death matters: understanding gameworld experiences. In: Proceedings of the International Conference on Advances in Computer Entertainment Technology (ACE) 14–16 June 2006, Hollywood CA. Association for Computing Machinery, New York (2006)

25. Tørnquist, R.: Prophet Without Honour. Online novel at http://www.anarchy-online.com/anarchy/frontend/files/CONTENT/download/documents/prophet_without_honour.pdf, p. 320 (2001)

26. Tørnquist, R.: Prophet Without Honour. Online novel at http://www.anarchy-online.com/anarchy/frontend/files/CONTENT/download/documents/prophet_without_honour.pdf, p. 252 (2001)

Chapter 5
Entropia Universe

The planet Calypso is in a class by itself. It is not the playing field for an online combat game, or the electronic embodiment of an existing fantasy. Rather, it presents itself as a new world that people can explore and where they can build a real economy. On Calypso, two large continents are accessible, Eudoria and Amethera, plus a small space station and a resort on an asteroid. All four areas are populated with hostile beasts and possess mineral resources. Originally opened for colonists in 2003, *Entropia Universe* underwent a major geological upheaval in August 2009, and for many months the aftershocks were still being felt. This virtual world is admirable for pioneering a new economic model for online environments, and for being a plausible simulation of real extraterrestrial colonization, but it is also socially problematic and problematizes the future of humanity in outer space.

Calypso's challenges are chiefly economic. How can individual pioneers make a living in the new world? Will they progress beyond mere survival to support a prosperous economy in which individuals trade resources and manufacture goods? What social forms serving what goals for their members can arise on this initially fragile economic basis? Will the economy of colonists provide profits for the company that transported them to Calypso? Over the 7 years of its existence, Entropia Universe has often been the focus of publicity implying it had achieved a breakthrough for virtual worlds, leaping to a higher level of economic success – a real success, not a virtual one. Disappointment has often followed enthusiasm, and yet Entropia has survived. Actual interplanetary colonization, of Mars to name the most likely example, would need to find good answers to the same questions.

Exploring Calypso

A promotional video, often shown on large-screen displays at settlements on Calypso and supposedly produced by the Entropia Broadcast Network, begins: "Are you feeling unfulfilled? Bored with life on Earth? What would you say to a new life, filled with adventure, where you can live out your dream and claim your fortune? We

W.S. Bainbridge, *The Virtual Future*, Springer Series in Immersive Environments,
DOI 10.1007/978-0-85729-904-8_5, © Springer-Verlag London Limited 2011

can give you that new life inside Project Entropia! Project Entropia is a virtual universe where thousands of pioneering settlers are creating a new identity, making new friends, and building wealth, all inside a vast virtual world... We will transport you to the beautiful planet Calypso, where your Project Entropia life begins. Calypso is the first planet after Earth to be safely inhabited by humans. As a pioneer there, you have the opportunity to claim real estate, have its resources, and tame its wild life" [1].

A moment later, the broadcast is interrupted by an angry colonist who warns the viewer not to believe the upbeat advertising, because the new planet is extremely dangerous. "Yes, there are large sums of real money changing hands here, millions of dollars and you can take that money back to your Earth-bound bank account. There's no doubt there are riches here, but they're lying to you about everything else!" Video footage then shows the rampaging animals, supposedly more danger-ous than dinosaurs, and the escaped robots that kill settlers on sight.

The broadcast then switches back to the official channel, showing the tools the settler will use "to explore and conquer this gorgeous plant... As you can see, life on Calypso offers so much more than your boring life on Earth." This is an extremely clever advertisement, because the net effect is suggesting that colonizing this world will be both fun and profitable, and yet by including the message that the advertise-ment itself is a lie, it does not really promise that many people will earn a real-world profit, while holding out the hope that they might.

I originally signed up for Entropia in September 2007, and occasionally logged in over the following winter, spent a few hours exploring territory around the entry point of Port Atlantis, but did not accomplish much. There was no cost to do so, because the way *Entropia Universe* makes money is to charge for virtual tools and resources in Project Entropia Dollars (PEDs) which themselves can be bought for external currencies, at a rate of 10 PEDs per US dollar. Entering the world with only a jumpsuit, the avatar cannot do much without money, and eventually I invested $100 to get nearly 1,000 PEDs (less the currency conversion charge). In the spring of 2008, I learned that there were plans to shift to the more advanced CryEngine 2 graphics engine that summer, so I delayed doing any serious research, but when it seemed this was not going to happen, finally in March 2009 I started exploring actively.

My Entropia avatar, William "Bill" Bainbridge, set himself the goal of surveying the potential for scientific research on the planet Calypso, chiefly in geology and zoology, but also looking at how technologies based on these sciences could support colonization of this new world. He did not try to get rich, and the $100 investment was well spent in terms of many hours of interesting exploration with what I believe to be sufficiently valuable intellectual payoff.

Like other Calypso pioneers, Bill bought some cheap armor, a cheap gun that did not require much skill, and a few 1,000 rounds of ammunition, then began hunting animals. This allowed him to learn about the environment while increasing his skills, but progress was exceedingly slow, and occasionally he was defeated and needed to be resurrected at the nearest outpost. Damage to armor and equipment sometimes needed to be repaired, at measurable cost. After a couple of months, he switched to mining and drilling for other natural resources, which also was costly but gave him resources he could begin to use to develop skill crafting virtual equipment.

Unlike most gameworlds, *Entropia Universe* does not have a single ladder of increasing experience, with some subsidiary skill ladders, but a whole host of ratings that relate to distinct activities. Bill developed 19 of his skills past 50 on scales from 1 to a reported or hypothetical 18,000 [2]. By these measures, his performance was pretty pathetic, but even these levels took a very long time to achieve, and his first priorities were exploring and gaining knowledge rather than accumulating points in a game. He reached 282 in laser weapon technology and 225 in rifle use. Three other combat related skills were weapons handling (58), evade (57), and combat reflexes (53). Especially after he quit hunting animals, and studied them instead, he developed the dispense decoy skill to 86. Figure 5.1 shows him brandishing his Omegaton Distractor DD-20, which drops decoys that may lure the animal that was chasing him, as so many animals did.

In his zoology work, he used a LifeScanner to collect data about animals, approaching as close as he dared and running away when they attacked. Indeed, at 329 his scan animal skill was his highest. Related skills were anatomy (186), biology (103), and botany (92). Researchers cannot actually scan the visually fascinating plants on Calypso, because there is no tool to do this and the plants seem only to be displayed in graphics but not represented in the part of the database the user interacts with. He gained botany points indirectly by scanning the animals. Use of some tools gave him rather low computer skills (51). Another science skill was analysis (104), "a measure of how well you are able to interpret seemingly unrelated information," and he also gained a general perception skill (122), "the ability to stay observant and aware of the surroundings" [3]. Bill also invested much energy gaining skills in earth sciences: drilling (147), prospecting (143), mining (108), surveying (124), geology (95), and probing (73).

Fundamental to all this research was exploring the geography of Calypso. Figure 5.1 shows Bill at Billy's Spaceship Afterworld, a relatively short but dangerous trek north from Port Atlantis. Although the name similarity was a pure coincidence, he used this junkyard of wrecked rockets as his headquarters for a while, as he trekked on many expeditions all across the continent of Eudoria. The Afterworld, like Port Atlantis, had a teleport station, so he could hop back and forth quickly at no cost, whether to visit the auctioneer at the Neverdie Bank, or to check out the stores in the mall. He could not teleport to a station until he had once walked to it, and there were 35 of them on the continent, so it took him about a month to reach them all. Even a short distance took a long time to hike, because it was constantly necessary to be on alert for the locations of ferocious animals, and detour around herds of them, often winding up surrounded and needing to retrace many steps back to safety.

A teleport link to New Oxford in Amethera was already available, and in May 2009 he went there to see an exhibit of 41 paintings by players on display in the Academy of Fine Art, where there also were pictures showing what Entropia would look like after the projected switch to the CryEngine 2 game engine. In mid-June, he

Fig. 5.1 An explorer visiting Billy's spaceship afterworld in *Entropia Universe*

toured the lavish mansion of the owner of Treasure Island, who was actually a student at University of Sydney, Australia, named David Storey, but used the moniker Deathifier in Entropia. From the elegant wall tiles and blazing fireplace, to the statues of Calypso wildlife, to the numerous paintings on the walls, it was a splendid home. Bill was especially fascinated by a display of 19 diary notes from the records of Dr. Almon Duchev on a Calypso expedition, telling the story of his encounter with mysterious orbs that consumed the other members of his party then captured him.

As Bill explored deeper and deeper into Amethera, the monsters became more fierce and more formidable. He felt proud when he reached New Switzerland in the far north, which actually looks the way he imagines Switzerland to be, in terrain as well as architecture. His biggest challenge, however, was in the southwest corner of the continent, after he had reached 20 Amethera teleporters and had only four to go. At great effort, he had trekked westward from Palm's Corner to Nea's Place to Omegaton West Habitat, where his next goal was Memorial Island to the southwest. Seeing that there was a direct water route, he decided to swim, hoping there were no rippersnappers in the water. Comparable to tuna-sized piranha, these fish were a terror, but he found none. Instead, he ran into dinosaurs along the beach and made the very bad decision to try to circle around them by land. In a few moment, he was dead and resurrected at a station deep inside the peninsula.

The place was owned by a group of players called Menace to Society (M2S) who had set up a fertilizing station which M2S supplied with great quantities of energized fertilizer made from growth molecules and common dung. This was the nearest thing to agriculture yet found on Calypso, and its chief effect was attracting large numbers of itumatrox, an archaic predator that "spouts four barbed tentacles to inject a powerful toxic into its prey, then mounts the carcass to feed through its bellyside mouth." Also attracted were swarms of bristlehogs (kills with long-distance electrical charges), and araneatrox ("catches prey with its hooks and rips them apart"). Bill tried to sneak past these monsters, but after several failures was forced to admit defeat. Two other players found themselves trapped as well, so the trio tried to fight their way out. Again: failure.

Not ready to abandon poor Bill, I googled "Entropia" with words like "rescue" and discovered a group of players called the Calypso Rescue Team. Bill joined their forum with the appropriate username Catastrophe, and begged for help. "Coordinates (X,Y): 11300, 8282… As you may know, this is a revival site on some land owned by Menace to Society, that is absolutely surrounded by nasty creatures. My gun and armor are both weak, and I'm running low on decoys… Is there a fee for this work, or are you people just heroes?" The next morning, he checked the forum and found a message from Coachman setting up a time for the rescue.

At the appointed hour, Coachman showed up, wearing formidable yellow armor, accompanied by Magam who wore sports clothes and a jaunty top hat that looked like it had been made of burlap. Coachman told Bill, "Let's go to the direction against Nea [i.e. west], and go behind me. I will avoid killing many mobs. I have only 16,000 ammo with me." Bill discovered he was totally useless in the fighting that followed so he stayed a good distance behind Coachman. They tried to avoid monsters, but often one would attack Coachman who would battle it fiercely, while Magam remained a few paces behind him operating a healing device to offset the damage the monster was doing to Coachman. Another player, named Vallkyria Thorssen trailed along for a while, and then a third member of the rescue team, Lars Sebra, showed up for the final breakthrough. The team would not accept any payment for rescuing Bill, and Coachman explained, "We do this for fun, to see happy faces."

Near the end of July, after visiting the Club Neverdie asteroid station and completing all the prospecting and crafting work he had planned to do, Bill decided to risk once again reaching the last four teleporters in Amethera. He returned to Omegaton West Habitat, but this time swam westward, skirting the coast of one island to reach Oyster Isle, and from there swam south east to Memorial Island, expending fully 182 decoys to escape swarms of rippersnappers. For a while he was trapped again at a different station on the peninsula below Omegaton, but this time was eventually able to work his way south to Akmul Island, and head westward through the dangerous contaminated zone that required taking an anti-toxic shot and bewaring other players who could kill him and loot his corpse in this lawless area. By the skin of his teeth he survived, to reach the last teleporter on Myrene Island and complete his thorough exploration of the planet Calypso.

Scientific and Philosophical Basis

Humanity evolved on the savannahs of East Africa, and waves of colonization washed outward. The European Colonization of the New World was only the most extensive tsunami well-documented in historical records. Most of human migration was very slow, a matter of a single long hike per generation. By one estimate, agriculture spread westward across Europe from the Middle East at something like a kilometer per year [4]. In the spring, farmers would plant crops in one additional field, gradually creeping across the landscape. The original colonists of the Americas hiked over from Asia and down the long west coast, in an uncounted but undoubtedly long series of steps, one per generation. When Europeans burst into the Americas long afterward, they did so on the basis of a complex seagoing technology they had developed for centuries in their own waters [5]. How could people conceivably creep to the planets, or develop the extensive space technology required for a great leap?

One part of the equation, who would want to be a colonist, has already been studied, at least in preliminary research stimulated by a British social scientist named Michael Young. In 1948 he urged the United Nations to undertake an ambitious space program, for sake of world peace as well as human advancement, but the UN did not respond. In the following decades, Young became one of Britain's leading intellectuals, publishing scholarly books in urban sociology, writing an ironic book on social class and technical skills titled *The Rise of the Meritocracy*, and helping to found the innovative Open University [6]. In 1984, he was inspired to return to space exploration by the visionary book, *The Greening of Mars*, in which Michael Allaby and James Lovelock describe the transformation of Mars into a more earthlike planet – what is called *terraforming* – in an environmentally conscious and peace-oriented movement that also improved the Earth [7]. Young immediately launched a private project called Argo Venture, collecting around him a group of like-minded intellectuals including Lovelock and myself, with the immediate goal of establishing a simulated Martian colony here on Earth to demonstrate its feasibility [8].

Thirty volunteers would live for a year under conditions similar to those on Mars, doing the kinds of work and research that real Martian settlers might do. The actual locale might be a remote Scottish lighthouse that happened to be for sale, Quonset huts placed at the edge of the Arctic, or even, according to one controversial plan, inside an abandoned warehouse on the London docks where television cameras could easily be installed. One member of the team, John Percival, had already completed a similar project on a somewhat smaller scale, in which a group of people lived for several months under the conditions that Iron Age Britons experienced thousands of years ago, for a BBC reality-TV documentary series [9]. Mass media publicity attracted a flood of inquiries from potential volunteers, and Lord Young asked me to prepare a questionnaire to send to them, both to learn about them and to use as the application form.

Who are the Martian settlers? Who would be willing to leave terrestrial society behind to live on a far-away world? One theory is that they would be alienated people, who disliked the society around them and wished to flee its noxious influences. Benjamin Zablocki had done a study of people who joined American communes, exploring whether alienation from conventional society had encouraged them to build their own radical alternatives to it. His questionnaire had used a number of items from a June 1974 Harris poll of ordinary citizens, designed to measure alienation, so I included these items in my Argo Venture questionnaire. The ordinary citizens were much more likely to agree with statements like: "I feel left out of things going on around me." "What I think doesn't count very much any more."

Neither the Argo Venture volunteers nor the commune members seem as alienated from conventional society as are ordinary citizens! Perhaps this is because both visionary groups believe they can take charge of their own fates and achieve a superior life. They do worry that social inequality is increasing, and this was factually true in many societies over the two decades after the questionnaire was administered. It may also be factually true that societal leaders are selfish rather than seeking to meet the needs of the respondents, as other questions asked. So, many Martian volunteers may be alienated from the government and economic elite of their nations, but not demoralized in their own lives. Even this form of alienation is less common among them than in the general population.

In the end, Argo Venture failed. It proved impossible to collect the donations needed to pay for the effort, and potential sponsors lost interest when they learned that the somewhat similar Biosphere 2 was in the planning stage. This American project was more ambitious, but oriented toward terrestrial environmental preservation rather than Martian colonization, and it was carried through to completion with frankly ambiguous scientific results [10].

In the following years, I included Mars items in questionnaires administered to other specialized groups, cognizant of the fact that these respondents were not a random sample of the population and probably much more positive about science and technology than the general public. In a 1986 survey of Harvard students, males were more interested in going to Mars and more supportive of a government project to send an expedition, than were females [11]. Enthusiasm also correlated with interest in these academic subjects: astronomy, geology, physics, engineering, and – surprisingly – anthropology. Students who liked the following subjects were less enthusiastic than average: art, sociology, and foreign languages. Fully 74% of students who love "fiction based on the physical sciences" would go to Mars, compared with 39% of those who hate it. This difference of 35 percentage points is the largest positive correlation. Other strong connections are with "science fiction," "stories about scientific progress," and "stories about new technology."

A decade later, I was invited to join the team that created one of the first really large online questionnaire projects, Survey2000, which ran from late September through early November 1998 and which recruited especially technology-savvy respondents through the National Geographic Society [12]. Fully 3,185 children aged 13 through 15 responded to this statement: "If I were asked to go along on the first rocket trip to Mars, I would go." Now, of course, this is a hypothetical question, and we were not selling tickets on an actual rocket ship. However, the responses certainly say something about the real level of enthusiasm, and how it correlates with other variables. For example, 39.9% of boys agreed, compared with 26.0% of girls.

One part of this online questionnaire asked the young teenagers to check which of 53 different activities or interests were among their favorites. Not surprisingly, interest in astronomy correlated most strongly. Of those who listed astronomy as a favorite, 47.1% claimed they would go to Mars, compared with only 27.0% of those for whom astronomy was not a favorite. In descending order of correlation, these other interests had a significant positive correlation with Mars: archaeology, science, rock climbing, martial arts, scouts or guides, history, sailing, geography, mathematics, computers, skateboarding, U.S. football, video games, camping, skiing, hiking, fishing, and soccer football. Notice that this is a combination of scientific or technical interests, including video games, plus the outdoor activities that might prepare a person to explore the Martian landscape – recognizing that sailing and fishing cannot literally be done on the Red Planet, although skiing at the poles is a distinct possibility.

Questionnaire studies such as these have two obvious flaws. First, they measure verbally-expressed attitudes about interplanetary colonization, not actual behavior with all the personal costs that may be involved. Second, they ignore the question of where the colonists could possibly find the resources to fund their space travel and establish viable colonies. Perhaps some insights can be derived from the history of actual colonization efforts in past centuries, here on Earth. I say *perhaps*, because the costs of establishing a viable economy of Mars will be so much greater than the cost of establishing colonies in the Americas, and the return on investment is dubious at best. There are no natural resources on Mars that could justify the costs of mining them and shipping them back to Earth, like the gold, furs, and cotton that could be shipped cheaply back to Europe from the Americas. The geology of the Earth is almost certainly more differentiated than that of Mars, because of the much greater tectonic activity here, and the eons-old action of our seas, so deposits of minerals are much more readily exploitable here, quite apart from the vastly lower cost of shipping. Setting aside such doubts, what can history tell us, especially if we apply it to the planet Calypso rather than Mars?

On September 12, 1962, in a speech in Houston, Texas, where NASA was building its Manned Spacecraft Center, President John Kennedy referred to outer space as "this new ocean" [13]. He compared the future Apollo mission to the moon with the founding of the Massachusetts colony, and connected it as well to the history of Texas: "What was once the furthest outpost on the old frontier of the West will be the furthest outpost on the new frontier of science and space." Many Americans conceptualize space as "the final frontier," assuming that like Texas and Wyoming it will become the domain for homesteaders and high-tech cowboys, on the way toward becoming fully civilized. However, in a recent analysis technology historian Alex Roland pointed out that this hope would be vain so long as we continue to lack seaworthy "ships for this new ocean" [14]. Roland said the best analogy was the few small Viking ships that touched North America, but could not stay. In any case, Kennedy's frontier comparison expresses the conception of space exploration that many people still possess.

The great theorist of the American frontier, Frederick Jackson Turner, suggested several reasons why the wave of colonization moved so swiftly westward. The availability of cheap farmland was a major attraction: "When wild lands sold for 2 dollars an acre, and, indeed, could be occupied by squatters almost without molestation, it was certain that settlers would seek them instead of paying 20–50 dollars an acre for farms that lay not much farther to the east-particularly when the western lands were more fertile" [15]. The introduction of steamboats on western waters as early as 1811 provided a cheap way farmers could not only reach points near their future homesteads, but also ship their agricultural produce to market. As the years passed, more and more transportation routes developed across the land. The essentially military conquest of the indigenous Native American inhabitants made colonization easier for settlers of European descent. Some settlers were impelled to move by difficult conditions where they were, such as the especially harsh New England winter of 1816–1817 following the War of 1812 that sent many New Englanders westward. Well-to-do southerners went westward, because they saw the possibility of increasing their wealth still further, so migrants were not limited to those experiencing economic hardships.

A later historian summarized Turner's central thesis thus: "It was the free lands of the West that constituted a safety value for discontented Eastern masses and furnished the nationalizing impulses that bound the loose confederation of states into a strong government" [16]. So, Turner was more concerned with the consequences of the frontier, and indeed of the ending of the Wild West at the end of the nineteenth century, than in the causes of the migration. However, he did note that dissatisfaction with society in one place can motivate people to move to another place. Another commentator saw two sides to Turner's definition of frontier. On the one hand it was "open space, lands disposed to settlement, lands that were always cheap and frequently free," and on the other hand it was "disruption or change or evolution" [17].

When Turner originally presented his frontier thesis, he emphasized that open lands are an opportunity for people to set up their own governments, experimenting with new forms [18]. There has been much debate among historians about whether religious persecution and the longing for political freedom really impelled people to escape to new lands, such as the Puritans who settled Massachusetts and the British colony at New Providence off Nicaragua, or whether the motives were much broader and merely became clad in religious or political veneer [19]. One could just as well argue that the freedom of religion demanded by the Massachusetts colony was the liberty to set up their own religious tyranny, consolidating political power in the religion that could then be exploited for economic advantage [20].

Colonizing Calypso

There is as yet no agriculture on Calypso, only hunting and forms of mining that do not require elaborate installations. While Entropia supports the emergence of groups of players who cooperate together, they tend to be very small and do not need the level of political development required by agricultural societies. Thus, colonization of Calypso is in a very early stage, more analogous to the hunting and trade system established in North America by the Hudson's Bay Company in 1670 than to the frontier described by Turner. While the fur trappers may have been malcontents, and Europe may have been glad to get rid of them, they were few in number and had little political consequence for the home country. Indeed, we learn essentially nothing about the society from which Calypso's colonists have come, and given that their numbers appear to have been only a few thousand, they were at best a very small safety valve.

For its first three centuries, the Hudson's Bay Company was a monopoly managing the trapping and trade in furs across much of North America. It would recruit men from the colder parts of Britain, send them to Canada with supplies, and ship the furs back to Europe for sale. Among its problems were how to prevent either the trappers or the local managers from engaging in private trade for their own profit, with a corresponding reduction in the company's profit. Among the solutions to this multi-facetted problem were paying the managers well, strictly controlling the shipping system, and negotiating mutually-acceptable standards under conditions of limited information [21]. The analogy on Calypso is that the Swedish MindArk company that created *Entropia* has absolute control over the sale of some goods necessary for hunting, such as ammunition, and for mining, such as the probes and explosives needed to find deposits. It has the ability to adjust which things colonists are physically able to make for themselves from local resources, thereby balancing customer satisfaction with income when they need to buy PEDs. MindArk also has the power to adjust the rate at which animals spawn, thereby avoiding the problem of resource depletion like the decline of beaver populations that afflicted some Hudson's Bay outposts [22]. Fundamental to all these capabilities is the fact that MindArk can know anything it wants to about the current state of the economic system, because every transaction take place through its Internet server.

A real company managing settlement of a real planet might not have all these powers, but could exert power by monopolizing some products needed by the colonists. We could imagine that whatever organization managed colonization would provide some manufactured goods that were infeasible for a small colony to make for itself, such as computer chips and nuclear fuel rods. However, the Hudson's Bay experience illustrates one of Turner's points that seems very different from interplanetary colonization, namely that the business could grow incrementally after an initial investment that was well within the capabilities of a seventeenth-century corporation. Calypso is supposedly the first Earthlike planet discovered, and clearly it is not inside the Earth's solar system, and most likely a dozen or more light years away.

The only model of interstellar colonization that makes sense is for non-economic factors to develop deep-space travel, and then settlement of an hospitable planet comes as an unintended benefit. I modeled this theory in a computer simulation study published in the *Journal of the British Interplanetary Society* [23]. Without trying to specify what unusual motivation might drive a civilization outward, I looked at what happened if one planet did have a spacefaring culture, colonized the nearest habitable worlds, and then they developed cultures that were based on the original one but which differed in colonization propensity due to cultural drift. Two key factors were the rate at which the propensity to colonize drifted downward, and how many habitable worlds were within spaceship range. A natural selection effect could work against this downward drift, because random factors made it possible for some offspring societies to have higher propensity to colonize, even if the majority of offspring had lower propensities. In another simulation study imagining colonization of Mars, I looked at an issue similar to that faced by the Hudson's Bay Company, how individual colonists would learn to cooperate and build a viable economy despite scarcity and danger [24]. Calypso can be conceptualized as another such simulation, but incorporating actual human beings.

Among the most significant challenges a colonist has when exploring Calypso was dealing with the indigenous fauna, and among the most common of these is the snablesnot. These are weak but unpleasant animals that squirt toxic liquid from their twin trunks. They are also the easiest animal to train for a pet, so they illustrate domestication of animals, a crucial step in human evolution. But Bill failed in several attempts to do so. First one needs a whip, and to develop some skill with it. Then one must repeatedly whip a snablesnot, without killing it, to beat it into submission. Unfortunately, the only whip available on the auction system when Bill began was too powerful, and many snablesnots died in his attempts to pacify them. Then a weaker whip appeared for sale, so he bought it and tried again. Now the problem was that the snablesnots would come close to killing him. He tried running away to regain his health, then turn and whip the pursuing snablesnot a few times before running again, but he could never find the right balance between running and whipping. Finally, a passing stranger offered to help by healing Bill while he stood and trained a snablesnot, but on the verge of success he became impatient and killed the poor beast. In his travels, Bill documented fully 64 different species, and as in the case of snablesnots, there were often two genders to study and various age or aggressiveness categories.

A new colonist who has no money cannot yet kill animals, because guns and ammunition are expensive. However, it is possible to sweat them, and the perspiration of the creatures native to Calypso has special properties. One stands at a moderate distance, for example from a snablesnot, and engages in a rather mystical movement of the hands and focus of the spirit, hoping to harvest a couple of units of *vibrant sweat*. This may irritate the beast, so one must be prepared to run away. Over many attempts, Bill gathered 652 units, finding that they had no PED value at all with vendors but could be combined in equal quantities with *force nexus* to make *mind essence*. A number of *mind force* technologies employ this substance to operate brain implant chips that confer special abilities, including teleporting the avatar over short distances. The question then becomes where one can obtain force nexus, and Bill found most of his 2,136 units by drilling for it on one of the islands in Amethera.

Figure 5.2 shows the results of Bill's mining and drilling activities, which gained him minerals and *enmatter* resources that were distinctive to Calypso's geology. Both activities are costly, because mining expends explosive charges and drilling uses up probes. In addition, the equipment shown must be purchased and repaired when it wears out. Minerals were gathered by these tools: Ziplex Z1 OreSeeker, Omegaton Seismic Bomb, and Genesis Star Earth Excavator ME/01. EnMatter Substances were gathered by these: Ziplex JU10 Matter Seeker, Omegaton Survey Probe, Matter Driller MD-101. Bill tried two different strategies for prospecting, but never found a good way of predicting exactly where he should concentrate his efforts. One strategy was to carry his equipment wherever he went and take a shot at it whenever he was bored with other activities. The other

Results of 200 Attempts to Mine for Ore	
319 Blausarian Stones, 6.4kg, value: 12.76 PED	Sold for 12.76 PED
139 Belkar Stones, 2.8kg, value: 2.78 PED	Combined with refined oil produced 100 Basic Pumps
5498 Lysterium Stones, 110.0kg, value: 54.98 PED	Combined with refined oil produced 1690 Basic Filters
27 Lytairian Dust, 2.7 kg, value: 5.13 PED	Sold for 5.13 PED
156 Ganganite Stones, 15.6kg, value: 18.72 PED	Sold for 18.72 PED
88 Copper Stones, 26.4kg, value: 14.08 PED	Sold for 14.08 PED
206 Narcanisum Stones, 4.1kg, value: 16.48 PED	Sold for 16.48 PED
7 Megan Stones, 2.1 kg, value: 1.26 PED	Sold for 1.26 PED
Results of 300 Attempts to Drill for EnMatter Substances	
1540 Crude Oil, 30.8kg, value: 15.40 PED	Refined and combined with Lysterium, Copper, and Zinc ingots to make components
298 Alicenies Liquid, 11.9kg, value: 14.90 PED	Refined to produce 149 units of Alicenies gel
70 Garcen Grease, 7.0kg, value: 7.00 PED	Refined to produce 35 units of Garcen lubricant
1251 Melchi Water, 25.0kg, value: 25.02 PED	Refined to produce 625 Melchi crystals
83 Typonolic Steam, 8.3kg, value: 12.45 PED	Refined to produce 41 bottles of Typonolic Gas
10 Ares Head, 1.0kg, value: 2.60 PED	Refined to produce 5 units of Ares powder
3 Acid Root, 0.3kg, value: 0.96 PED	Refined to produce 1 bottle of root acid
524 Sweet Stuff, 5.2kg, value: 5.24 PED	Combined with 103 Bombardo fruit produced 103 Nutrio Bars
2136 Force Nexus, 21.4kg, value: 21.36 PED	Combined with 652 Vibrant Sweat produced 652 units of Mind Essence

Fig. 5.2 Results of mining and drilling for natural resources

strategy, which worked with the force nexus, was to get advice from other colonists then concentrate his efforts systematically across a well-defined area.

The figure states what Bill did with the bulk of his resources, chiefly combining them, or adding resources bought on the auction system, to make components for machines or other manufactured goods. He labored at crafting stations inside the Neverdie bank at Port Atlantis, because this put him near the auctioneer, vendors from whom he sometimes bought a manufacturing blueprint, and vending machines to which he could sell his surplus materials, like all his extra force nexus. This crafting increased his skill level, but he never really achieved the point at which the products of his work were useful to him. It did seem plausible, however, that advanced players could profit from the economic system.

Social Implications

In late October 2005, the mass media reported the stunning news that a piece of Entropia property had sold for a fortune in real money, becoming a resort and commercial hub called Club Neverdie. As *The Guardian* expressed the news: "Project

Entropia has made the virtual world headlines again, not long after wow-ing the mainstream media streams with news of a $26,000 virtual island sold via auction to a player in its digital universe. This time they've quadrupled the stakes with the sale of a space station for $100 K to a player called Jon NEVERDIE Jacobs" [25]. The BBC announced the story thus:

> A virtual space resort being built in the online role-playing game, Project Entropia, has been snapped up for $100,000 (£56,200). Jon Jacobs, aka Neverdie, won the auction for the as yet unnamed resort in the game, which lets thousands of players interact with each other. Entropia also allows gamers to buy and sell virtual items using real cash. The space station is billed as a "pleasure paradise." Last year, a gamer bought an island for $26,500 (£13,700). The space station is described as a "monumental project" in the "treacherous, but mineral rich" Paradise V Asteroid Belt and comes with mining and hunting taxation rights. With the price tag also comes mall shopping booth and market stall owner deeds, a land management system, a billboard marketing system, and space station naming rights [26].

As soon as the story appeared on the scholarly virtual world blog, Terra Nova, bloggers began expressing skepticism [27]. The first one even used the name Skeptical, writing: "The buyer is named Jon Jacobs. This sounds like a fake name. (There is even a children's song with this name in it.) Is it possible that this is a publicity ploy for Project Entropia? Is there any way of verifying the legitimacy of this transaction?"

Psyae asked a deeper question: "Quick, fun legal question here: What if, one day after the $100,000 purchase, Project Entropia goes permanently offline and closes up shop? (ignore bankruptcy implications) Does Jon Jacobs have any recourse, or is he out 100 large? In short, although there's obviously actual 'value' in virtual property, is the property at all protected by the law like real property?"

Van Mardian defended the possible veracity of the news: "Not to completely validate the story, but BBC claims: Neverdie is a popular and well-known in-game character. He and another character, Island Girl, appeared in a 2003 dance music movie Hey DJ!, which starred Jon Jacobs, Charlotte Lewis, and Tina Leiu. Furthermore, I don't see any skeptics on the PE forum."

Luc Praetor added: "As a player of Project Entropia (15 months now), I'm familiar with the likes of Jon "Neverdie" Jacobs (btw… of course it's not a real name… it's the name of his avatar). In real life he is a DJ and actor, and he has always voiced interest in bringing clubbing and music to PE in a greater way than it's been to date. As far as I can recall from internet research, he is American, and Deathifier (from last year's purchase of Treasure Island in Entropia) is from Australia."

Calistas took the skeptical stance to a new level: "Wow, I'm surprised you all fell for this one. It looks like a complete and utter marketing stunt. Jon Jacobs is very very closely tied to the company; US Spokesperson and marketing guy close. Check my blog for a bit more info on this case."

Logan Blackmoore rushed to the defense: "Mindark has stated several times that they use players as spokespersons for Entropia around the world. I guess it has to do with the fact that they are small and don't have the money to have company reps all around the globe. Jon Jacobs, with other prominent PE players, was attending E3 for instance, speaking about Entropia. Nonetheless, they are players and are not employed by MindArk. MindArk operates differently compared to other companies, as they have close ties to the community and sees it as a real part in the creation of Entropia. Therefore collaboration with key players is a smart thing to do, it strengthens the community sense and it saves the company money. This is how I see it, anyway, being a lurking member of the Entropian community for a couple of years."

Neverdie himself then chimed in, saying his purchase of the space station was a genuine investment: "The Space resort allows me to bring my connections in the music business together with my experience as pioneer of Virtual Reality and make a real go of it. I genuinely think the resort will gross six or seven figures in 2006. I am the most thrilled and excited gamer in the world right now. And I'm not Rich, I'm using Game profits combined with cash taken from the equity in my house. I have a lot at stake here. And I'm gonna do my utmost to make it work."

In May 2007, according to several online reports, Entropia auctioned banking licenses to four others: [28]

- Avatar Janus JD D'Arcwire, representing a real life bank (more information to follow) – paid $59,060
- Russian Internet Payment Provider MONETA.ru, by avatar Yuri iNTellect Efremov – paid $99,900
- Famous cross-world virtual celebrity and entrepreneur Anshe Chung – paid $60,000
- The avatar "Jolana Kitty Brice" (veteran Entropia Universe participant and entrepreneur who wishes to remain anonymous at this time) – paid $95,000

However, Bill never encountered any clear evidence on Calypso about what these investors got for their money, if indeed they paid it. When he visited Club Neverdie three and a half years after it was bought, he discovered it was a marvelous place but difficult to reach. Figure 5.3 shows the busy teleporter at Twin Peaks in Eudoria where spaceship pilots connect with passengers. Watching the local text chat, Bill found a pilot, but the man's ship was located on faraway Amethera. An hour was required to negotiate the fee and travel to the launch point. The trip cost 25 PEDs, as did the return flight with a different pilot.

The central area of Club Neverdie holds a working model of the station's solar system, with the stars shining through a transparent dome roof. Bill also visited a smaller space station which had opened back in 2004, the Crystal Palace, which was represented as an actual station floating in space, whereas Club Neverdie was built on a virtual asteroid. Both had normal gravity, and could just as easily have been built on the planet. Both also were designed to combine an area for shopping with animal-stocked domes for hunting plus other facilities, and an area where spaceships could land. Ringing the central area of Club Neverdie, accessed by a long, circular corridor, were 66 shops. Only 16 of them seemed to be in operation, and one of those was empty. The other 50 were locked, and signs outside reported that their rents were overdue. Four of the shops, three of them having overdue rents, were assigned to Jon Neverdie Jacobs.

Given that the commercial potential of colonization has not yet been fully realized, what can we say about the motivations, values, and norms of colonists?

Fig. 5.3 The busy teleporter at Twin Peaks

A questionnaire study of *Entropia* colonists would be interesting but very difficult to carry out, unless the research project had a substantial budget and the full cooperation of Entropia's creators, as a recent highly successful study of *EverQuest 2* demonstrated [29]. However we can gain some insights from the public statements of the formal groups of colonists, called *societies*, accessible at *social terminals*. In the first week of February, 2010, Bill manually copied data from several datafields for 183 societies founded from 2003 to 2010 and having at least 20 members.

Even before analyzing what the societies say about themselves, a valuable perspective is provided by the descriptive categories suggested by Entropia's creators. The society page lets each one select a primary and secondary activity from this list, beginning with three economic areas: Mining (subcategories: All, Energy Matter, Minerals), Manufacturing (subcategories: All, Weapons, Armor, Clothes, Equipment, Attachments, Tools), and Hunting (subcategories: All, Animals, Humans, Robots, Mutants, Outlaws). Then follow these diverse motives in the order shown: Exploring the new world, Commercial business, Industrial business, Trading, Landowning, Having fun, Keeping the peace, Research, Uphold the law, Partying, Survival, Protect the meek, Fame seeking, Mindforce usage, Personal development, Be helpful to newcomers, Fight evil, Fight the power, Offer security, Conserve nature, Join the highest bidder, and None. Also, a society is asked to select one of these descriptors: Traders, Mystics, Basic, Corporate, Military, Miners, Crafters, Hunters, Mercenaries, Order, Scientists, Outlaws, Security, and Explorers.

In addition, each society is encouraged to write something in each of six text boxes, of which three are of interest here: Motto, Goals, and Rules. The most obvious fact about these statements is that they were written in many different languages, often two at once. While the official language of *Entropia* is English, the 183 societies included some whose languages were Chinese, Czech, Dutch, Finnish, French, German, Hungarian, Italian, Japanese, Polish, Romanian, Russian, Serbian, Spanish, and of course Swedish which is the language of the *Entropia* developers. In many international online environments today, users tend to mix their native language with English. Who would have guessed that Goth Nation is a Spanish-language society, Happy Noobs is Russian-language, and Fox Hunt combines German and Polish speakers? The name of a Polish group was what English-speakers think pigs say: "Oink Oink Oink!" The motto of Sweden Web Rangers is in three "languages," Swedish, English and the online abbreviation system called Leetspeak: "Ha kul i den mysiga entropia världen... 'may the 100 t be with you' :D" An automatic translation of the Swedish, using FreeTranslation.com, is "Have fun in the cozy entropia world." "100 t" is one-zero-zero-t or "virtual loot," the motto plays off an English phrase in *Star Wars*, and ":D" is a smiley face.

Five of the societies chose dramatic Latin mottos: *per aspera ad astra* (to the stars through difficulties), *nec temere, nec timide* (neither rashly nor timidly), *si vis pacem, para bellum* (if you want peace, prepare for war), *post proelia praemia* (after the battle, the rewards), and *oderint dum metuant* (let them hate, so long as they fear). Others took their mottos from popular culture, for example "Leben und Sterben lassen" (*Live and Let Die* from the James Bond series, but in German) and "One for all, and all for one!" (from *The Three Musketeers*). The Galactic Jedi Force used the *Star Wars* motto "May the Force be with you," and a society calling itself just Jedi expressed part of the worldview of Jedi masters: "There is no emotion." Some mottos were humorous yet had a philosophical edge to them: "Peace is our profession. Mass murder is just a hobby." The name of the Raumschiff Titanic Crew combined the German word for *spaceship* with an English word and the name of a British ocean liner. Its motto is: "Wir sind unsinkbar!! und doch ist das schiff untergegangen: (" (We are unsinkable! And yet the ship sank. Frown!).

One society, DSV Game Education, was created by a group at Stockholm University, whose website proclaims, "We are the department that focus on bridging the gap, between on one hand information technology, and on the other hand the social sciences, the behavioral sciences, and the humanities. The focus in the field is in design, construction and use of IT systems in their context in relation to people, organizations and society" [30]. Its motto is, "Reality is all in the mind." The mottos of many other groups expressed serious moral ideas: "Every Saint has his past, every Sinner has his future!" "Wer aufhört besser zu werden, hat aufgehört gut zu sein." (Who stops getting better, has stopped being good.) "You don't have to be the biggest or the strongest to be the best." "Even the weak become strong when they are consolidated." Others were more equivocal: "Aimlessly wandering for mankind!" "Our motto is 'Avoid having a motto.' Logically our goal is to have no goal."

Common goals were expressed by many groups, of which these are typical: "To make profit within the society, and to help new comers to feel at home." "Support, guide and help your society family and fellow citizens." "You must be active, logging in once a month doesn't count." "Take over the world or just have some fun." "To gain skill and knowledge about the Universe, have fun and make friends." "Der Weg ist das Ziel" (The path is the goal.). Sharing of information was prominently mentioned, reflecting Entropia's mentoring program, in which newcomers apprentice to experienced players. The goal of Brotherhood of Mentors is "Teaching, advising and helping in any way we can to make the transition as smooth as possible for the new generation of calypsonians." Some groups mentioned trading virtual goods among themselves, rather than using the auction interface. Across the various languages, similar sentiments were expressed: "Dobra zabawa" (Polish: good fun). "Prijateljstvo i dobra zabava" (Serbian: friendship and good entertainment). "Prietenie bazata pe respect, bun simt si responsabilitate!" (Romanian: friendship based on respect, common sense and responsibility!)

Although written in Russian, the rules of the Berkut (golden eagle) Squad are typical: "Запрещены: 1. Нецензурные выражения в чате; 2. Попрошайничество; 3. Скам" (Are forbidden: 1. Obscene expressions in a chat; 2. Begging; 3. Scam.). The first rule of a French-speaking group was "Fair Play." Similarly, a German group began its rules with an English word: "Fairness und Teamgeist einhalten, jedes Mitglied sollte für seine Kameraden da sein" (Keep fairness and team spirit, each member should be there for his comrades.). One German word has gained universal currency in the gaming community, *über* (often: *uber*) originally meaning *over* or *above* and used to mean *very* or *superior* among gamers. For example, one of the Russian groups valued becoming "уберами" ("uberami") which means *superiors* or *the best*. Thus, fair play becomes extremely important in a competitive system, in which becoming *uber* is paramount. A Spanish group was rather authoritarian: "El lider es Dios, y su palabra es la palabra de un ser supremo y ha de ser escuchada y llevada a cabo" (The leader is God, and his word is the word that is supreme and should be listened to and carried out.) In contrast, other groups expressed revolutionary or even anarchist rules: "Fight oppression on all levels. Especially oppression of individual rights." "There are no rules." "Die beste Regel ist keine Regel" (The best rule is no rule.). "Erlaubt ist was Spaß macht – solange es keinem schadet. ;)" (Whatever makes fun is permitted, so long as it harms no one. Wink.).

Conclusion

Immediately after the geological upheaval that remade Calypso in August 2009, Bill visited many of his familiar haunts, finding them radically changed. Much of New Oxford had disappeared, including the art museum and the monumental statue of a reindeer, as had a friend's apartment building at nearby Bilton Towers. The commercial malls at Port Atlantis and Twin Peaks no longer existed, although the Emerald Lakes Mall teleporter was at least still in operation. Bill spent 50 PEDs to visit the asteroid again, and out a window he could see Club Neverdie, but he could not actually enter it. Billy's Spaceship Afterworld still existed, but the wrecked spaceships had vanished, perhaps recycled as scrap.

Six months later, some but not all of the old features had been restored, including the reindeer, and social life had returned to normal but in a more modern graphics environment. How *Entropia Universe* evolves as it adapts fully to the new and very demanding graphics engine will be interesting to see, and truth to tell neither of the computers I use for exploring virtual worlds can handle it properly. Despite all the controversy about *Entropia Universe's* economic model, Bill and I find it really fascinating, similar to a game but also similar to exploration of a real alien world. Perhaps its fundamental lesson is that the human future is precarious. Many experiments of a social, economic, and technological nature must be tried, and it will be hard to predict which few will succeed.

References

1. http://www.youtube.com/watch?v=gDYpVn3vzGo
2. http://www.entropiadirectory.com/wiki/Skill_Ranks
3. http://www.entropiadirectory.com/wiki/Skills
4. Cavalli-Sforza, L.L.: Genetics of human populations. Sci. Am. **231**(3), 80–89 (1974); Genes, peoples and languages. Sci. Am. **265**(5), 72–78 (1991)
5. Cipolla, C.M.: Guns and Sails in the Early Phase of European Expansion, 1400–1700. Collins, London (1965)
6. Young, M., Willmott, P.: Family and Kinship in East London. Free Press, Glencoe (1957); The Symmetrical Family. Pantheon, New York (1974); Young, M.: The Rise of the Meritocracy, 1870-2033: An Essay on Education and Equality. Thames and Hudson, London (1958)
7. Allaby, M., Lovelock, J.: The Greening of Mars. St. Martin's, New York (1984)
8. Lunan, D.: Lord Young of Dartington and the Argo Venture. Space Policy **18**, 163–165 (2002)
9. Percival, J.: Living in the Past. British Broadcasting Corporation, London (1980)
10. Vergano, D.: Brave new world of Biosphere 2? Sci. News **150**(20), 312–313 (1996); Cohen, J.E., Tilman, D.: Biosphere 2 and biodiversity: the lessons so far. Science **274**, 1150–1151 (1996)
11. Bainbridge, W.S.: Goals in Space: American Values and the Future of Technology. State University of New York Press, Albany (1991)
12. Bainbridge, W.S.: A question of immortality. Analog **122**(5), 40–49 (2002)
13. http://www.historyplace.com/speeches/jfk-space.htm
14. Roland, A.: Ships for this new ocean. Futures **41**, 523–530 (2009)
15. Turner, F.J.: The colonization of the west, 1820–1830. Am. Hist. Rev. **11**(2), 303–327 (1906). p. 306
16. Lee, E.S.: The turner thesis reexamined. Am. Q. **13**(1), 77–83 (1961)
17. Coleman, W.: Science and symbol in the turner frontier hypothesis. Am. Hist. Rev. **7**(1), 22–49 (1966). p. 23
18. Turner, F.J.: Western state-making in the revolutionary era. Am. Hist. Rev. **1**(1), 70–87 (1895); Western state-making in the revolutionary era II. Am. Hist. Rev. **1**(2), 251–269 (1896)
19. Langdon Jr., J.D.: The franchise and political democracy in Plymouth colony. William Mary Quart. **20**(4), 513–526 (1963); Demos, J.: Notes on life in Plymouth colony. William Mary Quart. **22**(2), 264–286 (1965); Kammen, M.: The meaning of colonization in American revolutionary thought. J. Hist. Ideas. **31**(3), 337–358 (1970); Kupperman, K.O.: Errand to the Indies: Puritan colonization from providence Island through the Western design. William Mary Quart. **45**(1), 70–99 (1988)

20. Osgood, H.L.: Connecticut as a Corporate colony. Polit. Sci. Q. **14**(2), 251–280 (1899); Erikson, K., Wayward Puritans: A Study in the Sociology of Deviance. Wiley, New York (1966)
21. Carlos, A.M., Nicholas, S.: Agency problems in early chartered companies: the case of the Hudson's Bay Company. J. Econ. Hist. **50**(4 Dec), 853–875 (1990); Carlos, A.M., Hoffman, E.: The North American fur trade: Bargaining to a joint profit maximum under incomplete information, 1804-1821. J. Econ. Hist. **46**(4), 967–986 (1986)
22. Carlos, A.M., Lewis, F.D.: Indians, the Beaver, and the Bay: the economics of depletion in the lands of the Hudson's Bay Company, 1700-1763. J. Econ. Hist. **53**(3), 465–494 (1993)
23. Bainbridge, W.S.: Computer simulations of cultural drift. J. Br. Interplanet. Soc. **37**, 420–429 (1984)
24. Bainbridge, W.S.: Sociology Laboratory. Wadsworth, Belmont (1987)
25. http://www.guardian.co.uk/technology/gamesblog/2005/oct/27/100000realus
26. http://news.bbc.co.uk/1/hi/technology/4374610.stm
27. http://terranova.blogs.com/terra_nova/2005/10/the_winner_and_.html
28. http://web.archive.org/web/20070513022518/http://www.marketwire.com/mw/release_html_bl?release_id=249893; cf. http://en.wikipedia.org/wiki/Entropia_Universe
29. Huh, S., Williams, D.: Dude looks like a lady: gender swapping in an online game. In: Bainbridge, W.S. (ed.) Online Worlds. Springer, Guildford (2010)
30. http://dsv.su.se/en/

Chapter 6
Star Trek Online

The original 1966 *Star Trek* television series spawned movies, books, and a number of solo games for computers and videogame systems, but only on February 2, 2010 did it give birth to a massively multiplayer online game. Importantly, the entire *Star Trek* franchise was largely supported by the loyalty of a fan subculture, and fans themselves have created both extensive additional culture plus a set of expectations for new commercial offerings. Set in the year 2409, *Star Trek Online* (STO) involves both space battles in which the user is represented by a spaceship, and land missions in which the user is represented by a humanoid avatar. The primary conflict pits the multi-species United Federation of Planets against the Klingon Empire.

The fundamental principle of *Star Trek* is cultural diversity, and the stories often concern how members of different groups can develop mutual respect. In addition to suggesting this optimistic view of humanity, *Star Trek Online* illustrates how information technology may be used in real life over the coming decade or two. Indeed, all the games described here have that quality, plus serving as training grounds to give people command over the evolving technology, but as the most recent example STO offers the newest insights. In addition, it connects to the *Star Trek* mythos which embodies a distinctive ethical system and clear notions about how human social relations may evolve in the coming centuries. Even the obvious technical and aesthetic faults of STO can be valuable in this context, suggesting some of the hazards that humans will face in the real world.

Memory Alpha

All of the gameworlds described in this book exist only in a universe of information, connected via Internet, and composed of recently created cultural elements. *Star Trek Online*, however, illustrates best the modern conceptions of *cultural informatics*, and *human-computer interaction*. At the time of this writing, it was the most recent massively multiplayer online role-playing game, so it had the advantage of learning from all the previous ones. On the other hand, during its first two months

Fig. 6.1 Rho Xi's Ship, the Carbondale, at Memory Alpha

when I explored it, STO had many programming bugs, data errors, and design flaws which had not yet been corrected. The fact that its action took place in two very different environments added complexity. In addition, it experimented with new ways of spontaneously building teams of players and non-player characters. Thus, internally it was extremely complex and presented its designers and players with a host of challenges. But it was also complex externally, linking to 726 episodes of a television drama, to 11 movies, and to innumerable books and Internet resources. For example, the *Star Trek* cultural complex connects three things called "Memory Alpha."

The first is a base in *Star Trek Online* belonging to the United Federation of Planets. It is the base in the form of a series of interconnected domes on the planetoid in Fig. 6.1, and was a frequent port of call for my main STO avatar, the Bajoran scientist, Rho Xi. His last visit there will illustrate this gameworld's space travel command and control system, as well as the cultural-informatic heritage represented by Memory Alpha.

Immediately after completing the "Big Dig" mission, Rear Admiral Rho Xi returned to Earth Spacedock in the Sol system, and happened to visit the lecture hall where a discourse on astrophysics was in progress. To his embarrassment, the students saluted him even though he was merely observing them from the back of the room, and they whispered: "Did you hear about Rho Xi?" "Rho Xi is the best of the best." "I overheard Admiral Quinn recounting Rho Xi's last mission… impressive." The instructor, Commander Menn Hilo, proclaimed, "Impressive work, Rho Xi!" A science officer exclaimed, "Here, here!" To be sure, the Big Dig was an important mission, rescuing archaeologists and artifacts from Romulans and Remans, in the huge excavation of an ancient pyramid on a distant planet. But Rho Xi knew that his own contribution to victory was minor since he was only one of two dozen members of the Federation involved, although he had been one of the four who defeated the last Reman captain, thereby completing the mission. Apologizing for interrupting the class, Rho Xi walked clockwise along the corridor that circled the station to the shipyard.

At that point in his long career, six ships were at his disposal. Five were the science vessels he had commanded, at increasing levels of capability: the Oberth, Goddard, Tsiolkovsky, von Braun, and Korolyov. For his next voyage, he decided to take the U.S.S. Carbondale, a light cruiser of the original Enterprise class. He opened the ship selection interface and clicked on the button for the Carbondale, which brought up a display of the ship's special equipment. Clicking "Set as Current," he then closed the shipyard window, clicked the "Beam to Ship" button on his interface, and the transporter on the Carbondale beamed him to its bridge. The next step was to click the "Warp to Sector" button on the ship's interface to leave the Sol system. Over the video communication link, a traffic control officer announced, "U.S.S. Carbondale, this is Earth Spacedock. You are cleared to warp to Sector Space." In response, Rho Xi clicked the "Warp to Sector Space" command button, and a graphic of the Carbondale going to warp speed filled his display.

A sector space is displayed as a luminous, lined surface with solar systems suspended above it, over which the spaceship flies, depicted as a small model. Sectors are assembled, three or four at a time, into a sector block. The Sol system is in the Vulcan Sector of the Sirius Sector Block, which also contains the Orion Sector and the Risa Sector. The Vulcan Sector contains these systems, in addition to Sol: Wolf 359, Kei, Beytan, Andoria, P'Jem, Pellme, Bhea, Pico, and Vulcan. In *Star Trek* lore, Wolf 359 is where a major battle raged between the Federation and the Borg [1], but it is also a real star which because of its proximity and small size has attracted the interest of astronomers [2].

Rho Xi had explored all accessible sectors of the galaxy at this point, and there was no need to explore to get this list of systems. He could press the "M" key on his keyboard to get the navigation system, which included a system list, a galaxy map, and a local map. To head toward Memory Alpha, he opened the system list and double-clicked the bar for the Alpha Centauri Sector Block. This immediately told the ship to start moving, and very soon Federation Traffic Control reported, "You are clear to warp to the Alpha Centauri Sector Block." Clicking "Warp," he waited a moment for the display to clear, indicating that he had warped to the new sector, then he opened the system list and double-clicked "Memory Alpha System." The Carbondale zoomed across sector space toward his goal.

Then, unexpectedly, two serious problems hit, one right after the other. First, a priority one message came in from Starfleet: "A Crystalline Entity has been sighted near your coordinates. All available ships are needed to respond to this threat. The entity is on a course that will take it to a populated system. It must be stopped now!" Reluctantly, because he had faced crystalline entities before and never been able to defeat them, he joined a few other ships in battling this one. Instantly, the second problem occurred: A complete loss of communications, not only cutting the Carbondale off from Starfleet messages, but making it impossible for him to operate the ship!

After repeated attempts to log back in, Rho Xi returned to the battle a half hour later, saw that no progress had been made by the other captains, and returned to his original course in disgust. Finally, "Enter Memory Alpha System" placed him at the location shown in Fig. 6.1. He turned the ship to point directly at the planetoid, pressed the "E key" to increase engine power and briefly used his mouse to set impulse to maximum. Soon, a message came in from Orbital Control: "Welcome to Memory Alpha, Carbondale. You can beam down when ready." He clicked the "Beam Down" button on his command interface, and immediately appeared in the transporter room of the base. A short walk through twisting corridors, and he had reached his goal.

In the main central room, beneath the great, gold-colored rotating globe, he sold loot to Commander Jenna Romaine, the chief vendor at that location, increasing his store of money to 957,423 energy credits. I suspect she is the granddaughter of Mira Romaine, mentioned below. He walked a few paces to one of the bank interfaces, where he deposited many new research samples and trading commodities, then checked how his 19 tribbles were doing. Exiting from his own account, he checked that of the fleet he had recently joined, the William Shatner School of Acting, which at that time had 31 members. He deposited a science kit that was too low a level for him to use himself, thinking that somebody else might like it. Seeing that the fleet had only 18,011 energy credits, he added 20,000 from his own account. He could have sold some of his research samples to Romaine, because she was always seeking anomalous data to add to Memory Alpha's digital library, but she used the anomalous data bytes merely to upgrade people's armor, weapons and equipment, and all his stuff was already top grade.

While Rho Xi was visiting the bank in his Memory Alpha, I myself was visiting a second and even more valuable Memory Alpha, the online *Star Trek* wiki. Its welcome page explains: "Memory Alpha is a collaborative project to create the most definitive, accurate, and accessible encyclopedia and reference for everything related to *Star Trek*. The English-language Memory Alpha started in November 2003, and currently consists of 31,684 articles" [3]. Memory Alpha is one of the very highest quality information sources on the web, because so many people have labored long and hard not only to post data but to discuss and critique everything in the service of accuracy. Many of the articles are quite long, but care is invested in starting each one with a brief summary that gives a wandering reader an accurate quick impression.

For example, here is how the page about the first problem Rho Xi faced in his journey begins: "The Crystalline Entity was a powerful, spaceborne creature characterized by a crystalline structure that resembled a large snowflake. It had warp speed travel capability, formidable size, and the ability to consume all life on a planet or starship (TNG: 'Datalore')" [4]. The parentheses hold a link to the episode about the entity, "Datalore," in the series, *Star Trek: The Next Generation*. The page related to Rho Xi's destination begins:

Memory Alpha (also called The Memory Planet) is a planetoid. Memory Alpha is also the name of the library complex set up on the planetoid, containing an archive of the total cultural history and scientific knowledge of all planetary Federation members. The library was assembled for academic purposes only. No defensive shielding was installed, as the information was available to anyone in the galaxy.

In 2269, The USS Enterprise was en route to transfer newly-designed equipment to Memory Alpha. Lieutenant Mira Romaine was on her first deep space assignment to supervise the transport from the emergency manual monitor. Before the arrival of the Enterprise, Memory Alpha was attacked by the non-corporeal Zetarians.

While the Zetarians were attempting to take over the bodies of the personnel of Memory Alpha, they managed to cause extensive damage to the complex. The memory core of the computer, called the central brain, was burned out. The energy generator was rendered inoperative. All occupants of the complex died from brain damage caused by resisting the mind control efforts of the Zetarians. After the Zetarians were destroyed, the Enterprise returned to Memory Alpha to begin repairs. (TOS: "The Lights of Zetar") [5]

"The Lights of Zetar." was first broadcast January 31, 1969, and a remastered version with enhanced special effects was broadcast June 7, 2008. Thus, just as there are multiple versions of Memory Alpha, there are two versions of the episode. In the original, the planetoid was depicted as a blurry circle, but STO used the enhanced version for its model, as depicted in Fig. 6.1. The wiki page gives far more details about the episode, including a romance between Mira Romaine and Scotty, the chief engineer of the Starship Enterprise. Because of her especially empathic abilities, she is not killed when the Zetarians take over her mind, and they speak through her, telling the story of how their planet was destroyed and they are seeking a new home [6].

"The Lights of Zetar" foreshadowed two features of modern information technology: digital libraries, of which Memory Alpha is an early example, and the use of one "person" by another as an avatar. Of course, spirit possession is an ancient religious idea, and avatars in Hindu religion were the source of the term. But there is another source of this idea. The chief author of the script was Shari Lewis, a puppeteer, ventriloquist, and *Star Trek* fan. In the 1960s, she became famous through very modest but high-quality children's television programs, often centered on a hand puppet of a sheep named Lamb Chop [7]. As her Wikipedia article notes, "Lamb Chop, who was little more than a sock with eyes, served as a sassy alter-ego for Shari" [8]. Mira Romaine became an avatar for the Zetarians, but she was also an avatar for Shari Lewis, and an actress named Jan Shutan gave life to the character on the screen [9]. The profusion of overlapping identities in online role-playing games has a long heritage and is rooted in primary facts of human nature, through which every mentally healthy is able to play the role of another.

So there are three versions of Memory Alpha: the virtual place in *Star Trek Online*, the *Star Trek* wiki, and a setting in the original 1969 episode of the television program. All three are accessible online, including the television program, because CBS has made it available for free with only very brief advertisements [10]. This illustrates two points that may seem obvious once they are mentioned but represent profound transformations of civilization.

First, all forms of digital communication are merging, so that the differences vanish between computing, television broadcasts, telephone calls, news reporting, book publishing, music distribution, and many information-related functions in private life such as picture-taking and diary writing. For example, the Memory Alpha wiki publishes news stories, such as this one from February 9, 2010 that reminds us again of the mysteries of human identity and links to a newspaper obituary: "Actor Bernard Kates, who portrayed Sigmund Freud in the *Star Trek: The Next Generation* episode 'Phantasms', passed away on 2 February 2010 from pneumonia and sepsis. He was 87 years old" [11]. Coincidentally, the day of the actor's death was the day *Star Trek Online* was born.

Second, building on the centuries-long traditions in printing and the arts, modern information technology is able to preserve vastly more knowledge than ever before and provide it as needed in real-time to serve a great variety of human purposes. The question then becomes: What does *Star Trek* mean?

Scientific and Philosophical Basis

In his book, *The Physics of Star Trek*, Lawrence M. Krauss shows that beaming down to a planet and traveling at warp speed are not really feasible in our physical universe, and they are really just dramatic conventions that allow the story to jump from one scene to the next [12]. Journalism professor David Hajdu has argued that *Star Trek* was never really about the future, but about the past, recycling popular culture clichés from western movies and police shows. As evidence, he cites "Sigma Iotia II, the gangster-movie planet" and observes:

> Certainly, few living astronomers expect to find Planet 892-IV, the gladiator-movie planet, where Spock and McCoy were forced to battle in Roman games. Or Ekos, the Nazi-movie planet, where Spock ended up discomfortingly sympathetic to the fascists. Or the unnamed orb in Melkotian space, the Western planet, where the crew literally re-enacted the gunfight at the O.K. Corral. Or Tarsus IV, the Shakespeare-movie planet, where everything was just frightfully dramatic [13].

I prefer to see this as *Star Trek's* way of anchoring its visions of the future in our human heritage, rendering it humanly meaningful. This is difficult to do for space travel, because the real universe is so different from the universe science fiction fans wish they lived in. It is possible, however, that *Star Trek* and the virtual worlds considered in this book can prepare humanity to become something different from what it traditionally has been, giving it a longer and higher vision. Today's civilization simply is not prepared to "boldly go where no one has gone before," especially if there will be no quick returns on financial investments. In a review of the 2009 *Star Trek* movie, Dave Itzkoff commented:

> It takes a certain mix of optimism and frustration to contemplate the possibility of space travel. To dream of navigating the cosmos is to assume that man has the resources and the know-how to propel himself into the heavens, but also some compelling reasons to exchange his home planet for the cold vast unknown [14].

Closer to home, the original *Star Trek* can be understood on two levels: (1) as a standard continuing one-hour television series in which most episodes tell complete stories, and (2) as a visionary subculture that expresses the social idealism and technological optimism of its decade, the 1960s. These two combine in the central philosophical concept, *IDIC*. Memory Alpha explains: "The Vulcan IDIC is an abbreviation for Infinite Diversity in Infinite Combinations, the basis of Vulcan philosophy, celebrating the vast array of variables in the universe" [15]. Wikipedia puts it this way: "The phrase 'Infinite Diversity in Infinite Combinations' (IDIC) refers to the infinite variables (or forms of intelligence) in the universe and the infinite ways in which they may beneficially combine" [16]. IDIC symbols are worn by some *Star Trek* characters, in the form of a triangle pointing to a small disc surrounded by a large offset ring. Several large sculptures of the IDIC symbol stand on the grounds of a Vulcan monastery on the planet P'Jem in STO.

Gene Roddenberry presented his plan for *Star Trek* to the NBC network in 1964 as "Wagon Train to the stars" [17]. In the 1961–1962 season, the NBC series *Wagon Train* was the highest-rated TV program, depicting a group of pioneers going from Missouri to California in the old days of the wild west [18]. A set of stock characters interacted with guest characters from episode to episode at different locales during the journey. Each episode was a separate story, divided into scenes punctuated by advertisements, and the over-all story of a given season was rather vague. This allowed the producers to air the episodes in any order. Crime shows on television generally use a different metaphor to accomplish the same thing, starting each episode when a crime is brought to the attention of the authorities who always can be found in their offices. When the *Wagon Train* pattern was adopted for *Star Trek*, the conceit that time was measured according to stardates allowed Captain Kirk to identify what day it was without clarifying how that day related to different episodes.

Thus the first meaning of IDIC is that many quite different stories can be linked under a set of unifying concepts, with a continuing cast consisting of actors in the case of the TV series and the players in the case of the game. In creating *Star Trek Online*, Cryptic Studios explicitly adopted the episode concept:

> In Star Trek Online episodes are player mission chains (also known as "quests"). They were called episodes rather than mission chains or quests mainly due to the *Star Trek* TV series and how they impacted Cryptic's influence on how to design and tell a story in-game. They stated that their content writers approached the content as if they were writing an episode from the TV shows. This seemingly allowed Cryptic to develop better stories for the game in relation to how they play, look and feel. Episodes in the game are written to advance the overall story; however, some episodes will be standalone and will not have much to do with the main story. This is by design as Cryptic has stated that the TV series often featured side-stories that were not directly part of the main storyline [19].

The episode and scene structure is not unique to television, but has been employed in the theater for centuries. Shakespeare's histories tell a vast story in segments at three scales: play, act, and scene. STO exploration episodes follow a freer pattern, sending the player to investigate three solar systems apparently at random in a given sector or nebula, doing either space or land missions that are limited in duration and may not be conceptually related to each other. Still others require the player to participate in three space battles against the same enemy, different only in the random placement of enemy ships and different allies depending upon who has joined or left the fight.

The second more visionary meaning of IDIC was illustrated in the episode that introduced the concept, "Is There in Truth No Beauty?" Broadcast October 18, 1968, the story concerned an alien species so ugly that to gaze upon it caused madness, yet the one human who did go insane was actually a victim of his own jealousy. Thus, the perception that aliens are ugly merely reflects the ugliness within us. A *Star Trek* fan advertisement of the same year explained, "Infinite Diversity in Infinite Combinations represents a Vulcan belief that beauty, growth, and progress all result from the union of the unlike. Concord, as much as discord, requires the presence of at least two different notes. The brotherhood of man is an ideal based on learning to delight in our essential differences, as well as learning to recognize our similarities" [20].

Many *Star Trek* episodes and a few in STO mention the Prime Directive, the strict rule in the United Federation of Planets against interfering in the natural cultural evolution of intelligent species across the galaxy who have not yet developed the advanced technology needed for interstellar travel. Despite endless debates about how to apply it in particular circumstances, the Prime Directive expresses the central theme of *Star Trek*: Technological progress and ethical progress must be achieved together [21]. The Prime Directive serves IDIC by preserving the cultural uniqueness of developing societies, until such time as they would naturally blend with the others in the galaxy.

Numerous STO missions involve four very different societies with different relationships between citizens: The United Federation of Planets, The Klingon Empire, The Borg Collective, and the Mirror Federation. Initially, users could create characters only in the Federation or the Klingon empire, the former enjoying all the most complex episodes since the television program was always told from the Federation perspective. The Klingons occasionally battled each other in combat between competing *houses* in their feudal society, but destruction was the goal of all the Klingon missions I tried. Figure 6.2 shows Korbette, receiving praise from the Klingon High Council, after defeating many enemies in simple combat missions.

While the other three groups were in the original series, the Borg were introduced in *Star Trek the Next Generation*. They are a technically advanced collectivist society that assimilates other species and controls their minds centrally, but except for rescuing a few prisoners from the Borg in land-based shootouts, their culture is not depicted in STO. Rather, on numerous occasions one must destroy Borg machinery in space battles: probes, spheres, and cubes.

Similarly, the game does not yet fully exploit the Mirror Universe concept. The original series of *Star Trek* drew heavily upon the science fiction subculture, and a number of experienced writers in that field wrote scripts for it. A notable example was Jerome Bixby who wrote four of them, including "Mirror, Mirror." Beamed up from a planet during a magnetic storm, Captain Kirk and three crewmates find themselves catapulted into a parallel universe, where everything is the same except human morals. They struggle to play the roles of their counterparts, with whom they have exchanged places, until they can beam back into their own version of the

Fig. 6.2 Female Warrior Korbette at the Klingon High Council

universe. Leaders in the mirror universe are harsh, sadistic, and selfish, belonging to an empire based on those principles. In STO, the player gets to battle ships belonging to the mirror empire, that look exactly like Federation ships, but subtle lessons about mercy and morality are absent.

Political issues of the 1960s often shaped *Star Trek* episodes, including the precarious balance of terror that existed between the Soviet Union and the United States. "The Doomsday Machine," written by prolific science fiction writer Norman Spinrad, concerns a robot weapon destroying one planet after another. This episode includes two direct references to the hydrogen bomb and only slightly more indirect references to the mutually assured destruction (MAD) that encouraged both sides to keep the peace, because they knew that war would lead to annihilation. Apparently, a civilization outside our galaxy created the doomsday machine under similar circumstances, but it failed to preserve peace and after destroying that civilization began wandering the cosmos in search of additional victims. STO ignores the philosophical meaning of the device, and the fact that no single ship can destroy it, so Rho Xi had no trouble putting it out of action on his first attempt.

Of the many species in the galaxy, the ten listed in Fig. 6.3 could be selected for a Federation avatar, and Klingons can also be played more conventionally as avatars in the Klingon Empire. Each species has distinctive traits, which increase one of the character's mathematical parameters, and players can add two or three more from a list. Players actually have an eleventh species option, crafting their own Alien with one of ten head styles and selecting four traits from a long list. In addition, it was possible to purchase the right to have a Ferengi or Tellarite avatar, for 80 or 200 Cryptic Points respectively, in which 1000 CPs can be bought online for $12.50 [22]. Note that three of the well-known characters in the table are actually mixtures.

Species	Description	Traits	Example
Human	"a great deal of diversity both in their culture and in their appearance"	leadership, teamwork	James T, Kirk, original series
Andorian	"a militaristic species that settles disputes through ritual combat... passionate and emotional but not overly concerned with sympathy"	acute senses	only minor characters
Bajoran	"a deeply spiritual race dedicated to their gods, the Prophets"	creative, spiritual	Kira Nerys, Deep Space Nine
Benzite	(no behavioral peculiarities)	natural armor, natural immunities	only minor characters
Betazoid	"Because of their telepathic abilities, Beatzoids are open about their emotions and they value honesty."	empathic, telepathic	Deanna Troi, Next Generation
Bolian	"highly outspoken and jovial"	corrosive blood	only minor characters
Klingon	"a proud species that values tradition, honor and strength"	honorable, warrior	Worf, Next Generation
Saurian	"renowned traders, and most of their early interactions with other species were related to commerce"	circulatory redundancies, acute senses	no named characters
Trill	"generally friendly and many serve the Federation as ambassadors or politicians"	hyper metabolism	Jadzia Dax, Deep Space Nine
Vulcan	"Known for their logical minds and stoicism"	logical, physical strength	Spock, original series

Fig. 6.3 Ten playable species in the United Federation of Planets

Both Kira Nerys and Spock are half-human hybrids, and Jadzia Dax is a combination of a Trill woman named Jadzia with a nearly immortal slug-like symbiont named Dax who had already outlived five other hosts.

I decided to create Rho Xi as a Bajoran scientist, something of a contradiction because Bajorans are perhaps the most religious of the ten species. All STO Federation characters have the same experiences, and the missions near the planet Bajor are not reserved for Bajorans. I chose the name Rho Xi because it plays off Chi Rho, a Christian religious symbolism, yet Rho has many uses in science, including representing density and a correlation coefficient. I chose Xi rather than Chi, because I admired the 1950 science fiction story, "The Xi Effect," by Philip Latham (a pen name for astronomer Robert S. Richardson) that imagined what would happen if a fundamental constant of nature changed.

Rho Xi quickly assembled a crew of secondary avatars, representing diverse species cooperating on his away team that carried out many land-based missions. He relied heavily upon Thuvia, a female Andorian tactical (combat) officer, named after the central character of *Thuvia, Maid of Mars*, a 1916 novel by Edgar Rice

Burroughs. Azura, a female Vulcan science officer, was named after the Martian Queen in the 1938 movie serial, *Flash Gordon's trip to Mars*, and was responsible for healing injured team members. Tonga, a female Trill engineering officer, named after the Lady of Diamonds from the early 1950s television program *Space Patrol*, strengthened the shields of individual team members and could create a large force-field shield for the entire group. Initially I had a second engineering officer, a male Human named Flash Gordon, but for practical reasons I replaced him with a second tactical officer, a male Ferengi named Marx after Karl Marx, a play on the fact that Ferengi are devout capitalists.

Episodes

Three STO episodes illustrate very close connections to famous episodes of the original series: "The Ultimate Klingon," "City on the Edge of Never," and "The Tribble with Klingons." The first derived from the episode of the original series, "Space Seed," which first aired on February 16, 1967, and which also led to the 1982 movie, *Star Trek II: The Wrath of Kahn*. The Enterprise finds an ancient space-ship slowly traveling between the stars, with six dozen passengers asleep in suspended animation. Their leader, Khan Noonien Singh, slyly avoids explaining who he is and why his people were fleeing Earth, until he has mastered the command systems of the Enterprise, at which point he attempts to seize control.

Kahn was the dictator of one quarter of the Earth's population, from India through the Middle East, in the mid-1990s. The result of eugenic selective breeding, he was a superman, physically as well as mentally, one of a set of nearly a 100 such elites who controlled many parts of the planet before being defeated in the Eugenics Wars. He hopes to enlist the crew of the Enterprise to conquer some inhabited planet, where he can prove his superiority by creating a perfect society.

Selective breeding could not really create a superman so quickly, and today the slightly less implausible science fiction explanation would be genetic engineering that changes the DNA code. In the 1960s, the "master race" pretentions of the Nazis were fresh in everybody's mind. In the original story, Marla McGivers, the ship's historian, develops a crush on Khan, because she admires great male leaders of the past, such as Alexander the Great. For a while she helps Khan, then turns against him at the last minute, allowing Kirk to retake command of the Enterprise. Surprisingly, Kirk does not deliver Khan over to Starfleet authorities, but settles him and his followers (including McGivers) on an uninhabited planet where they can prove what supermen can accomplish when they have nobody to dominate but themselves. Spock comments, "It would be interesting, captain, to return to that world in a 100 years, and learn what crop had sprung from the seed you planted today."

"The Ultimate Klingon" begins as starfleet tells Rho Xi that Klingons have been raiding shipments of medical supplies. He is sent to the Korvat system to meet Ghee P'Trell, a medical researcher who can analyze what the medical supplies could be used for. There, he encounters Gorn allies of the Klingons, and the first scene of the episode requires destroying two of their patrols. The second scene begins as Rho Xi beams down to P'Trell's medical research facility with an away team consisting of Tonga, Thuvia, Azura, and Flash Gordon. There they must kill many Klingons and Gorns in hand-to-hand combat, then rescue P'Trell. He explains the Klingon commander demanded information about Earth's Eugenics Wars, hoping to develop technologies to augment the abilities of his warriors. P'Trell mentions the 30 million deaths in the wars and the dark age that followed, then recounts the Klingons' own dismal experience in an earlier augmentation effort that led to a devastating epidemic among their people. The third scene consists of another space battle; the fourth rather brief scene involves sneaking past Klingon ships through a nebula, and the fifth scene is an extended battle through a Klingon laboratory complex.

There, Amar Singh, grandson of Khan, proclaims, "Combining several different species will create the perfect race! We will rule the galaxy!" When the away team finally defeats augmented Gorns, Rho Xi reminds Singh that genetic modification is illegal. He scornfully replies, "I don't recognize the laws of your petty, judgmental Federation. You mouth pretty words about morality and diversity and peace, but you fly around in death machines that could obliterate a planet! You talk about personal freedoms, but impose your will on everyone in your grasp! The Federation is a collection of tyrants!"

Rho Xi learns from Singh that the Klingon who is most vigorously promoting the war, B'vat, was especially interested in learning about a Federation officer named Miral Paris, a Human-Klingon hybrid. She is the daughter of two major characters from the fourth television series, *Star Trek: Voyager*, and her DNA is the basis for a cure of a fatal Klingon disease [23]. B'vat was also seeking information about time travel. This provides a transition to the episode, "City on the Edge of Never," which is a sequel to "The City on the Edge of Forever" from the original series.

This award-winning episode was written by science fiction author Harlan Ellison. Catapulted into the past through a portal called the Guardian of Forever, Kirk and Spock find themselves in New York City in the year 1930 trying to undo harm that time travel has done to the fabric of history. They meet an idealistic social worker named Edith Keeler and gradually discover that she is the key, but their broken tricorder cannot access the data they need. Disguised as ordinary men in this early year of the Great Depression, they gratefully accept jobs from her. As Memory Alpha says,

> After their third day of work, Kirk returns from shopping with radio tubes, wires and other items. Spock is noticeably frustrated at the lack of technology in the 1930s. He spends many hours building circuits and connections. Eventually, after several setbacks, the tricorder reveals its wealth of information. Spock sees Edith Keeler's imminent obituary. Then he plays the recording for Kirk – and they see a report about Edith Keeler's meeting with United States President Franklin D. Roosevelt 6 years hence. She cannot have two futures; they've discovered the point where McCoy altered the past. But did he save her? Or kill her? And how? "What if Edith Keeler must die?" Spock asks the troubled Kirk [24].

The sad answer is that she must die, because in her naive idealism she would convince Roosevelt to delay American entry into the Second World War, allowing the Nazis to develop nuclear warheads and long range missiles with which they conquered the world.

The sequel in STO sends the Carbondale to the Hromi Sector to meet the USS Kirk, to follow up on this hint of time travel. The first scene of "City on the Edge of Never" is a space battle helping the Kirk fight Klingons, and the second beams the away team into the Kirk to fight some who have boarded this historically-named ship. The captain of the Kirk tells Rho Xi that the enemy kidnapped Miral Paris: "Miral's ties to the Klingons have always been trouble. Half of them think she's a traitor, the other half think she's a savior, and now this bunch thinks she can cure some crazy virus!" The next scene is a brief space battle, followed by travel to the Gateway System where the fourth scene is another space battle. Then the Carbondale's team beams down to the planet where the Klingons used the Guardian of Forever. When asked what happened to Miral, the Guardian says,

> The one known as Miral Paris finds her future in the time before her time. She is the kuvah'magh. Her people follow her footsteps before she has made them. Her presence in her past alters the river of time. Those who took the kuvah'magh are conquering before the warriors arrive. They have brought the weapons of your world to a time that will be helpless to resist them. Your reality, your world, your beginning? All that you know is gone.

Transported back to the year 2270, the team first assists the original Enterprise, commanded by Spock. This concludes the episode, but leads into a sequel, called Past Imperfect, to rescue Miral and stop genetically augmented Klingons from altering the timeline, in scenes with evocative names like "Through the Looking Glass" and "Time Savior."

"The Tribble with Klingons" is based on the comic episode, "The Trouble with Tribbles," first broadcast December 29, 1967. To his great displeasure, Kirk is ordered to take the Enterprise to Space Station K-7 and protect a shipment of grain seeds destined for a planet claimed both by the Federation and by the Klingons. The variety of grain, quadrotriticale, is a wheat-rye hybrid that will grow well on the planet, thus strengthening the Federation's claims of ownership. Klingons arrive at K-7, arousing suspicions that they plan to sabotage this plan, but under the terms of a recent peace treaty they are allowed to enter.

Serious issues beneath the surface of this farce concern relations between different nations and species. The Russian member of the Enterprise crew, Chekov, makes several questionable assertions that key scientific discoveries had been made by Russians. This was a standard joke of the period in America, casting scorn on the delusions of grandeur of the Soviet Union, and it is worth noting that the episode was produced exactly a decade after the Soviets launched the first space satellites. Later in the episode, Federation and Klingon personnel exchange insults, and they react in exactly opposite ways to the tribbles.

Ah, tribbles! A traveling salesman offers these furry, featureless creatures as the ideal pets, and Lieutenant Uhura of the Enterprise takes one as a gift when the salesman see that she likes it so much that she will get her friends to buy some. She caresses it as it coos at her, little realizing that as soon as it gets into her ship it will begin eating them out of house and home, and reproducing faster than the proverbial rabbits. Humans adore tribbles, Klingons loathe them, and Spock the Vulcan thinks they are impractical and thus uninteresting. Back on the space station, they begin eating the quadrotriticale, but when some tribbles die it is revealed that the Klingons are poisoning the grain. In the end, Scotty, the chief engineer of the Enterprise, beams the tribbles into the departing Klingon ship, commenting that they will be "no tribble at all."

"The Tribble with Klingons" sends Rho Xi in command of the von Braun to the Minos Korva system, where the first scene, "Enter the Tribble," involves battling a Klingon Threat Eradication Force intent upon destroying what they consider to be an extremely dangerous environmental hazard, namely tribbles. Scene two, "Wack a Tribble," and scene three, "Tribble Savior," require an away team to protect tribbles and kill Klingons in and around a Federation exobiology lab where the furry animals have taken up residence. At the end, the head of the lab explains that Klingons view tribbles as a menace rather than an endangered species, and tried unsuccessfully to breed a predator to cull their numbers. "They sent warriors to hunt tribbles throughout the galaxy, and they destroyed the tribble homeworld with an orbital bombardment."

A month later, noticing that he had a variety of the adorable creatures throughout his storage spaces, Rho Xi decided to breed them scientifically, feeding them particular food items that would stimulate them to produce rare offspring. Tribbles are useful, because caressing one gives a character increased abilities for a time on away missions, how much and which ability depending upon the particular variety of tribble. Rho Xi never was able to afford three of the rarest tribbles, or the expensive food required to breed them from other varieties he already possessed, but others had posted online the results of their research, documenting 25 types and how to produce them [25]. For example, he had a Mattson tribble, which improved health regeneration and damage per second (DPS) and which if fed a *tranya* would give birth to a Velasquez tribble, which had double the benefit for DPS. But the cheapest tranya cost 84,000 credits on the auction system! At the end of his labors, he realized that all four of his personal storage spaces contained tribbles, so he checked the ten members of his crew and discovered the same was true of them. All 66 slots of his inventory, and all 96 slots of his bank vault were likewise totally tribblized!

Korbette's last mission required her to lead a Klingon team into an outpost infested by tribbles, exterminating them all and not being allowed to collect any of them. She found she was able to buy a couple of these obnoxious critters from Federation players on the auction system and breed them just as Rho Xi had. But when she held one in her hand, they recoiled from each other. Given that she was a tactical warrior rather than a scientist, she decided to leave research on these abominations to Klingons who specialized in such loathsome labor.

Social Bugs

Many new virtual worlds contain programming bugs and data errors, and *Star Trek Online* seemed to have more than its share. Some were just typographical errors and misspellings in displayed text, such as *tacticle* for *tactical* in one place. Others prevented missions from being completed, as when Rho Xi destroyed four groups of enemy ships but could never find the required fifth, or when one of the enemies he was fighting was just outside the boundaries of the instance he was in and would take no damage. Minor errors get corrected in time, but many reviewers and players complained that the game possessed major design flaws. My own view is that it is a very interesting virtual world, well worth the investment of time and money, and that the complaints about it might just as well be directed at the real human future.

People came to *Star Trek Online* with very strong preconceptions about what it should be, yet perhaps no game could really succeed in going "where no one has gone before." Notably, the many *Star Wars* games are generally considered better than the many *Star Trek* games – although I rather liked *Deep Space Nine: The Fallen* and *Voyager Elite Force: Set Phasers to Frag. Star Wars* is about combat, and combat games are relatively easy to create, but *Star Trek* has elements of soap opera and psychological drama, which do not lend themselves easily to "gamification."

For example, early in April 2010, one of the STO wikis featured a very critical article by a player using the name JadeEnigma: "When those of us who have grown up with *Star Trek* think on it, we experience a very particular sensation, one that the Great Bird of the Galaxy, Mr. Roddenberry himself, had wanted, designed, and planned for. Hope. A bright and fulfilling future. There will be conflict, since that is the nature of existence, but in *Star Trek* there was always purpose to it... a reason and an ambition and meaning that was better for the whole if not for the individual. In that, there was heroism" [26]. STO, in contrast, features one meaningless battle after another, in JadeEnigma's view.

About the same time, a player using the name Angelus exclaimed in the game's text chat, "I just want to say that this game sucks! (waits for the flames about: 'Well don't play it then.')." Another player made an obscene comment about Angelus's mother, a third offered sound effects, and a fourth respectfully asked Angelus to explain further. "Well, I don't like the fact you don't have a death penalty, or how they've turned *Star Trek* into an arcade game. It's not even as good as an R-Type, yet all you do is shoot constantly." R-Type is a primitive side-scrolling shooter arcade game from the 1980s, which had a futuristic theme. "You die, respawn. Die, respawn. There is no fear of losing your ships or xp [experience points]. There is no point to healing... you might as well keep going. When you rank up, you find that everyone else in the game is Rear Admiral. And you have five Rear Admirals running around on away mission. The in space battles are repetitive, if pretty. And the away missions are dull, with a very poor third person interface." Another player told Angelus to quit the game calling him a loser, but he continued his tirade: "They don't have elements on the bridge like they originally advertised... and they instead just made it into the most non-tactical, non-thinking brain dead shoot em up. I would move on, but I fell for the adverts and bought a lifetime subscription."

Other criticism focused on STO's economic system. Early in his career, Rho Xi posted three unneeded mark-II weapons on the system for selling virtual goods, which is shared by the Federation and the Klingons. K'mpok bought his disruptor sniper rifle, T'Hrathen bought his disruptor split beam rifle, and Kah-lel bought his disruptor arcwave assault gun, each for 215 credits. A discussion in the zone chat debated the viability of the exchange system, noting that many of the posted prices were ridiculously high, not prices of a few hundred credits, but hundreds of thousands. Dearth said this was the case "because there are no real ways that a substantial amount of Energy credits leave the system… they just keep stacking up." Cortharis mentioned ship buying as a counter-example, but Dearth replied that this "is a onetime deal and not that substantial."

Zutty chimed in: "I think if Cryptic had made more vendors accept energy credits instead of freaking medals and badges, things wouldn't be so bad." There are many separate currencies in STO, which cannot readily be converted into each other, one of which can be used only to upgrade equipment, and another that can be used only to complete certain missions. The exchange system does not permit auctions, as *World of Warcraft* and *Lord of the Rings Online* do, because potential buyers cannot bid competitively, thereby efficiently setting the market price. As Dearth noted, there could be other solutions like "a repair system for gear that required Credits, or countless other methods, something to get a constant stream of creds out." The discussion turned to "gold spammers," the people reputed to be Chinese gold farmers or credit card scammers who sent advertisements like the following over the chat and email system: "Sto_Energy_Credits <<www.ignmin.com>> 100 K = 3$ Star Trek Online Coupon Code 'STO' 100 K sale 3$, Powerleveling 1–10 15$, Supper [sic] Best Services !"A given advertisement appeared many times, purportedly sent by different characters.

It is difficult for any economic system to stabilize if outsiders are constantly disrupting it. One reason the STO designers created multiple currency systems was precisely to damp down tendencies for money to dominate the action. And action is what this game is about. Many of the space battles are extremely fast-paced, so much so that players cannot pause in firing their weapons and adjusting their shields to type messages to the others on their team. Setting up voice chat takes time and effort, so it was seldom used, given that the membership of teams was constantly changing.

STO pioneered real-time automatic team building. When Rho Xi entered a solar system, he never knew if he would be alone, fighting against spaceships automatically set to be appropriate for his level, or automatically combined with as many as four other players fighting more difficult enemies. While most away missions on the surface of a planet involved a team of five, sometimes the other four were members of his bridge crew of secondary avatars, and sometimes they were other players, automatically assembled into an appropriate team. Because it was so fast-paced, STO used innovative methods to combine players into teams, but this may have eroded the ordinary mechanisms of social trust that take time and effort to build teams that may endure long after the battle.

In the early weeks of STO, players often expressed skepticism about the value of *fleets*, the persistent groups of players generally called *guilds* in fantasy games. So many STO missions automatically combined players into teams, or adjusted automatically to be suitable for solo play, that few players worried about fleets until they had reached very high levels of experience.

Over three weeks into his own career, Rho Xi noticed this message in the text chat: "Now… Recruiting… For… The William Shatner School of Acting. New

Fleet… looking for… Casual members. If you… want… to learn… to play lead… roles… in… Rescue… 911, or price line negotiator." This message parodied the "method" acting style of William Shatner, the actor who played Captain James T. Kirk in the original series. The *method* is a system developed by acting teacher Lee Strasberg based on principles proposed by Konstantin Stanislavski, in which the actor achieves the most lifelike acting style by really feeling the emotions of the character. *Star Trek* merged with Shatner's real life profoundly, although he was more successful than others of the original cast in finding a range of roles in later years. He was nominal author of some of the *Star Trek* novels [27], hosted the dramatic reenactment series *Rescue 911* that blurred reality with fiction, and played the Priceline Negotiator gangster in TV commercials which used high-emotion drama to sell a real service.

Rho Xi asked if this was a real fleet or a joke, and when told it was real he joined it. At its peak, it had 33 members, but few were ever online at the same time, a web-based forum never really got going, and the fleet folded when the founder quit playing STO a month later. Soon afterward, Rho Xi was doing business at Memory Alpha when he saw a message asking if anybody had tetryon particles to sell. He replied that he had 17 and was immediately offered 50,000 credits for them. He gave them to the other player for free and then inquired about the fellow's fleet, named Starfleet Consoritium [sic]. It seemed both large and active, so he joined, but he had already reached Rear Admiral rank and maximum level 45, so he never became active in it. Fleets may have value for advanced players who have completed all available missions but want to continue battling with social support from comrades, often in PvP combat against other groups of players. Early in STO's history, they did not seem to evolve into role-playing groups of dedicated *Star Trek* fans, although that could happen with the passage of time.

Thus, I believe the criticisms of STO are literally misplaced, because they may in fact reflect problems that real society will face. Using mobile and ubiquitous computing, often in computer-supported cooperative work, may preclude the development of traditional social bonds between people. If events are always moving too fast for the individual to keep up, and technologies are developed to handle the chaos and complexity of future life, we may lose our humanity in a way we never anticipated. To use a phase-change metaphor from physical science: The solid institutions of society may melt; society itself may boil, and we will wind up living in a gas or ionized plasma is which social atoms churn at a rate far beyond the ability of any person to comprehend.

Conclusion

I named my replica of the starship Enterprise the "Carbondale" and gave it a serial number ending in "1972" because it was in Carbondale, Illinois, in 1972 that I met Gene Roddenberry, the creator of *Star Trek*, while doing research for my Harvard doctoral dissertation and first book about the spaceflight social movement [28]. He was attending the first Syncon conference staged by the Committee for the Future, which had the goals of uniting humanity, transcending the current human condition, and becoming a universal species that would expand throughout the galaxy. Its wealthy leader, Barbara Marx Hubbard was considering investing in a new television series about a lunar colony, but Roddenberry's three attempts to create another science fiction series in the 1970s never got beyond the pilot stage. The nearest Roddenberry ever got to real spaceflight was after his death, when some of his ashes were placed in orbit a quarter century after I met him.

I met Nichelle Nichols, who played communications officer Uhura on the Enterprise, at a Los Angeles spaceflight convention in 1981, while I was visiting Jet Propulsion Laboratory to study the encounter of the real spacecraft Voyager II with the planet Saturn. She was part of the revolution in Hollywood that improved the career opportunities for African Americans like herself, and her character's name was based on the Swahili word, *uhuru*, which means *freedom* and was the name of an African liberation movement. Her Wikipedia article explains: "After the cancellation of *Star Trek*, Nichols volunteered her time in a special project with NASA to recruit minority and female personnel for the space agency, which proved to be a success. Those recruited include Dr. Sally Ride, the first American female astronaut, and United States Air Force Col. Guion Bluford, the first African-American astronaut, as well as Dr. Judith Resnik and Dr. Ronald McNair, who both flew successful missions during the space shuttle program before their deaths in the Space Shuttle Challenger disaster on January 28, 1986" [29]. I was at JPL again at the time Resnik and McNair were killed, which coincided with Voyager II encounter with Uranus, and the trauma inspired me to write another sociological book, *Goals in Space* [30]. The first *Star Trek* movie, in which Nichols again played Uhura, had been released in 1979, and concerned a Voyager spacecraft that had been captured and augmented by an advanced machine civilization and returned to threaten Earth.

Repeatedly, *Star Trek* has linked to real space exploration, providing popular cultural support for this vast enterprise, even as it promotes Infinite Diversity in Infinite Combinations. The first space shuttle was even named after Captain Kirk's ship. Its Wikipedia article notes, "On September 17, 1976, Enterprise was rolled out of Rockwell's plant at Palmdale, California. In recognition of its fictional namesake, *Star Trek* creator Gene Roddenberry and most of the cast of the original series of *Star Trek* were on hand at the dedication ceremony" [31]. As it moved slowly across the pavement on its wheels, the program's theme music played. Perhaps symbolically, this Enterprise never flew in space, but was used merely for glide tests to perfect landing techniques, and it currently rests in a museum at Washington Dulles International Airport. Thus, looking at a conflict-ridden world in the post-shuttle years, we can wonder whether either of *Star Trek's* utopian dreams can be fulfilled, spaceflight or human unification, through respect for diversity.

References

1. http://memory-alpha.org/en/wiki/Battle_of_Wolf_359
2. http://en.wikipedia.org/wiki/Wolf_359
3. http://memory-alpha.org/en/wiki/Portal:Main
4. http://memory-alpha.org/en/wiki/Crystalline_Entity
5. http://memory-alpha.org/en/wiki/Memory_Alpha
6. http://memory-alpha.org/en/wiki/The_Lights_of_Zetar_(episode)
7. http://memory-alpha.org/en/wiki/Shari_Lewis
8. http://en.wikipedia.org/wiki/Shari_Lewis
9. http://memory-alpha.org/en/wiki/Jan_Shutan
10. http://www.cbs.com/classics/star_trek/video/index.php?pid=LReT2xBMg_cSm8t71VDkF3__9PqUxTBK
11. http://articles.latimes.com/2010/mar/08/local/la-me-passings7-2010mar07
12. Krauss, L.M.: The Physics of Star Trek. Basic Books, New York (1995)
13. Hajdu, D.: Exploring the universe, one B-movie at a time. New York Times, 9 May 2009. http://www.nytimes.com/2009/05/10/opinion/10hajdu.html?_r=1&hp
14. Itzkoff, D.: The two sides of 'Star trek'. New York Times, 9 May 2009. http://www.nytimes.com/2009/05/10/weekinreview/10itzkoff.html
15. http://memory-alpha.org/en/wiki/IDIC
16. http://en.wikipedia.org/wiki/Vulcan_(Star_Trek)
17. http://memory-alpha.org/en/wiki/Star_Trek_is…
18. http://en.wikipedia.org/wiki/Wagon_Train
19. http://stowiki.org/wiki/Episode
20. http://www.statemaster.com/encyclopedia/IDIC
21. Rushton, C.: Fables of the prime directive. In: Star Trek Corps of Engineers: Wounds, pp. 207–251. Pocket Books, New York (2008)
22. http://www.startrekonline.com/store
23. http://memory-alpha.org/en/wiki/Miral_Paris
24. http://memory-alpha.org/en/wiki/City_on_the_Edge_of_Forever
25. http://sto-intel.org/wiki/Tribble
26. STO Geekipedia, March 17, 2010; on April 3 this was the featured news article at http://sto-geek.com/wiki/Main_Page
27. Shatner, W., Reeves-Stevens, J., Reeves-Stevens, G.: Star Trek: Captain's Glory. Pocket Books, New York (2007)
28. Bainbridge, W.S.: The Spaceflight Revolution, p. 167. Wiley-Interscience, New York (1976)
29. http://en.wikipedia.org/wiki/Nichelle_Nichols
30. Bainbridge, W.S.: Goals in Space: American Values and the Future of Technology. State University of New York Press, Albany (1991). http://mysite.verizon.net/wsbainbridge/system/goals.pdf
31. http://en.wikipedia.org/wiki/Space_Shuttle_Enterprise

Chapter 7
EVE Online

Created by a small group of innovators in Reykjavík, Iceland, *EVE Online* has a well-deserved reputation for being challenging, immense, and different in many respects from the typical online game. It shares with *Jumpgate* the feature that the user's avatar is a spaceship, and all the action takes place in space rather than on the surface of a planet. The pilot is represented by a small picture with personal possessions and a set of skills rather than a human body. For new players, *EVE* offers many training missions, but the main action is created by the players themselves as they set up corporations that occupy regions of the galaxy and fight battles against each other. Although my two main characters visited about a hundred solar systems, reportedly *EVE* spans 7,500 of them.

Of all the virtual worlds described in this book, *EVE Online* offers the most detailed projection of what human space technology might be like, in the distant future. It shares with *Anarchy Online* a history of rebellion against tyranny, with *Entropia Universe* a social structure that is largely created by the inhabitants rather than by game designers, and with *Star Trek Online* a focus upon direct team-based combat between competing forces. While dwellers in the EVE galaxy can never descend to the surface of a planet, this has the effect of liberating them from the oppressive force of gravity, leaving them free to seek or create their own destinies.

Republic Versus Empire

The two chief spies I sent into *EVE's* galaxy, Cogni Tion and Theo Logian, completed well over 150 missions, earned more than 2,000,000 skill points, and explored many different technology-oriented activities. They were equally intelligent but had markedly different personalities. Cogni was even-tempered and analytical, preferring to start with the facts and then induce general principles when it was possible to do so without contradicting her empirical data. Theo was far more emotional and doctrinaire, always beginning with a set of axioms and deducing their applications

W.S. Bainbridge, *The Virtual Future*, Springer Series in Immersive Environments,
DOI 10.1007/978-0-85729-904-8_7, © Springer-Verlag London Limited 2011

to particular situations, where he then enforced them with great passion. Thus, it made sense to send Cogni into the Minmatar Republic, and Theo into the Amarr Empire.

The planets Matar and Amarr were two of the four seedling worlds that survived the great isolation and are available for players to join. Humans from Earth had discovered a wormhole they called *EVE*, and voyaged through it to a galaxy so distant they could not even discover which direction it lay in the cosmos. They had nearly completed colonization of several worlds, when the wormhole unexpectedly collapsed, cutting the new worlds off not only from home, but from some of the supports required for a galactic civilization, so a Dark Age set in.

Amarr was the first world to re-establish interstellar travel, so it imposed its rule on others, enslaving the Minmatar. In time, war between Amarr and the mysterious Jovians allowed Matar to break away from the empire and establish a republic, but many Minmatar remain slaves within Amarr's realm, while others are refugees. The two other playable races that reestablished interstellar civilization, Caldari and Gallente, originally shared the same solar system, Luminaire, and have their own histories of turmoil and progress. But it is the competition between the individualistic Minmatar and the theocratic Amarr that defines the *EVE* universe.

Cogni Tion is a Minmatar of the Sebiestor bloodline with Tinkerer ancestry. Anyone who checks the information in her file can read:

> Widely respected as being among the most innovative thinkers of the cluster, the Sebiestor are an ingenious people with a natural fondness for engineering. For the last millennium, they have been pioneering advances in applied sciences despite laboring under chronic material shortages. Sebiestor engineers believe they can build anything, with anything, out of anything. Veritable masters of deriving solutions from impossible circumstances, they are most commonly found working in shipyards, assembly lines, terraforming projects, outpost construction, and aboard starships.

The history of enslavement suffered by Cogni's ancestors, and by millions of fellow Minmatar even now, provided a motivation for applying this engineering skill, that she would not admit was a sea of subconscious rage. Even-tempered though she naturally was, she responded to the militia's appeal:

> Millions of souls cry out for emancipation, begging to be freed from a life where they are treated no better than captive animals. The Minmatar heart sings for freedom and the Minmatar soul strives for open skies, but the Minmatar heart withers away in captivity. It is now up to you, the capsuleer. You hold the power to free our people. You are the heroes of your generation. It is finally time to make the Amarr pay for their atrocities. We will find those who called themselves "masters," and we will bring them to their knees! Look to your heart, look to our people. Join us! Death to Amarr!

Cogni began her training at the Republic Military School in the Ammold system, flying a poor quality ship called a *Reaper*, that looked like a random collection of junk lashed together with bailing wire. All the Minmatar vessels are improvisations built from whatever materials happened to be at hand. Her first two missions, assigned by an agent named Geil Ustegokkur, involved eliminating a saboteur to retrieve stolen documents from him, and then repairing the security breach by delivering a new codebook to Republic Fleet Logistical Support in the Minmatar capital system, Pator. She then transferred to the Republic Military School in the Hadaugago system where she repeated that two-session course with Alfiker Maliddar.

Next Cogni completed three much more substantial courses. "Balancing the Books," taught by Latorfani Aldimund, was a ten-mission business practicum, in which she learned how to mine valuable ores from asteroids and also how to protect the trade routes against criminal cartels. Second, she took "Cash Flow for Capsuleers," a military class taught by Fykalia Adaferid, eliminating pirates, rescuing civilians, resisting an invitation to join the pirates, and finally destroying a narcotics warehouse with its boss. Pilots in *EVE* are called capsuleers because whenever their ship is destroyed they survive in an escape capsule, as happened to Cogni once during this course.

Finally, she completed "Making Mountains of Molehills," a ten-lesson industrial course taught by Stedad Yrmori in which she mined ore, refined it to extract the useful resources, then employed a Capacitor Booster blueprint with the manufacturing system on the space station to create 25 of these valuable pieces of equipment. Many systems on a spacecraft draw power from a capacitor, which constantly recharges but can run dangerously low during combat, so a booster can be the difference between victory and defeat. The mid-term exam, so to speak, was constructing a small shuttlecraft with materials she collected herself, and the final exam was crafting a small frigate called a *Burst*.

Having completed 34 training missions, Cogni made what proved to be a serious mistake, imagining she was ready for any challenge. Sister Alitura of the Sisters of EVE in the distant Arnon system recruited her to undertake a 50-mission epic arc, beginning with an assignment to search for the wreckage of a ship called the Damsel. Intermittently battling pirates, she rescued crew members from the doomed vessel and gathered data, with the growing sense that the Damsel's fate was part of a much larger problem. A key fact was that control had been lost over a number of drones, robot spacecraft that were formidable weapons. In two missions she rescued people, once from drones and once from pirates, by zooming in, grabbing her target, then zooming away without doing battle. This tactic may have seemed clever at the time, but it provided no insight about how well she would do if she were forced to stand and fight.

Mission 27 of the arc was her downfall. Having discovered the hive where the drones were being controlled, the Sisters of EVE told her to wipe them out. Three times she attempted to do so and three times her ship was destroyed. When she bought a new one for the next attempt, she added more advanced technology to help her escape and planned new tactics – but to no avail. Disheartened, Cogni retreated back to Minmatar space.

Theo Logian saw what had happened to Cogni, and vowed it would not happen to him. He would prepare better, and he would never lose a ship. However, his extreme self-discipline was a form of arrogance, and his pride that he would never become overconfident was merely another kind of overconfidence. Theo is not only a citizen of the Amarr Empire, but also belongs to the pure Amarr bloodline, described in this paragraph on the Info description other players see when they check his data:

> True Amarrians – direct descendants of an ethnic group that conquered all the civilizations of its home world – are proud and supercilious, with a great sense of tradition and ancestry. They are considered arrogant and tyrannical by most others. The Empire's defeat at the hands of the mysterious Jovians, and the Minmatar uprising that followed, left an indelible

mark on Amarrian culture. This double failure, a turning point in their history, has shaped an entire generation of policy and philosophy among the imperial elite.

In his own mind, Theo sees both past and future in fundamentally religious terms. When he was visiting the Theology Council Tribunal in the Amarr system itself, heart of the Throne Worlds, he read with approval the following propaganda for the Militia Office:

The Amarr Empire used to shine as a beacon to humanity of what it meant to be civilized: To be strong, and to lead by example. Through God's words we spread civilization throughout the stars and it is by our leadership that New Eden achieved its wings. It is up to you to carry this example, the lessons of God's chosen, and reinstate the Empire of Amarr to its former and rightful glory. We need to reclaim the Minmatar from the drudge, chaos and inhumanity in which they currently dwell, and into God's light. We are their angels. We must be their saviors. By your power they shall be rescued from the dark. God wills it, and so it shall be.

At the Imperial Academy in the Deepari system, Theo took classes essentially identical to the ones Cogni had taken, but with different teachers. Always guided by spiritual concerns, he decided to christen his spaceships with the names of the astrologically-significant old planets of the now-lost Earth system, quickly working his way through Mercury, Venus, Earth, Mars, Jupiter and Saturn. The last of these was his favorite, a beautiful cruiser with powerful armaments and even decent cargo capacity. He planned to name his future battlecruiser Uranus, and his battleship Neptune.

When the Sisters of EVE sought his aid, he very carefully did the first ten missions, paused while gaining experience elsewhere, then did 13 more missions before pausing again. Priding himself on his caution, he decided that the epic arc could be completed only with a battleship outfitted with heavy defenses and using long rage artillery and cruise missiles. This would require much training and investment of much money, so he returned to Amarr space intending to accomplish that thorough preparation while doing missions for the Theology Council and other imperial agencies.

Unfortunately, while he was able to get assignments that earned him money, they often seemed trivial or unrelated to Amarr's sacred goals. One mission involved recovering the stolen formula for the Quaff company's new soft drink, for example. Perhaps the most disillusioning mission was assigned to him by Hansa Anuf in the imperial Court Chamberlin Bureau, and was called "The Heir's Favorite Slave." A slave girl had escaped from one of the five heirs to the imperial throne, and her owner naturally wanted her recaptured, while keeping the whole incident quiet. Anuf explained that slaves should obey their masters: "Most of the difficult labor in the Empire is performed by legions of uneducated slaves, who serve at the beck and call of those who are both clearly and naturally above their station. From conquered nations to hereditary servants, Amarrian slaves are diverse and numerous, and they spend their entire lives working toward enlightenment under the guidance of their rightful masters."

An online novella titled *Theodicy*, by Tony Gonzales, begins with the words of God from the *Book of Reclaiming* in the Amarr scriptures: "I give to you the destiny of Faith, and you will bring its message to every planet of every star in the heavens. Go forth, conquer in my Name, and reclaim that which I have given" [1]. It then quotes the Minmatar reaction from the *Sebiestor Tribe Chronicles*: "How, dear God, did it come to this? Were these invaders not of flesh and bone like us? What evil is this that compels men to commit such horrors against each other?" The story begins as an Amarrian guard tortures a slave, confident that every blow by his shockwhip benefits the slave, because dying in infinite agony would bestow spiritual enlightenment. It is doubtful that Theo would have behaved this way, had he been assigned to supervise slaves.

By this point in his career, Theo had developed his own scriptural interpretations, and he could imagine a devil's advocate argument that the slave was not worth the effort of hauling her back. But Anuf offered him 104,000 inter-stellar credits to do the job, with an 88,000 credit bonus if he did so within 6 hours, so he immediately launched. However, he quickly encountered a technical problem. The acceleration gate he needed to reach the runaway could not handle a ship as big as his Saturn, so he forfeited the 758 credits he had placed as collateral to ensure successful completion of the mission.

After many missions in which he gained skills, Theo was able to handle enemy fleets as large as 30 ships, hitting them in skirmishes with time to repair before the next one. Even when a mission did not require him to destroy every enemy, he did so because he could use his skills in salvaging from the wrecks materials that were often far more valuable than the prize for completing the mission. His doom came when Delabet Adiam at the Imperial Academy School in the Sarum system ordered him to harass some drones that had been bothering the miners in a nearby asteroid field. He immediately attacked what seemed to be the lead ship in the first of several groups, a Strain Infester Alvi. Three ordinary Invester Alvis and a Splinter Alvi began firing at him as well, while five other enemy ships waited at a safe distance of 50 kilometers.

His recent experience with other multi-group battles convinced him that he could defeat the first group, then recover shield and capacitor strength before engaging the second group. If necessary, he assumed, he could warp out for repairs and then rejoin the battle. He soon discovered that his opponent was both webifying and scrambling his ship, so he could not warp out and his weapons were ineffective. He struggled to break through the enemy shield, and briefly thought he might succeed, but then his capacitor was exhausted and his own shields failed. In utter disgrace, he piloted his escape pod back to the Imperial Academy School where he had wisely kept his old ship, the Jupiter. Chastened, he tried mining with the Jupiter to get money for a new ship, but its pathetic cargo capacity was only a quarter that of his Saturn. The only bright note was that he had insured the Saturn, and the company dutifully paid him 2,263,750 credits.

Swallowing his pride, he bought a cheap industrial ship with huge cargo capacity, and named it Uranus. The sales brochure explained, "The Bestower has for decades been used by the Empire as a slave transport, shipping human labor between cultivated planets in Imperial space." It looked to him like an old shoe and could initially support only one mining laser, compared with the four that his lost Saturn

Fig. 7.1 Theo logian's battlecruiser, Neptune, at the heart of the Amarr Empire

could handle. But with cargohold expansions it could carry 10,000 m³ of ore, ten times the Saturn's 1,000, and he settled down to the sordid business of grubbing in the dirt of asteroids.

Figure 7.1 shows the result of Theo's pious labors. Blazing across the sky is his battlecruiser, Neptune, armed with a thousand cruise missiles of Paradise class. Speeding at 3,750 meters per second, for a flight time of 20 seconds, their range is fully 75 km. These are extra heavy assault weapons, described by the manufacture in almost supernatural terms: "The mother of all missiles, the Paradise delivers a tremendous payload, guaranteed to get its victims acquainted with their personal god in a quick, but painful manner." In the distance at the right is the ringed planet, Amarr VI, otherwise known as Zorast. At the top is the planet's second moon, and in the lower right is one small part of the Theology Council Tribunal, the vast, city-sized space station where the Amarr Empire's judicial matters are judged.

Scientific and Philosophical Basis

EVE Online is the best gameworld to help us think though the realities of interstellar travel and colonization. Space is much more vast than many people imagine, and those who do know the facts still have difficulty fully comprehending them. Personally, I think about this in terms of the 2 week-long research trips I took to NASA's Jet Propulsion Laboratory, to observe scientists communicate with journalists during the times when the Voyager II robot spacecraft encountered the planets Saturn and Uranus. Voyager II launched from Earth in July 1977, reached Saturn in

Planet	Amarr Solar System				Pator Solar System			
	Name	Radius	Orbit	Temp.	Name	Radius	Orbit	Temp.
I	Mikew	2,086 km	0.267 AU	292 K	Istin	1,864 km	0.420 AU	148 K
II	Mikeb	1,844 km	0.388 AU	242 K	Belogor	3,350 km	0.782 AU	108 K
III	Amarr	3,751 km	0.465 AU	221 K	Huggar	5,769 km	1.723 AU	73 K
IV	Tamiroth	4,035 km	0.729 AU	176 K	Matar	3,253 km	2.663 AU	58 K
V	Sek	6,296 km	1.241 AU	135 K	Vakir	9,913 km	3.674 AU	50 K
VI	Zorast	14,307 km	2.017 AU	106 K	Varkal	3,323 km	4.629 AU	44 K
VII	Nemantizor	9,992 km	3.565 AU	80 K	Kulheim	8,204 km	5.910 AU	39 K
VIII	Oris	47,775 km	7.789 AU	54 K	Orinn	7,897 km	9.421 AU	31 K
IX	Derdainys	18,268 km	19.900 AU	33 K	Sylo	2,563 km	11.743 AU	28 K

Fig. 7.2 The home solar systems of the Amarr and Minmatar

August 1981, and Uranus in January 1986. To go from Saturn to Uranus – from our seventh planet to our eighth – took about 1,613 days. I just asked Theo Logian to make a similar voyage in the Amarr solar system from Nemantizor, the seventh planet which even looks like Saturn because it has rings, to Oris, the eighth planet. He made the journey in less than a minute, implying he was travelling something like two million times as fast as Voyager. I also asked him and Cogni Tion to give me data about their solar systems, shown here in Fig. 7.2.

We see that the radius of Amarr Prime, the mean distance from its center to its surface, is 3,751 km, which is about 2,330 miles. This makes it rather smaller than the Earth, which has a radius of about 6,371 km, and just slighter larger than Mars, which has a radius of 3,396 km. Its orbit, or orbital radius, is the mean distance from the planet to the star at the center of its solar system, which is 0.465 AU. Presumably, "AU" stands for Astronomical Unit, which in conventional astronomy is the mean distance from the Earth to the Sun or about 150,000,000 km. However in *EVE* an AU equals 100,000,000 km, which means Amarr Prime orbits 46,500,000 km from its star. This is almost exactly the closest distance that our own system's planet Mercury comes to the Sun on its somewhat eccentric orbit, which we might think would make Amarr rather hot. However, the mean temperature of the planet's surface, 221 K (Kelvin), is the equivalent of −52°C or −62°F, well below the freezing point of water.

Other information in the database about the planet gives a fuller picture. Amarr Prime is described as a solid planet with very low atmospheric pressure. A solid planet, as opposed to the two other categories of ice and gas, makes sense for a planet near its star, because a star's radiation tends to clear ice and gas out of the region close to it. A thin atmosphere means that the heat of its star does not get trapped on the planet, nor does wind disperse the heat away from the equator. Thus like Mercury, Amarr is probably very hot in the center of the equator exposed to the heat of the star, but very cold at the poles and on the night side because there is too little atmosphere to hold the heat. We do not know how long Amarr's day is, so we cannot guess whether rapid rotation evens out the temperature between day and night. However, the database tells us that its orbital period – its year – is 25 days. Amarr goes around its star much faster than Mercury, which takes 88 days on a slightly longer orbit, implying that Amarr's star is more massive than our own Sun.

Most of these planets lack substantial atmospheres. In the metric system, the atmospheric pressure on the Earth is just over 100 kilopascals (kPa); a pascal is a force of one newton per square meter. Two Amarr gas planets have thin atmospheres, Zorast with a surface pressure of 21.22 kPa and Nemantizor with 4.03. Only three of the Pator planets have measurable atmospheres: Vakir is a gas planet, with a pressure of 15.94 kPa, while Kulheim and Orinn are ice planets with surface pressures of 10.34 and 2.63 respectively. Just two of the 18 planets, both in the Amarr system, have something we might call *air*.

Derdainys has an atmospheric pressure comparable to that of the Earth, 142.06 kPa. An ice planet, it is so cold that all the oxygen and nitrogen would have frozen out of the atmosphere, so I wonder what foul gases it consists of! Even chlorine would be hard as a rock. The answer probably is hydrogen and helium, both of which would still be gasses at that cold temperature, benign enough, but it does no good to breathe them. Given the lack of free oxygen, at least the hydrogen will not explode. Shouting for help in this atmosphere would produce a squeaky high-pitched voice, so people's last breaths might be wasted in laughter.

Oris is the monster world of both systems, smaller than both Jupiter and Saturn, but larger than Uranus and Neptune. Its atmospheric pressure is 1,032.78 kPa, ten times that on the Earth but not nearly so great as the pressure on the surface of Venus. The acceleration of gravity on Oris is 30.5 meters per second per second, more than three times that on the Earth. So, people would be unable to move, and it is doubtful whether their bodies could stand the gravity for long. The database gives the escape velocity as 54.0 km; this is the speed a bullet would need to be fired straight up – ignoring the effects of the dense atmosphere – to escape the planet. This is nearly five times the 11.2 kilometers per second for the Earth, suggesting that anybody who landed on Oris would have great difficulty leaving.

Both solar systems possess asteroid belts, 15 in Amarr and 4 in Pator, where miners get the raw materials for the economy. These are not like the one asteroid belt in our own solar system, where the asteroids vary from Ceres – which has recently been redefined as a dwarf planet because it has a 475 km radius – down to gains of sand spread entirely around the sun over a wide range of distances between the orbits of Mars and Jupiter. An asteroid belt in the EVE galaxy is always associated with a planet and consists a 50 km arc of boulders that are set closely together. This is convenient for mining, because when one asteroid is exhausted another is ready to be mined near at hand, but not astronomically realistic.

In order to complete a picture of the worlds from which the current galactic society expanded, I briefly created a third character, a Caldari named Gala Xy, and sent her to the Luminaire system. The planet Gallente Prime turned out to have a radius of 37,753 km, and Caldari Prime was nearly as big at 30,217 km. Both had surface temperatures only a few degrees above absolute zero, and they were no more attractive places to live than our own Uranus and Neptune. Like Amarr, Luminaire has 15 asteroid belts. In all three solar systems, human society had survived among the moons and asteroids around large, inhospitable worlds.

The key point about these three solar systems is that none really contains an Earth-like planet, suitable for easy colonization by human beings. No wonder that the Amarr Empire and the Minmatar Republic prefer to remain in orbit! Doing so saves them the heavy fuel costs of launching from large planets, so naturally they look to the moons and asteroids for mineral resources. The Amarr and Pator systems realistically make a valid point: The majority of real solar systems are likely to be inhospitable for the evolution of intelligent life, and colonizers from outside will face grave difficulties. Thus, interstellar voyages will need to go greater distances on average than between one star and its nearest neighbor.

Voyager II is not going to any particular star, but by some definitions is has left our solar system. As of July 30, 2010, Voyager II was 13,891,000,000 km from the Sun, moving outward at 15.479 kilometers per second [2]. That sounds far and fast, but it is nothing compared to the numbers that would be required for interstellar travel. The Sun's light, traveling as it does literally at the speed of light, takes 24 hours and 37 minutes to reach Voyager II. That is just a little over a day, so we could correctly say that Voyager II had moved one light-day in the 32 years since launch. A light-year is 365 times as far, and Alpha Centauri which is the closest other probable social system is 4.4 light years distant. Do the math, and Voyager would take on the order of 50,000 years to go from one solar system to the next. And we don't even yet know whether Alpha Centauri has planets!

Science fiction writers have invented a host of fantasies to explain how their ships can travel faster than light, let alone faster than real spacecraft [3]. *EVE* makes use of three of them, warp speed within solar systems, stargates to jump from one solar system to another, and a wormhole to get everybody into the *EVE* galaxy in the first place. Despite all the nice stories, there is no scientific basis for any of these ideas. They are no more realistic than to say that Cupid shoots his arrows at a young couple to make them love each other. There is however one way in which people could "travel" to distant stars at the speed of light. They could go as packets of information transmitted by a galactic Internet, just as the *EVE* packets zoom between my home near Washington DC and the *EVE* server farm in London, England!

Technology of the EVE Galaxy

In *EVE Online*, spaceships can either be made or bought, but in neither case do we learn much about their propulsion systems. For example, the rockets they use for short distance travel do not apparently require fuel. They can warp swiftly across a solar system, and as Theo found to his distress an enemy can disable this ability. However, we know nothing about the machinery they use to accomplish these billion-kilometer jumps. Every player is given a free starter ship, like the Impairor that Theo named *Mercury*, and will get another one if his only ship is destroyed in combat. Figure 7.3 shows all of Theo's ships, along with information about their capabilities and requirements.

The cargo capacity of Mercury, a measure of how much ore or equipment it could transport, was only 135 cubic meters (m^3), but that of Uranus was 4,800, even before Theo added a number of cargohold expansions that more than doubled its capacity.

Type	Statistics	Training Required
"Mercury" Impairor-class Rookie Ship	120 m^3 1,148,000 kg 0 ISK	Spaceship Command 1 Amarr Frigate 1
"Venus" Tormentor-class Frigate	235 m^3 1,180,000 kg 15,000 ISK	Spaceship Command 1 Amarr Frigate 2
"Earth" Sigil-class Industrial Ship	3,000 m^3 11,000,000 kg 371,000 ISK	Spaceship Command 3 Amarr Frigate 3 Amarr Industrial 1
"Mars" Executioner-class Frigate	135 m^3 1,124,000 kg 50,000 ISK	Spaceship Command 1 Amarr Frigate 2
"Jupiter" Punisher-class Frigate	135 m^3 1,047,000 kg 178,000 ISK	Spaceship Command 1 Amarr Frigate 3
"Saturn" Omen-class Cruiser	450 m^3 11,650,000 kg 4,000,000 ISK	Spaceship Command 3 Amarr Frigate 4 Amarr Cruiser 2
"Uranus" Bestower-class Industrial ship	4,800 m^3 13,500,000 kg 514,000 ISK	Spaceship Command 3 Amarr Frigate 3 Amarr Industrial 1
"Neptune" Prophecy-class Battlecruiser	350 m^3 13,665,000 kg 23,900,000 ISK	Spaceship Command 4 Battlecruisers 1 Amarr Cruiser 3 Amarr Frigate 4

Fig. 7.3 Theo Logian's ships

The mass of each ship is given in kilograms, a factor that combines with the power of the engines to determine how rapidly a ship can accelerate. The third statistic for each ship was its cost, when Theo bought one from the elaborate market system. The currency in *EVE* is called ISK. This is the standard abbreviation for the currency of the game's home country, the Icelandic Króna or Crown, but in *EVE* it means Inter-Stellar Kredits. To put this in context, a full mining run for Uranus could take as much as 4 hours and netted about 1,000,000 ISK. About 16,000,000 of the cost of Neptune was covered by mining, during something like 32 hours spent floating among the asteroids.

The final column in the table shows the training Theo needed before he could operate the ship. He began at level 1 on both Spaceship Command and Amarr Frigate, but needed to train Amarr Frigate to level 2 before he could get the Venus. Training takes time, and training an entirely new skill also requires buying or being given the right to train in it. At any given moment, either Theo or Cogni – but not both – would be training by having a skill in a training queue. Practicing a skill has nothing to do with training in *EVE*, although it does in many other games. About every 3 seconds, the skill at the top of the training queue gains one point.

Here is what Theo needed to do to gain the ability to operate Paradise cruise missiles. He needed to reach level 3 in both Standard Missiles (16,000 skill points) and Heavy Missiles (24,000), and level 5 in Missile Launcher Operation (fully 256,000 skill points), before he could even begin to train Cruise Missiles. This took about ten full days, but the training progressed whether or not I was logged into *EVE*. He needed to train Cruise Missiles only to level 1, but decided to go right away to level 2 to increase their effectiveness. This required training 7,072 skill points. To add level 3 would have taken 21 hours, and level 4 would have added 5 days. Of course, before he could do any of this training, he needed to buy the rights from the market. The three preparatory skills costs a total of 128,000 ISK, and Cruise Missiles itself cost 315,000 ISK.

Manufacturing an item requires training necessary skills, getting a blueprint plus raw materials from mining different kinds of asteroids, then using the manufacturing system at a space station. One can also develop research skills, as Cogni did, that can be used to increase the quality of goods manufactured with the blueprint. All kinds of equipment and even light ships can be manufactured efficiently, but really powerful ships seem far too costly. Theo checked what would have been required to make his Prophecy-class Neptune rather than buy it. The minerals required were isogen (27,028 units), megacyte (1,058), mexallon (168,822), pyerite (660,168), zydrine (2,664), and tritanium (3,078,189). Note that *tritanium* is different from *titanium*, and *EVE* has both. Theo had mined a good deal of tritanium to earn the money for Neptune, obtaining it from asteroids composed of dense veldspar. But when he checked the market for buying all these materials, they added up to more than 300,000,000 ISK, and the cost of the blueprint would have been 229,500,000. It was hard to see how Theo could have afforded to set up his own ship-building business, and that was not his goal.

Despite its silence about ship propulsion, *EVE* probably uses more metaphors from advanced technology than any of the other games, in explaining how various devices work. This is especially obvious for weapon ammunition. A laser gun requires a crystal that regulates the wavelength of the beam it fires, each with a distinctive range to target and damage effect. Standard crystals operate in the visible light range, that one octave of radiation that humans can see. Others operate in the gamma, X-ray, ultraviolet, infrared, microwave, and radio wavelengths. As its online catalog description says, the special multifrequency crystal "randomly cycles the laser through the entire spectrum."

Laser weapons deplete the capacitor of one's own ship, thus competing with the ship's energy shields, so many pilots prefer projectile weapons instead, despite the fact that they require costly ammunition. These offer a range of options, including nuclear warhead shells, although the catalog says these "are considered by most races to be crude and primitive." Depleted Uranium slugs, which have actually been used by the American military and are merely heavier than lead rather than nuclear, are said to have good penetration of armor. Titanium sabot rounds penetrate armor with their explosive cores that shoot fragments into an enemy ship, whereas EM shells deliver an electro-magnetic pulse that fries the enemy ship's electronic shields. Alternately, one may use rockets and cruise missiles that can hit the enemy at extreme distances.

Travel between solar systems is accomplished through jumpgates that connect particular pairs of systems. Figure 7.4 shows what four of them look like. Whenever a ship jumps, a ball of light appears inside the gate, expands into something like an

Fig. 7.4 Some of the many designs of jumpgates for interstellar travel

arrow of light, and shoots away. The physics involved is unknown. Users do get much experience in the control system, however, and a ship's autopilot can handle several jumps in a row, to any given destination. Indeed, the navigation system in *EVE* is complex, functional, and realistic, allowing the user to look at the galaxy, rotate it, focus on particular systems, and search for the best routes. Many space-flight games unrealistically expect the user to fly the vehicle like an airplane, and some even recommend joysticks. Real space navigation is accomplished by switching on the correct program in a computer, and that is how *EVE* does it.

Social Life Between the Stars

EVE Online stresses conflict between people even more than many of the other examples do, leaving much of the galaxy wide open for player-versus-player (PvP) combat. A fictional organization called *Concord* enforces a truce only in the areas where new players gain the skills necessary to navigate PvP. This is evident in the rhetoric used by the four official factions. We have seen the recruitment appeals of the Amarr and Minmatar, and here is comparable propaganda from the two others:

> Gallente: The Federation is the standard, indeed the only example, of equality, justice, freedom and sanity in today's universe. While the rest of the Empires seek to expand in willful acts of destruction, the Federation seeks to protect its people and its borders from the deprivations of the Caldari who have shown unprovoked aggression against us. We attempted to be civilized, to talk, to travel the road of peace, but they refused.

> Caldari: The state had lost its way. The corporations forgot the principles upon which they were founded. The people suffered. The State suffered. We were an embarrassment. Our

forefathers turned in their graves at the depths to which our leaders had allowed our State to fall. No more. We are strong once again. We are Caldari once again. We are the State once again, and our homeland is ours at last. We are at war.

These two civilizations originally shared a single social system, Luminaire, and the reestablishment of space travel naturally led to a war. The Gallente conquered the Caldari home world, but not before a fleet of refugees escaped to establish their sovereignty elsewhere. What the Gallente call "unprovoked aggression," may have seemed to the Caldari as simply an attempt to recover their stolen territory. Thus, once conflict has begun, it continually reignites when aggrieved peoples seek to reverse history.

Anger and revenge are powerful motives, as the following example from an Amarr text channel illustrates. Lee JaeDong is alone in low sec space – low security space where a powerful ship can attack a weak one – and runs into serious trouble, including scrambling that prevents the ship from escaping by warping:

Lee JaeDong: I'm in 0.2 space and there is a guy flashing red at me. Should I run?

Aetara Baeldeth: Run.

Princess Amalia: That means he's hostile, get out of there!!!

Delilah Narthex: Means he might have friends.

Asherdonis: Flashing red means thief.

Geema: Or sec rating lower than −5, right?

Lee JaeDong: It says something about warp scramble. What do I do?

Delilah Narthex: Try and warp.

Asherdonis: Ask for a ransom. If they wreck your ship, keep warping.

Princess Amalia: You'll have to abandon ship.

Mamluk Fayeh: Put your boxing gloves on.

Uritori: Kiss your asteroids goodbye.

Asherdonis: Pods are hard to scramble.

Princess Amalia: Just get out of there, abandon ship and get out of there. You never go into low sec space alone.

Delilah Narthex: Or fight if you don't have expensive implants and don't mind showing up at a station where your clone is at (assuming your clone has skillpoints higher than current). Make the bugger work for the ship if you can't warp out.

Princess Amalia: Delilah, are you nuts?

Delilah Narthex: No. I had an Amarr ship and took out two Hurricanes before they podded me.

Uritori: Of course she is.

Delilah Narthex: Save them to your future "hit" list.

Princess Amalia: The rules of engagement state quite clearly, "If the hostile vessel is stronger than your current loadout and they don't ask for ransom money then the only option is to abandon ship and retreat."

Delilah Narthex: That was written by pussies.

Princess Amalia: That was written by smart fleet admirals. Discretion is the better part of valor, missie.

Delilah Narthex: There is a point to running. But if you can't, you fight.

Princess Amalia: So you'd rather get killed than live to fight another day.

Delilah Narthex: Depends.

Uritori: Why should anyone assume they'd be honorable about anything?

Delilah Narthex: Did the Russians like burning cropland when fleeing Nazis? Did Churchill really want to let Nazis bomb Coventry when England had broken the Enigma code?

Princess Amalia: That's ancient Earth history ladies.

Delilah Narthex: If you're scrambled and have no way out. Don't leave the asset, it's lost anyway. Make the buggers pay.

FaFneir: Agee. Take them with you.

We don't have the testimony of the pirate attacking Lee JaeDong in this case, but some pirates have boasted in other online channels. A character named UberNero posted a video on YouTube, proclaiming 20,796 views when I found it, "How to be a EVE-Online Pirate." His text read:

Warp in on target, lock, proceed to warp scramble and Web. Begin to orbit at optimal range, and open fire. Now sit back and watch the fireworks. And hope your ship can kill your target before he kills you. As soon as you notice your target is about to pop, be prepared to lock and warp disrupt the pod. Start a conversation with your now ship-less target. If the target accepts, get straight to the point, "Good fight, and ask for your desired ransom amount." If the target declines, simply blow up his pod. Ransom amount varies on the age of pilot, corp he is in, and just what you think his life is worth. Older pilots = Demand a higher ransom. Younger pilots = Demand a lower ransom. Don't waste time, give the target between 30 and 60 s to come up with the money, last thing you need is to get jumped. Although sometimes, a little reassurance is needed. If local is empty and the target doesn't seem to trust you take your time. Any ISK is better than none. Once the target has paid, warp to safespot, sure you can still pod him, but it is frowned upon. As well, if the target doesn't pay up, feel free to send a few more volleys into him. Walked away with five million ISK. Not bad off a 20 day old character. Don't forget to go back and see what you can get out of the wreckage.

The threat of piracy is one motivation that impels people to join corporations, the chief voluntary organizations in the galaxy. Briefly, Theo Logian was attracted to a pure Amarr corporation with a religious name: Sanctus Ordo Luminarium Amarri. Led by a Grand Inquisitor named Pawel Minutor, this corporation quoted in its advertisements what Emperor Heideran III said in the year 21,290 when he opened the first modern stargate: "In God's name, the Amarr have reclaimed the entirely of our world. Now, blessed with the divine mandate of God, we spread our reach unto other worlds. From nearby Hedion, to the distant Misaba, to the burning southern star Penirgman, and all lands in-between. They are our birthright, our duty, our Domain." Theo hesitated to join, however, when he saw that the membership was only 35, hardly enough to defend him against all the enemies they faced.

Checking the list of advertisements available in the user interface, Theo saw that a corporation called EVE University had fully 882 members. That was more like it! Its advertisement was less thrilling, but impressive in its own way: "For over 5 years, we have trained players who are new to the galaxy, and taught them all they need to know in order to make a good start. We always have position available for both new students and experienced teachers who are willing to pass their experience on to new generations." Visiting the university's chat channel, he learned that students often graduate and join other corporations once they have been fully trained, or remain to become mentors of new students. That sounded right for him. Unfortunately, when he examined the procedures for applying to the university, he read: "Due to a recent rash of corp thefts, Uni recruitment is currently closed. Please bear with us as we work out the details. Have a nice day."

The highest level of social organization among players is the elected Council of Stellar Management, which advises the creators of *EVE* about improvements and problems. 40 candidates competed in the May 2009 election, 16 from the United States, 5 from the United Kingdom, 4 from Canada, 3 each from Netherlands and Australia, 2 from Serbia, and one each from Austria, Belgium, France, Germany, Italy, Norway, and Romania. To run for office, they were required to give their real names, but here we refer to them by the names of their characters.

One candidate, Chip Mintago, posted two parody advertisements on YouTube, that boasted 1,456 and 625 views when I checked them out. The first video, "Chip Mintago Answers the Allegations," shows him sitting in his sleazy office, wearing a blue and white floral Hawaiian short-sleeve shirt, and trying to refute a long list of corruption charges. First he defends a charity founded by his brother, Sal Mintago, called the Jovian Children's Fund that solicits donations "to sponsor an adorable little Jovian boy or girl" in the war torn Autonomous Jovian Region, who will then write thankful letters to the sponsor. Chip notes that a disgruntled sponsor claimed the planet did not even exist, let alone the children, but Chip explained this was just hysteria from "the political lynch mob" that opposed his candidacy. "As to the accusations of black-market trading, bootlegging, misappropriation of Concord funds… that I shook down a children's hospital, that I stole essential shuttle parts and sold them on the black market, that I made up a planet and sold real estate there to the Amarr royal family…" All these were false accusations, Chip says, by his political enemies.

The second YouTube advertisement is titled, "Annual Statement to Shareholders (and litigants in The People of Osman-4 vs Mintago) – Chip Mintago Scrap Metal King. Director Chip Mintago." Mintago explains that investment in his company is not endangered during the current galactic financial crisis, because it is handled in his own currency, the Mintago. At this point a warning disk appears on the screen, bearing the legend, "We do not accept Mintago Dollars." He comments that the economic crisis is a "golden age" for the scrap metal business, and a graph appears on the screen showing that as scrap metal profits rise, human dignity falls. He then turns to the subject of the lawsuit: "As to the misunderstanding on Osman-4: Unfortunately, I wasn't there to supervise the operation personally, because a restraining order by my ex-wife prevented me from traveling within four AU of the Osman system. But I can assure you, that if I had been there, if I had known that you regarded that titanium statue as your god, we would never – never – have touched it." While he speaks, his equally-disreputable assistant is talking heatedly on the telephone in the background, beside a blackboard that proclaims, "22 days since an indictment." When the call is over, this flunky erases the "22" and replaces it with "0."

A total of 26,855 votes were cast in the May 2009 election, 766 of them for Mintago, including mine. However, only nine people won seats on the council, each of them having over a 1,000 votes. A good sense of what the voters value comes from analysis of the campaign platforms of the top three candidates. Dierdra Vaal, the leader and chair of the new Council with 2,967 votes, is a female avatar of a male player who lives in the Netherlands, and who proclaimed five main platform planks.

First, Vaal advocated major changes in the pioneer territories held by corporations of players. These are parts of the galaxy called 0.0 space because there is no protection preventing one player from attacking another. Normal space has a security status rating from 0.5 to 1.0, nominally held by one of the societies, such as the Amarr Empire or Minmatar Republic, and patrolled by the truce-enforcing organization called Concord. Vaal wanted the sovereignty holder to be able to increase the security status of their areas, seed asteroid belts so that the mining returns would be greater, and "invite NPC mission agents into their outposts" so people could undertake missions for them as in high-security space.

Second, Vaal wanted the early experiences for new players to be improved, largely by offering them a more gradual introduction into the complexities of the galaxy, commenting "Eve remains a very difficult game to start in." Third, Vaal suggested a number of improvements in the computer interface, which seemed too complex, and tended to get overwhelming for officers of corporations who had so many things to deal with. Fourth, there were several problems with the rules governing the bounty hunter and mercenary professions, and among the solutions Vaal offered was making kill rights tradable between players. Finally, Vaal wanted the rules of war between player corporations revised, to reduce the advantage of the aggressor.

Vuk Lau, with 2,020 votes, is a male avatar of a male player in Serbia. He also was concerned with the advanced experience in the low-security space: "Watching the first CSM session with great interest the most glaring problem to me was the lack of representation for the 0.0 side of EVE. I consider the 0.0 'endgame' and warfare in it to be the 'real' EVE. Empire space serves some essential services to this endgame, but its primary role should be to get players adjusted to EVE before they head out to 0.0 and enjoy the greatest player versus player combat available anywhere, in any game." He wanted improved customer support, a real effort to achieve consensus on what the long-term goals should be, and making the most costly capital ships harder to destroy.

Mazzilliu, with 1,983 votes, is a female avatar of a female player in the United States who had been playing *EVE* for 3 years. She stressed that despite being female she was "a 0.0 player interested mostly in the PvP aspect of the game, specifically guerilla warfare and alliance combat and seeing that they both have a place in the game." She identified a variety of technical issues, like what she saw as the poor quality of Minmatar ships, and the need for better automatic ways of detecting ISK farmers, who sell in-game currency for real-world currencies as a business.

The constituency for all three of these top candidates was advanced players who operate in low-security space, where conflict rules. To be sure, *EVE* and the others are online games, in which competition must therefore be emphasized, but people enjoy competing because our species evolved under conditions in which wandering bands competed for their hunting and gathering territories. War may not be exactly instinctual in humans, but the basis for it is certain ingrained. Once agriculture had been developed, and people began to hold territory even more fiercely, military institutions became essential to society [4]. *EVE* raises the possibility that the human future will be one of endless war over boundless territories. Note that citizens of the *EVE* galaxy could live in peace with each other, because they are too few yet to fill all the solar systems and thus are not really forced to compete for resources. However, conflict is endemic in human life, and the only question is what form it will take.

Conclusion

As we leave the *EVE* galaxy, and say farewell to Cogni and Theo, each of them is charting a personal future. Cogni Tion is methodically learning how to operate scanning drones, robot space probes that can explore wide territories for interesting sites that demand her personal examination. She may even learn the archaeology skill to allow her to find ancient ruins, whether left over from the first phase of human expansion, or belonging to alien species.

Theo Logian is brooding about whether he dares carry out any missions in the Neptune, which is really too small for cruise missiles, or should save up the 56,000,000 ISK required to buy an Armageddon-class battleship. He has already completed the preliminary training – taking to skill level 4 Spaceship Command, Amarr Frigate, and Amarr Cruiser – but training Battleship would cost him 3,600,000 ISK. He wondered what he should name his great ship. Ancient legends say that the original human solar system contained a ninth planet, Pluto, but more recent records list only eight. Perhaps Pluto was destroyed in a cosmic war. If so, naming his battleship after it would be a bad omen.

References

1. Gonzales, T.: Theodicy. CCP Games, Reykjavík, Iceland (2006). http://www.eve-online.com/races/theodicy/
2. http://voyager.jpl.nasa.gov/mission/weekly-reports/
3. Bainbridge, W.S.: Dimensions of Science Fiction, pp. 78–83. Harvard University Press, Cambridge, MA (1986)
4. Childe, V.G.: Man Makes Himself. New American Library, New York (1951)

Chapter 8
Star Wars Galaxies

Immediately after the destruction of the first Death Star, and across a number of familiar planets, *Star Wars Galaxies* (SWG) allows a player to experience the environment of the great saga without contributing to its events. In studying SWG, I found that it was essential to analyze the movies, several of the books, plus earlier videogames, most especially *Star Wars Episode III: Revenge of the Sith* which I completed. I ran an engineer character named Algorithma Teq up to level 20 in *Star Wars Galaxies*, and a Jedi named Simula Tion up to level 35, but insights seemed to come more from connecting aspects of the mythos across multiple media, rather than concentrating exclusively on the massively multiplayer gameworld.

Hardly a person in an advanced industrial society is unaware of *Star Wars*, yet few may have thought about what this series of movies, novels, and electronic games says about the future of its central topic: religion. Nor may they often think how elitist these stories are, in which one of the heroines is a queen, and the other is a princess. Luke Skywalker and Obi-Wan Kenobi are high priests of a religious cult that is open only to a very tiny fraction of the population who possess supernatural powers. The general public of the galaxy seems to have no faith at all.

A Galaxy Far, Far Away

The game begins with a familiar phrase: "A long time ago in a galaxy far, far away..." Then yellow lettering scrolls up the screen and away, over a black sky filled with stars: "Star Wars Galaxies: An Empire Divided. It is the height of the Galactic Civil War. Although the Rebel Alliance has destroyed the dreaded Death Star, the Emperor still holds thousands of systems in his grip. Throughout the galaxy, civil war rages. Innocents and heroes alike are swept into the conflict. The fate of millions shifts with every battle. On a distant Imperial Space Station, a smaller battle erupts over the fate of a single being's destiny, yours..."

This galaxy may be far, far away, but it is also very familiar. While carrying out some rudimentary training missions on the station, Algorithma was guided via

W.S. Bainbridge, *The Virtual Future*, Springer Series in Immersive Environments, DOI 10.1007/978-0-85729-904-8_8, © Springer-Verlag London Limited 2011 comlink by the humanoid protocol droid, C-3PO, and she actually met Han Solo and Chewbacca face-to-face. After she helped Solo fix the hyperdrive on the Millennium Falcon, he helped her escape to Mos Eisley spaceport on Tatooine, which Obi-Wan called a "wretched hive of scum and villainy" in the original 1977 movie. Soon she found her way to the famous cantina, the tavern where Han Solo originally met Luke and Obi-Wan. She watched the dancers, three of which were holograms of storm troopers in their white space armor. More of a concern were two real storm troopers who scrutinized the customers, in the belief this was a Rebel meeting place, but who became distracted by a pair of Jawas.

Because she was an engineer, Algorithma immediately accepted more training missions, began prospecting the rough terrain for mineral resources, and started crafting useful items. She gained no points when she had to kill someone, because unlike the case in most online role playing games, a character ascends the ladder of experience and status by practicing his or her specific profession, not by completing the same quests as other types of characters or by killing enemies, unless of course their profession specifically requires killing. Algorithma did face the issue of how to avoid being killed. For example, she heard that Jabba the Hut had his agents looking for her because of her connection to Han Solo. At this point in the saga, Han had already cheated Jabba, but Princess Leia had not yet strangled him.

Algorithma avoided invitations to work for the Empire, and to join the Rebels, instead focusing her attention on gaining technical skills, such as building components from which to assemble droids like R2-D2. She remained on Tatooine, but explored widely in search of resources and occasionally accepted a mission to make and deliver some product to a distant destination. Along the way, he visited a few of the historic sites that had been scenes of the original *Star Wars* movie.

Figure 8.1 shows Algorithma, riding her All Terrain Recon Transport walker, inside the crater that was the childhood home of Luke Skywalker, inspecting the moisture evaporator. His Uncle Owen and Aunt Beru were already dead and buried a short distance from this spot, while Luke was busy being a pilot for the Rebel Alliance half way across the galaxy. Tatooine was a very dry planet, not very different from Mars but at least with a substantial atmosphere. Thus it was necessary to extract water for agriculture or human use from the air. The original movie remarked that evaporators required constant maintenance. Technophile that she was, Algorithma also located the abandoned escape pod in which C-3PO and R2-D2 had landed on the planet.

Unlike Algorithma, Simula Tion was a born adventurer and trained to become a Jedi Knight. While Algorithma was puttering around with her minerals and her machines on Tatooine, Simula was gallivanting across several planets, killing bad guys and undertaking dangerous missions. Even when she reached level 35, her skills with the force were frankly rather weak, chiefly limited to wielding an improved model light saber. Her standard battle tactic was to scout a group of enemies from a distance to target one who was separate from the others. A shot from her rifle would wound the lone enemy and cause him to attack, at which point Simula would draw her light saber and make short work of him. However, if two or more enemy attacked at once, she was in deep trouble. This was especially likely

Fig. 8.1 Algorithma Teq at Luke Skywalker's home in *Star Wars Galaxies*

during the many missions that sent her into winding caverns deep under the surface of the planet, or into the maze-like corridors of underground bunkers.

On Tatooine, Simula killed womp rats just as Luke had done, hunted elephantine banthas, and tangled with Tusken Raiders. She zoomed across the dry desert in her souped-up landspeeder, not very different from Luke's, levitating just a few inches above the sand, visiting Mos Eisley, Tosche station, Anchorhead, Mos Espa, and many less familiar places. She walked along the street where Anakin Skywalker had lived with his mother, Shmi, and as best as I can tell the architecture was identical to that shown in the movies. She also photographed the krayt dragon skeleton on a sand dune, Obi-Wan Kenobi's home, and the immense octopus-like sarlacc monster.

Many missions came from Jabba the Hut or his associates. Jabba is a huge slug-like creature, who might be compared to a walrus at the risk of insulting the entire mammalian class of animals. He lounges in what amounts to a throne room, surrounded by lackeys and entertained by a dancing girl. In the 1977 move, Jabba was the head of a crime syndicate that had employed Han Solo to do some smuggling, and he reappeared to play a central role in the 1982 film *Return of the Jedi*. Although moviegoers did not actually see Jabba's headquarters until *Return of the Jedi*, it presumably existed long before, so it was not anachronistic to have it in *Star Wars Galaxies*, showing Jabba at the height of his powers.

Simula placed flowers at the grave of Shmi, Luke's enslaved grandmother, at Luke's boyhood home. When she spoke with the new owner of the place, Zef Ando, he begged her to accept a mission that ironically reflected the way R2-D2 behaved when Luke first acquired him. Ando had bought cheap droids from Jawas, just as

Luke's uncle had done, but these robots were so fastidious they had decided that the farm's moisture harvesters needed to be junked rather than repaired. Simula defused the explosives the droids had set, and in return got information about a mysterious shipment both the Empire and the Rebel Alliance were hunting for. Her next stop was a wrecked Jawa sandcrawler, a huge lumbering fortress on tank treads like the one that had belonged to the Jawas who captured C-3PO and R2-D2 and who were later slaughtered by imperial storm troopers. However, this time the bantha tracks were in single file, indicating that sand people were responsible. This was the exact opposite of the situation in the 1977 movie, where imperial storm troopers had wanted visitors to believe the Tusken sand people were responsible but had stupidly left tracks that were not single file.

A protocol droid looking very much like C-3PO but named FA-2PO sent Simula onward in this series of legacy quests. In Tusken caves, Simula encountered binary load lifters, so she finally got to see what this technical term referred to. In the original movie, C-3PO said he could program them, so many viewers may have assumed the "binary" part referred to the computer programming. No, it merely refers to the fact that these robot equivalents of forklift trucks use two (binary) hands to load warehouse objects. The next stop was the shop belonging to Watto, the flying slave master who had owned Luke's father, Anakin Skywalker, and his grandmother, Shmi. Watto presumably lived long after his scenes in the first prequel *The Phantom Menace* which dates from 1999 and covers events about 35 years before *Star Wars Galaxies*. Step-by-step, quests sent Simula in search of components of an R2 droid, to reassemble them and deliver the droid either to the Empire or to the Rebel Alliance. Whether this was really R2-D2, on an incidental misadventure, or a close cousin of his, may not make much difference. Simula chose to deliver the reassembled R2 unit to a Rebel agent on Naboo.

Simula took pilot training and visited the planets Naboo, Corellia, Endor, and Yavin IV. At Naboo, she toured the palace that had belonged to the late Queen Amidala, who was the mother of both Luke Skywalker and Princess Leia but died when they were born. She also went deep into the swamps to meet the Gungan leader, Nass, where she helped him by retrieving some artifacts from thieves. Corellia was mentioned but did not appear in the six original movies; Simula used it chiefly as a transportation hub when visiting other planets. At Endor she visited with the peaceful Ewoks in their tree house villages. Trekking deep into the jungles of Yavin IV on her speeder bike, she found the secret Rebel base and personally congratulated Luke Skywalker for having destroyed the Death Star just minutes before, as his X-wing rocket fighter cooled off from the mission beside them.

Scientific and Philosophical Basis

The *Star Wars* saga is what science fiction literary critics call *space opera*, an extravagant adventure set against a fanciful interplanetary background, in which little attention is paid to scientific realism, and where much of the technology functions as if by magic but usually wrapped in the rhetoric of machinery. The term is by analogy to the *soap operas* that began on radio decades ago and still infest daytime television, and to *horse operas* which were run-of-the-mill cowboy dramas that used to be popular decades ago.

The most direct science fiction influences on *Star Wars* were the three *Flash Gordon* movie serials of the 1930s [1]. The very opening of *Star Wars*, when paragraphs of text scroll up and away describing the previous episode of the story, is taken from the 1940 serial *Flash Gordon Conquers the Universe*, and the famous *Star Wars* music was directly inspired by the classical *Flash Gordon* soundtracks. Audiences may have been confused in the Death Star escape scene of the 1977 movie, when Luke accidentally destroys the controls for a light bridge and needs to hold Leia as they swing across a chasm on a cable like Tarzan and Jane on a jungle vine. Several scenes of the 1938 serial, *Flash Gordon's Trip to Mars* involve a light bridge, including one in which the heroes escape across it. The climax of the 1977 movie, in which Luke destroys the Death Star, is similar to the conclusion of *Flash Gordon Conquers the Universe*, in which Flash crashes his rocket ship into the citadel of Ming the Merciless, a scientific sorcerer equivalent to the emperor in the *Star Wars* saga.

The *Star Wars* movies begin with that famous phrase: "A long time ago in a galaxy far, far away." Yes, that long ago time may have been the 1930s when people falsely believed that other planets were earthlike biospheres where Flash Gordon could experience adventures of a kind familiar from other genres of heroic fiction. But that "long time ago" could refer to childhood in general, when the transition to adolescence unleashes all kind of dreams, both realistic and unrealistic. Much of the technology seems positively adolescent, speeder bikes like motorcycles and landspeeders like convertible cars. A constant theme in the stories is the relationship between fathers and sons, and the difficult time when the son replaces the father as the primary male adult. If space opera is a childish form of science fiction, *Star Wars* seeks to become mature.

Indeed, *Star Wars* has something that most space opera fiction lacks, namely a quasi-religious ideology. For a thousand generations the Old Republic was defended by a priesthood of Jedi Knights, but they were eradicated in the Clone Wars that ushered in the Dark Time. The clones were biologically mass produced soldiers who overwhelmed the Jedi with their very numbers. The Jedi were warrior monks who followed a transcendental spiritual discipline not unlike Zen Buddhism. Thus, the clone victory represented the triumph of materialistic technology over spiritual religion.

The chief principle of Jedi philosophy was called *the Force*, an energy field that permeates all existence and binds the galaxy together. It has no personality of its own, although sensitive humans can communicate through it, and thus it is not a god. The prequel films dating from around the year 2000 introduced a concept not found in the original 1977–1983 trilogy: *midi-chlorians*. These microscopic entities dwell inside living cells, and people who happen to have a high density of them are strong in the Force. Thus, after the *Star Wars* mythology was well established, creator George Lucas downplayed the religious quality that was at its core. Indeed, outside the ranks of the Jedi, belief in the existence of the Force was sparse and possessed none of the organization and practices that would allow it to be called a religion.

Even before the minions of the Emperor crushed the Jedi, therefore, the galaxy lacked wide-ranging religious denominations, much less an established church. Two factors seem likely to have created this situation. First, the galactic civilization was an amalgam of many highly diverse societies created by almost as many independently evolved intelligent species, so there may not have existed the common assumptions and institutions that could have been the basis of a universal religion. Second, the progress of science and technology, which had advanced furthest in areas that emphasized power and control, had driven traditional religions out of the thoroughly secularized interstellar society, to survive precariously only in isolated pockets of cultural rebellion in remote regions of backwater planets.

The victory of the clones over the Jedi was not merely a triumph of science over religion, however, because the Emperor had been aided by treachery within the ranks of the Jedi, themselves. Anakin Skywalker, talented student of two prominent Jedi Masters named Yoda and Obi-Wan Kenobi, allowed himself to be seduced by the Dark Side of the Force, largely from resentment over his mother's enslavement and murder. The Jedi believed that the Force was at their disposal to accomplish miracles, but this could be done safely only if they suspended their own desires and adopted a spiritual state of philosophical detachment. If a trained Jedi approached the Force with feelings such as fear, longing, or anger, the result could be catastrophic even if the Jedi's intentions were benevolent. For a highly adept Jedi to use the Force to satisfy his own personal lusts, would be disastrous in the extreme. After a duel nearly to the death against his teacher, Obi-Wan Kenobi, Anakin Skywalker became sinister Darth Vader.

The initial sign that the Force could be any more than a primitive superstition is some vestigial power, possibly only psychological, that Vader appears to possess. In a pivotal scene in the 1977 movie, Governor Tarkin presides over the war council in the Death Star conference room, as Darth Vader stands ominously to one side. Vader's grotesque respirator mask, part of the life-support system he has needed ever since Obi-Wan defeated him, gives him the appearance of a great beetle. Admiral Motti boasts about his Death Star, "This station is now the ultimate power in the universe."

Vader disputes this, saying, "The ability to destroy a planet is insignificant next to the power of the Force."

Motti scorns Vader's "sad devotion to that ancient religion," but suddenly he finds he cannot breathe, because Vader has used his paranormal powers at a distance of several meters to choke the admiral's windpipe. After teaching Motti a lesson, Vader releases his spell. Interestingly, the novelization of this scene has Mott refer to faith in the Force not in terms of religion, but as "sad devotion to that ancient mythology" [2].

Meanwhile, Obi-Wan is instructing Luke in the ways of the Force. Again, the movie and the novel differ somewhat, not merely because the text of the movie is much shorter, but also because the novel's ghost writer, Alan Dean Foster, may have shifted the metaphors slightly in the direction of orthodox science fiction. In the book, Obi-Wan explains that the Force is "in the mind" and can influence weaker minds. He says it is an energy field: "An aura that at once controls and obeys. It is a nothingness that can accomplish miracles... as much magic as science" [3].

For many years, Kenobi withdrew from the conflicts that raged across the galaxy. He had served honorably in the Clone Wars, but soon after Darth Vader betrayed the Jedi he entered anonymous exile in the Dune Sea of Tatooine. There R2-D2 found him. He has not lost all the powers of a Jedi knight and is still capable of clouding the minds of imperial storm troopers, but he seems a very powerless old man. Han Solo calls Kenobi's spiritual discipline a "hokey religion" in the movie and a "hocus-pocus religion" in the book, even as the elder seeks to train young Luke Skywalker in the ways of the Force.

While Obi-wan is teaching the boy to use his father's light saber, he feels a terrible disturbance in the Force that he later learns was the deaths of millions when the planet Alderaan was destroyed by the Death Star. Recovering his balance, Kenobi tries to explain to Luke that "a Jedi can feel the Force flowing through him" and use it to guide his aim in battle. In the end, Luke will become so sensitive to the Force that he can destroy the Death Star with an impossibly well-aimed missile, after switching off the automatic guidance system.

When a tremor in the Force tells Darth Vader that Obi-Wan has entered the Death Star, Tarkin is incredulous, convinced that Kenobi is long dead. Vader insists he must not underestimate the power of the Force. Tarkin replies, "The Jedi are extinct, their fire has gone out of the universe. You, my friend, are all that's left of their religion." This overconfidence leads shortly to Tarkin's death, but Vader escapes to battle for Luke's soul in *The Empire Strikes Back*, made in 1980.

In the original 1977 movie, much of the action of the Force seems to be purely mental, either a sixth sense that the three Jedi have, or the ability to influence weak minds. In the final battle, Luke wins because he trusts his intuitive feelings, so his victory could be one of philosophy or psychology, rather than religion. The one strikingly religious point is when Obi-Wan's body vanishes when Vader's light saber strikes it, and Obi-Wan's voice continues to speak to Luke after death. The 1980 sequel takes the ideology in an even more supernatural direction.

Much of the doctrine of the Force is taught to Luke by Yoda on the swamp planet Dagobah, which is not depicted in *Star Wars Galaxies*. When I first saw the film, after waiting in line a couple of hours outside the theater near midnight for its first Seattle showing, Yoda struck me as a Zen Master of the California sect. Japanese Buddhism actually made its highly-publicized American debut not in California, but at the 1893 Chicago World's Fair where a group of Swedenborgians organized the World's Parliament of Religions. To his largely Christian and thus perplexed audience, Horin Toki remarked: "Prayer or worship is like a finger which points to the moon; when the round face of the moon is once seen there is no need of the finger" [4]. My Chinese aristocrat aunt once told me, "Bill, my family has never been religious. We are Confucian!"

There are three related ways in which the religious traditions of major Asian civilizations are very different from Judeo-Christian-Islamic traditions [5]. First, and most obviously in this context, their intellectual elites tend to treat the doctrines as refined philosophies and downplay the supernatural elements we associate with religion. Second, ordinary people in these traditions tend to believe in much more magic, whether for healing or prognostication, than modern monotheists do, but often outside the official temples. Third, religious communities tend to be fragmented and highly pluralist, often mixing very different traditions of belief and practice. Although Protestantism and other movements in western countries created a degree of pluralism within Christianity, having one god and one book promotes conformity and centralization. There is no pope of polytheistic Hinduism. Yes, Confucianism was highly bureaucratic, but Chinese people simultaneously practiced Buddhism, Taoism and local magical cults. Yes, Shinto in Japan was connected to the imperial government, but people also practiced several varieties of Buddhism, and public shrines tend to be locally owned and operated.

There are many ways to interpret Zen: as a monastic retreat from the demands of a high-pressure feudal society, as a psychotherapy to treat anxiety under conditions of objective and inescapable external stress, and simply as the logical refinement of Buddhist principles. In the 1950s, this wave washed up on the California shore, just as the wave of enthusiasm for Psychoanalysis washed in from the opposite direction [6]. Daisetz Suzuki and Erich Fromm even famously debated what these very different movements had to say about each other, without coming to any firm conclusions [7]. In retrospect we can say that a significant fraction of the American population, especially among artists and intellectuals, had become literally *disenchanted* with their traditional religious faiths and were looking for a new way to deal with their emotional and existential problems. The pessimists among intellectuals soaked up Existentialism and became *Beatniks*, preparing the way for the drug counterculture of the late 1960s. Artists can find joy in their art, even when it contradicts the prevailing ideologies, and George Lucas was able to blend Zen principles into a remarkably optimistic space opera.

Yoda explains to Luke that a Jedi must become focused on the present, not fearful of the future, passive not aggressive, peaceful not impatient. This is Buddhist detachment, yet in Zen it also requires submission to a teacher. As Yoda said, "A Jedi must have the deepest commitment, the most serious mind... You must unlearn what you have learned." Japanese culture blends Buddhism with traditional animist beliefs, and the two really are compatible. If the world is in some sense not really real, allowing us to detach from it, then it can be conceptualized in spiritual terms rather than material ones. For most Christians, the soul exists apart from matter, and God rules the universe rather than being contained within it. But for pantheists, there is no difference between spirit and matter, and everything that is real has a spiritual essence. Yoda says, "A Jedi's strength flows from the Force." Yet this is not one of the forces of physics, but a force of psychics.

Near the end of Luke's training by Yoda, two incidents reveal more about the Force. Luke has been learning to levitate physical objects by channeling the Force through his mind. His spaceship, unexpectedly sinks into the swamp, and Yoda challenges him to levitate it. Luke struggles, raises it a short distance, then drops it back down into the muck. A spaceship stuck in the mud is a perfect metaphor of the failed human attempt to transcend the mundane limitations of life. Luke says the ship is too big for him to lift, suggesting that a physical quality can trump a spiritual quality. Yoda responds that size does not matter, and, immediately before levitating the ship himself, explains:

> For my ally is the Force. And a powerful ally it is. Life creates it, makes it grow. Its energy surrounds us and binds us. Luminous beings are we… (Yoda pinches Luke's shoulder)… not this crude matter. (a sweeping gesture) You must feel the Force around you. (gesturing) Here, between you… me… the tree… the rock… everywhere! Yes, even between this land and that ship! [8]

The second incident is when Luke breaks off his training, against Yoda's firm advice, to save his friends, when the Force tells him they are in danger on another planet. This triggers one of the many debates about the Dark Side of the Force, unleashed when adepts use it for their own purposes, typically polluting it with their personal passions. Of course this is the opposite of Buddhist detachment, but remarkably it does not reduce the individual's ability to use the Force. When Luke destroyed the Death Star, he was acting out exactly the climax of Eugen Herrigel's 1953 book, *Zen in the Art of Archery*, in which perfect detachment allows an archer to hit the bull's eye of a distant target [9]. However, once Anakin Skywalker had learned how to channel the force in his Jedi training, he retained that power when he turned to the Dark Side and became a disciple of the Sith.

Here, the story not only becomes a moral drama between good and evil, rather more Christian than Buddhist, but also connects to a major theme of science fiction: parapsychology. Over the century spanning the year 1900, a number of radical religious movements departed from Christian traditions, including Spiritualism and Theosophy drawing upon occult or Asian traditions to varying degrees, and began to use scientific rhetoric, not unlike the Force. Upton Sinclair wrote a book about telepathy, calling it *mental radio* [10]. Cults used apparently technical terms like *vibrations*, *rays*, *engrams*, *telekinesis*, *psychokinesis*, *clairvoyance*, *parapsychology*, and *extra-sensory perception*. At the same time the *Flash Gordon* serials were being made, J. B. Rhine reported laboratory research that seemed to provide scientific evidence for the reality of ESP [11]. The fact that academic researchers have been unable to verify the existence of any of these psychic phenomena weighs heavily against them, but many members of the general public still believe [12].

Magic and science are not clearly distinguished in the *Flash Gordon* serials, as they are not in *Star Wars*, but there are moments when magic prevails. The original 1936 serial ends as Emperor Ming immolates himself at the Temple of the Great God Tao (pronounced by the high priest *tay-oh*, not approximately *dow* as in Taoism). However, he magically survives the flames to become allied to Queen Azura of Mars in the sequel. A bona fide sorceress, she is able to teleport herself from place to place, and to cast spells, using magic gems. At the climax, they are rendered powerless when Flash, Dr. Zarkov, and the King of the Clay Men use high voltage electricity to zap her jewelry, which leaves open the possibility they were not magic but advanced technology.

Division of Labor

Sony Online Entertainment (SOE), the creators of *Star Wars Galaxies* faced a difficult problem. Presumably, every player would want to be a magical Jedi knight, yet for several reasons this would ruin the game. First of all, given that the gameworld is set in the period immediately after the destruction of the Death Star, long after most Jedi had been killed in the Clone Wars, or hunted down by Dark Vader's extermination squads, there simply were not supposed to be any Jedi, according to the *Star Wars* mythos, except for Luke Skywalker [13]. The 2004 novel connected to the game, *Star Wars Galaxies: The Ruins of Dantooine*, focused on more ordinary people, caught in the struggle between the Empire and the Rebel Alliance, and did not suggest any process that might quickly fill the galaxy with a new generation of Jedi [14].

Even more crucial, to create a rich virtual world, a large number of players would need to be motivated to play all the other roles in society, from smugglers and bounty hunters, to technicians and foot soldiers. Therefore, when the game launched in June 2003, it did not include any Jedi. Only by completing a large number of unspecified achievements at great difficulty could a player earn a "Force Sensitive slot" permitting creation of one Jedi character, which no player achieved until that November. Wikipedia reports:

> Media outlets and players criticized SOE for the substantial time commitment to unlock a Jedi, penalties for in-game death of a Jedi character which was permanent after three deaths, and monotonous game play required to acquire the Jedi character. Developers responded by changing the penalty for death to skill loss in January 2004 and creating a quest system to unlock the character. In November 2005, as part of the "New Game Enhancements" Jedi was changed to a starting profession and all players were allowed to play as one [15].

The New Game Enhancements (NGE) update included a major reformulation of the professions and effectively invalidated all the effort many players had invested gaining the right to have a Jedi character. In my research in other gamelike virtual worlds, I have encountered several people who are still angry at what they saw as a major act of betrayal. Reportedly, the NGE also interfered with a regular game expansion scheduled for the same time, and many players demanded refunds. Not having experienced the NGE myself, I am in no position to criticize Sony. 2005 was the year in which Sony's *EverQuest II* was overwhelmed by the popularity of *World of Warcraft*, which reached something like 20 times as many players, so I can imagine the company was desperately seeking the formula for success.

Truth to tell, most jobs in a real world are boring, and most workers may justly believe they are exploited by the elites. Thus it is difficult to create a virtual world that is both realistic and popular. To their credit, the people at Sony had originally designed an extremely complex economy with a vast division of labor following intricate rules. Clearly the intent was to find something interesting for each player to do, regardless of which roles they chose to perform, at the very least basking in the glory of living in a galaxy far, far away. The NGE was so sweeping that we can consider it only in outline, but it simplified the professions, made achievement

Original Professions		After New Game Enhancements	
Starting	Elite, Hybrid or Allegiance	Professions	Role
Artisan	Architect, Armorsmith, Chef, Droid Engineer, Merchant, Shipwright, Tailor, Weaponsmith	Trader	Crafts and sells items (domestic goods, structures, munitions, engineering)
Brawler	Commando, Fencer, Pikeman, Smuggler, Swordsman, Teräs Käsi Artist	Commando	A combat specialist who uses heavy weaponry and demolitions
Entertainer	Dancer, Image Designer, Musician	Entertainer	Uses dance and music to heal minds
Marksman	Bounty Hunter, Carbineer, Combat Medic, Commando, Pistoleer, Rifleman, Smuggler, Squad Leader	Bounty Hunter	Mercenaries who chase foes like prey
Medic	Bio-Engineer, Combat Medic, Doctor	Medic	Keeps others alive during and after combat
Scout	Bio-Engineer, Bounty Hunter, Creature Handler, Ranger, Squad Leader	Officer	Leads a squad
(Brawler and Marksman)	(Smuggler)	Smuggler	Moves stolen goods across the galaxy
Pilot	Privateer, Imperial Navy Pilot, Rebel Alliance Starfighter Pilot	Pilot	Privateer, Imperial Navy Pilot, Rebel Alliance Starfighter Pilot
Politician	(Master Politician)	Politician	(Master Politician)
No Equivalent		Spy	Sneaks up quietly on targets
No Equivalent		Jedi	Uses the Force to overcome and control enemies

Fig. 8.2 Two systems of professions in *Star Wars Galaxies*

easier, and may in so doing have debased the creativity of the designers. However, the original system may have had serious flaws. Given that fallible human designers were trying to do God's job – creating a world – complete success eluded them.

Figure 8.2 compares outlines of the system of professions before and after the NGE, arranged roughly to show similarities. The data come from a pair of guidebooks published in 2005, one before and the other after the NGE [16]. Some additional but more modest changes had been made by the time I entered the gameworld in December 2008. The original professions were so complicated that no chart can do them justice, but most of them fit one of three categories: starting, elite, and hybrid. As the name implies, a starting profession is what a player does at the beginning. A player who has completed the arduous training in a starting profession can than train in a related elite one. For example, an experienced artisan can learn to be an architect. A hybrid profession requires the player to have completed training in two specific starting professions. For example, a character who is both a marksman and a medic can train to become a combat medic. The NGE wiped away most of this structure, thereby making some players feel their prior labors had been invalidated. The history of the real world teaches that revolutions tend to do that.

Training up in the original professions required hard work, along four upward paths. For example, a marksman trained up these four status ladders: rifles, pistols, carbines, and ranged support. Each ladder required earning and investing skill points plus points representing experience performing the profession. For example, becoming a master marksman requires 77 skill points and 338,550 experience points. To start training as a combat medic, the player would need to invest similar effort climbing the four ladders of the medic profession: medical augmentation, ranged healing, medical support, and organic chemistry. Then, combat medic training would begin, using a similar skill tree. A character's skill points were limited to 250, so this system (like those in many other games) forced players to specialize with each character, and thus motivated having multiple characters if they wanted a range of playing experiences [17].

Originally, players could not pilot spaceships, but that ability was added in the Jump to Lightspeed expansion in October 2004, as was the elite shipwright profession. I have listed pilot as a starting profession, but really the system was rather different for this skill tree. To get training and to get a spaceship, a player needed to select one of three allegiances, either supporting the emperor, joining the rebels, or acting alone as a privateer like Han Solo. Any characters could become pilots, regardless of what other professions they practiced.

The politician profession was also open to characters practicing any other professions. Like the earlier game, *Anarchy Online*, *Star Wars Galaxies* allowed players to own houses, and to cluster them into their own cities. A politician could place a city hall, attract people to place their houses around it, and cooperatively develop various civic improvements. The four ladders of a politician's skill tree were: fiscal policy, martial policy, civic policy, and city customization. When Simula visited a city hall, she admired many heroic statues standing in the corners and flanking the doorways, gazed in awe at the many trophy heads of beasts on the wall, and contemplated the weighty decisions that must have been made at the elegant conference table. She inspected the city voting terminal, where politicians had entered their names in candidacy for mayor, and citizens of the city had voted one of them into office.

Notice that the new professions in Fig. 8.2 are related to the old ones. Bounty hunter is like the old bounty hunter elite profession building on the scout starter profession, and the new commando role is derived from the old brawler, marksman, and commando roles. An officer in the new system is like a squad leader in the old one, a trader is like an artisan, and smugglers remain smugglers, as is true for medics and entertainers as well. The new spy profession seems to be inspired by rogues in *World of Warcraft*, or stealth characters in other games who can render themselves unobtrusive or even invisible. Now, Jedi is a starting profession Given that players had already created all the other kinds of characters, adding a flood of Jedi to the mix may not have been as disruptive as had this quasi-religious profession been available from the beginning.

Each profession still had subspecialties and status ladders, but no longer embedded in quite so rigorous and complex a division of labor. I wanted to have an engineer character, in order to become familiar with the crafting technologies, but that was classified as a subspecialty of *trader*, a label that emphasizes its economic rather than technical functions. The post-NGE guidebook explained:

> While they can't fight their way out of a paper bag, Traders are an essential facet of the galaxy. Traders are the ones who craft all the really nice, non-generic equipment that allows you to excel at whatever you do. There are four varieties of Traders – Domestics (who craft food and clothing), Engineering (who craft droids and most weapons, but not explosive munitions), Munitions (all weapons and armor), and Structures (both groundside buildings and interstellar ships). All Traders start with the basics of Surveying and Business, and all of them learn Merchant skills, as well [18].

Algorithma found surveying very interesting. First, one needs a survey device, of which there are several kinds, most of which must she had to manufacture from raw materials, components, and schematics. Each survey device could be used to prospect for a particular natural resource, such as a given metal that was needed to build part of a machine. Algorithma would go out into the wilderness. She would set the survey device to detect the desired metal and push the *survey* button. In a few moments, a map of her vicinity would appear, showing the chances of finding the metal at each point on a grid, expressed as a percentage. She would see a range of numbers, often all zeroes but sometimes with higher numbers in one direction. She would walk in that direction, activate the survey device again, and see a new map telling her which direction she should walk next. When she found a spot with a fairly good chance of success, often above 70%, she would take a sample. At low experience levels, this is how an engineer gets needed materials, but at higher experience levels a second device would be used to extract greater quantities.

The assumption of the system was that engineers would act as traders, selling the raw materials and manufactured products that they alone can offer, and making a variety of useful things that contributed to a vibrant economic system. However, Algorithma found a leveling guide on the World Wide Web that quickly increased her experience in a thoroughly introverted manner [19]. First of all, manufacturing something in *practice mode* conferred a little more experience than manufacturing for sale, so she always used practice mode and never sold anything. Second, the guide identified the items that produced the most experience at least cost, so she practiced making the same things over and over: 7 survey devices, 56 crafting devices, and as many personal harvesters and droid frames as she could endure making. Periodically, she surveyed the wastelands of Tatooine for the needed materials, and pretty much the only things she needed to get from the wider economy were the schematics that allowed her crafting devices to make particular products.

In contrast, Simula Tion leveled up by taking on missions, mostly to kill specified numbers of local enemies or perform tasks inside their bases. She did occasionally receive Jedi training, but most of the time the fact she was a Jedi rather than a commando did not seem very significant. As Fig. 8.3 shows, she got to wear a Jedi costume and to visit the locale of the climax of the film *Return of the Jedi*. But other types of characters could just as easily have visited an Ewok village on Endor, riding a speeder bike.

Fig. 8.3 Simula Tion at an Ewok village in *Star Wars Galaxies*

One Jedi lesson involved understanding how the Force affects all life on the planet, whether connected to anger or to harmony. Amid a stand of trees at coordinates -5529, -3832 on Tatooine, she meditated in peaceful tranquility, soothed by the Light Side of the Force. Even animals lost all hostility, under this benign influence. At a ruined village at -7572, -1867, she destroyed ten twisted creatures that had been perverted by the Dark Side. However, a later Jedi quest required collecting crystals from within dark caverns, in order to upgrade the light saber, rather than having any philosophical significance. Other quests identify transcendent values that could be secular rather than religious. To gain the Mark of the Hero, a character must demonstrate altruism, honor, courage and intellect. Thus, the introduction of hordes of Jedi into *Star Wars Galaxies* did not seem to transform it into a religious drama.

The Future of Religion

In a pair of award-winning books titled *The Future of Religion* and *A Theory of Religion*, Rodney Stark and I examined the possibility that religion will continually reinvent itself, rather than be consigned by science to the dust-heap of history [20]. More recently, I have expressed doubts in my book, *Across the Secular Abyss* [12]. Science and technology may improve human life, but they are not solving the existential dilemmas of life, notably death and social deprivations like poverty and powerlessness. There is good evidence that religion serves some positive functions for society, sustaining the birth rate, suppressing some kinds of crimes, and supporting physical health in some ways. Religion is not an unalloyed good, of course, and it may at times do harm, and at other times be impotent. But on balance it seems to be beneficial.

But are religious faiths "true?" From a scientific perspective, are they correct descriptions of reality? Or, do existing religious doctrines contradict some solid findings of scientific research, while not offering any objective evidence that could convince non-believers? For a moment, please set aside your own answers to these questions, and consider this remarkable possibility: Religion may be factually false but necessary for human survival. If so, no matter how much respect they have for each other as human beings, clergy and scientists may be on a collision course, and we all face potential disaster if one or the other prevails. We cannot rely upon *Star Wars* to answer questions theologians and scientists have failed to resolve, but the mythos presents challenges to both.

Given that the empire, with its clones and Death Star, represents evil technology, and the Jedi represent good religion, what is the role of religion in *Star Wars Galaxies*? It is almost entirely absent, except among the Jedi. To be sure, a player who explores every nook and cranny of every planet will find a few religious references. On Corellia there is a Nyax cult and an Afarathu cult; the Witches called Nightsisters on Dathomir appear to be a cult; Krayr cultists on Tatooine collect bones, but these are all non-player character enemies, rather than members of player society. The ruins of Jedi temples can be found on Mustafar and Dantooine; there is a Gungan temple on Naboo; and two abandoned temples on Yavin IV, but players do not worship in them.

Star Wars Episode III: Revenge of the Sith is a fundamentally religious videogame, but set entirely outside the western traditions. This is the episode in which Anakin Skywalker is turned to the dark side, against the urging of his teacher, Obi Wan Kenobi. Until the final level, the player alternates between the characters of the two Jedi, battling enemies with light saber and occasional application of the Force. It can lift heavy objects that block the path, throw things at enemies, cast spells on enemies to facilitate using the light saber on them, allow the Jedi to jump great distances, and heal the Jedi when he has been wounded. Along the way, the player builds up the abilities of both Jedi, only realizing near the end that this makes Skywalker a more formidable opponent when he turns against Kenobi. In the final level, the two battle, with the player taking the role of Kenobi against Skywalker who is played by the game machine. Both can use the Force, and Kenobi must press his attack against Skywalker vigorously, to give him no time to heal himself with it. In the end, Skywalker is vanquished, but then transforms into Darth Vader, the formidable villain of the series. The values taught by *Star Wars* differ from Christianity not only in urging detachment rather than charity, but also in lacking a deity and suggesting that humans can acquire god-like powers.

In his novelization of this story, Matthew Stover quotes some of the Jedi wisdom Obi-Wan tried to teach Anakin. Detachment brings with it a sense of timelessness, or of existing in the present without fear of the future or anger at the past. To blame people, we must believe in both free will and causation, yet: "*Why* is meaningless;

it is an echo of the past, or a whisper from the future. All that matters, for this infinite now, is *what*, and *where*, and *who*" [21]. Yet Anakin is obsessed by guilt and
anger at the death of his mother, who might not have been killed by the sandpeople
if her son had not run away with Obi-Wan to become a Jedi. The Jedi rule by tradition rather than gaining their power through any kind of democratic process, so their
lack of sympathy concerning the death of innocent people seems self-serving: "It is
the way of the universe, which is another manner of saying that it is the will of the
Force," Obi-Wan has told him. "Everything dies. In time, even stars burn out. That
is why Jedi form no attachments: all things pass. To hold on to something – or someone – beyond its time is to set your selfish desires against the Force. That is a path
of misery, Anakin; the Jedi do not walk it" [22].

Since the Jedi form no attachments to others, it is only reasonable that others
form no attachments to them. They do not function as priests in the *Star Wars* universe; they do not minister to people's emotional needs, and they do not heal. In *Star
Wars Galaxies*, the characters who perform functions like those of a religious minister are the entertainers and medics. Not aloof from society like the holy Jedi, they
are deeply embedded in it, as Nic Ducheneaut and Robert Moore explain in their
detailed pre-NGE analysis of social relations in the game:

> Professions have an enormous impact on the interactions between players. Indeed all of
> them are essential to the game, and they were also purposefully designed to be interdepen-
> dent. To pick a simple example, marksmen need medics and entertainers to heal their
> wounds and battle fatigue. Medics, in turn, need wounded marksmen to heal and scouts to
> procure the resources needed to make drugs. Entertainers need tired combatants to relax but
> also tailors to manufacture their stage outfit [23].

This was written before Jedi became common, yet when I played a Jedi character
it felt perfectly comfortable to handle the quests alone, without bothering to join
a group or rely upon others to do what I could not. To the extent that Jedi can function well as solo players, they do not contribute to the social life, quite apart from
the mystical ideology that distances them from other people. The game does not
treat pilots who work for the Empire any less well than pilots who work for the
Rebel Alliance, so how can we distinguish the evil side in their conflict from the
good side? Time will tell whether the Rebel Alliance rules any more wisely than the
Empire, but it is certainly possible to argue that both the Jedi and the Sith to whom
Darth Vader belongs are bad guys. Given that they have no god, the Jedi cannot
logically argue that their powers are legitimate because they are god-given.

When Algorithma and Simula visited private homes in the player-created cities,
they cataloged the great variety of artworks on display, seeing very few that could
by any stretch of the imagination be called religious. A life-sized statue of the
emperor stood in the corner of one house, and a bust of Count Duku stood on a
pedestal in another house, sitting in front of a wall display of gigantic beetles. Many
homes had model spaceships of several designs, projected in the air as bluish holograms, or holograms of Luke Skywalker, Darth Vader, a Jawa sandcrawler, and even
the Death Star. One home proudly displayed a duplicate of the hologram chess set
for the original movie, in full animation. Many homes contained collections of
manikins dressed in clothing that might be worn by characters of different kinds.

Posters and paintings hung on the walls, a few of which even depicted the movies as movies, while most presented the mythos as if it were real.

Luxurious carpets covered the floors of more affluent homes, some of them carrying military symbols. In addition to much ordinary furniture, some houses had deluxe sarlacc trash cans, in which a replica of this tentacled desert monster presumably consumed the trash. A few had a large indoor fountain and a fireplace, complete with water and flames. There were also many fancy appliances that save the owner a trip to a non-player city to do various work: food and chemical crafting station; weapon, droid, and general item crafting station; clothing and armor crafting station. Other appliances which may not have been functional included: holonet tracking station; technical console; incubator unit; and droids of many types. Simula did not dare sit in Darth Vader's loveseat, for fear he would appear beside her. Conceivably, the two Wookiee totems she found in one home might have religious significance, but they were displayed on a coffee table rather than in a shrine.

All of these artifacts were provided by the game designers, often as part of special events and promotions over the years, rather than expressing the tastes and possible religious sensitivities of the players. Yet it is noteworthy that the objects embodied the arts and technology, but not religion. The Jedi cult may be a religion, or it may be an exotic reflection of science and technology, but in the mythos it seems to be a spiritual elite that bars ordinary people from membership. Its status comes from the fact that Jedi possess actual paranormal powers. Its moral ambivalence comes from the fact that no god exists to judge or discipline Jedi, and thus from a traditional perspective it is a defective religion. Given the social chaos that afflicts the entire galaxy, and the sinister qualities attributed to much of the advanced technology, it is remarkable that ordinary people have not created their own religions to fill the vast spiritual vacuum.

Conclusion

At the very end of *Return of the Jedi*, after Darth Vader and the emperor have been vanquished, the first night of freedom falls on Endor. Luke stands beside the celebrating Ewoks smiling at his friends, Leia, Han, Chewbacca, and the two robots. But he looks beyond them, into the Force. And there he sees his father, Yoda, and Obi-Wan Kenobi, smiling at him. He alone of the celebrants has the capacity to see them, but they truly exist, on a higher plane of being. The three Jedi are the only figures Luke perceives in this vision of the afterlife. He does not see his Uncle Owen or Aunt Beru, who were slaughtered by the storm troopers back on Tatooine, nor does he see the many fellow rebels like Biggs who died in the battle on Hoth or the assaults on the two death stars. Like the Norse Valhalla, this is an elite heaven, where only the most transcendent heroes may go.

The *Star Wars* myth states a very clear conception of the religion of the far future. The Force is not a god, although it clearly is supernatural. The Ewoks worshipped a God, and mistook C-3PO for that golden deity, because they were primitives. Religion had expired in the civilized parts of the galaxy, persisting only among savages, and only a real miracle could bring it back. This is the most challenging claim of *Star Wars*, by far. In advanced technological societies, religion will die, unless its beliefs are literally true. Only actual intervention by the supernatural can save religion from science. At least this is the implication of the *Star Wars* stories, and nothing in *Star Wars Galaxies* proves otherwise.

References

1. Gordon, A.: Star wars: a myth for our time. In: Martin, J.W., Ostwalt, C.E. (eds.) Screening the Sacred: Religion, Myth and Ideology in Popular American Film. pp. 73–82. Westview Press, Boulder (1995); Kinnard, R.: The flash Gordon serials. Films Rev. **39**(4), 194–203
2. Lucas, G.: Star Wars in the Star Wars Trilogy, p. 31. Random House, New York (1987)
3. Lucas, G.: Star Wars in the Star Wars Trilogy, pp. 77–99. Random House, New York (1987)
4. Barrows, J.H.: The World's Parliament of Religions, p. 547. Parliament Publishing Company, Chicago (1893)
5. Bainbridge, W.S.: The Sociology of Religious Movements. Routledge, New York (1997)
6. Suzuki, D.T.: Zen Buddhism. Doubleday, Garden City (1956); Reps, P., Senzaki, N.: Zen Flesh, Zen Bones. Charles E. Tuttle, Rutland (1957); Watts, A.W.: The Way of Zen. Pantheon, New York (1957)
7. Suzuki, D.T., Fromm, E., De Martino, R.: Zen Buddhism and Psychoanalysis. Harper and Row, New York (1960)
8. http://www.blueharvest.net/scoops/esb-script.shtml
9. Herrigel, E.: Zen in the Art of Archery. Pantheon, New York (1953)
10. Sinclair, U.: Mental Radio. A. and C. Boni, New York (1930)
11. Rhine, J.B.: Extra-Sensory Perception. Bruce Humphries, Boston (1934); Frontiers of the Mind. Farrar and Rinehart, New York (1937)
12. Bainbridge, W.S.: Across the Secular Abyss. Lexington, Lanham (2007)
13. Luceno, J.: Star Wars: Dark Lord, the Rise of Darth Vader. Ballantine, New York (2006)
14. Whitney-Robinson, V., Blackman, H.: Star Wars Galaxies: The Ruins of Dantooine. Ballantine, New York (2004)
15. http://en.wikipedia.org/wiki/Star_Wars_Galaxies. Retrieved 17 Oct 2009
16. The earlier system is presented in McCubbin, C., Ladyman, D., Frase T. (eds.) Star Wars Galaxies: The Total Experience. Prima Games, Roseville (2005); the newer version in McCubbin, C.: Star Wars Galaxies: The Complete Guide. Prima Games, Roseville (2005)
17. De Govia, M.: Star Wars Galaxies: The Empire Divided, Quick Reference Guide, p. 55. Prima Games, Roseville (2003)
18. McCubbin, C.: Star Wars Galaxies: The Complete Guide, p. 193. Prima Games, Roseville (2005)
19. http://forums.station.sony.com/swg/posts/list.m?topic_id=556841
20. Stark, R., Bainbridge, W.S.: The Future of Religion. University of California Press, Berkeley (1985); Outstanding book of the year. Award, Society for the Scientific Study of Religion (1986). Reprinted in Chinese, 2006, China Renmin University Press; A Theory of Religion. Toronto/Lang, New York (1987). (Rodney Stark and WSB); Outstanding scholarship. Award, Pacific Sociological Association (1993). Reprinted with new preface. Rutgers University Press, New Brunswick (1996). Translated into Polish as Teoria Religi. Nomos, Krakow (2000)
21. Stover, M.: Star Wars: Revenge of the Sith, p. 127. Ballantine, New York (2005)
22. Stover, M.: Star Wars: Revenge of the Sith, p. 25. Ballantine, New York (2005)
23. Ducheneaut, N., Moore, R.J.: The social side of gaming: a study of interaction patterns in a massively multiplayer online game. In: Proceedings of the 2004 ACM Conference on Computer Supported Cooperative Work, pp. 360–369. ACM, New York (2004), p. 361

Chapter 9
World of Warcraft: Burning Crusade

By far the most popular subscription-based massively multiplayer online role-playing game, *World of Warcraft*, is primarily a fantasy universe in which magic and mythology weave a rich tapestry of legend a visitor can experience directly through completing thousands of quests across vast realms [1]. However, the first of its two major expansions, the Burning Crusade, emphasizes science-fiction elements and offers a direct intellectual challenge to the idea that our own science and technology can progress significantly beyond their current levels of development. Beneath all the fun and delight offered by this marvelously crafted gameworld lurks a grim question: Is it possible that the natural laws of the world we actually inhabit are not capable of supporting the kinds of future we might want to create?

Every viable world, material or virtual, must be governed by natural laws, and *World of Warcraft* is no exception. However, its physical laws are very different from those of our world: planets are flat and the periodic table of elements begins "earth, air, fire, water." Yet, as in our world, conservation laws prevent magic from spiraling out of control, and it is not possible to wish things into existence. While some technologies work better in *World of Warcraft*, such as magic wands, others work worse, such as rockets. The balance of nature is maintained. The laws of social interaction seem very similar to those of our world, basing cooperation on a mixture of mutual trust and economic advantage, while the flourishing economic system seems practically identical to our own. Thus, one feature of this fantasy world is especially troubling: World peace is impossible because too many groups are competing for too few resources. Despite its fanciful good humor, World of Warcraft implies that we in our world face never-ending war in our own real future.

Two New Races

Of my 22 *World of Warcraft* characters, the four most experienced characters provide the observations for this chapter: Catullus the level 80 Blood Elf priest, Maxrohn the level 75 Human priest, Annihila the level 70 Undead death knight, and

Etacarinae the level 50 Draenei shaman. The user interface can tally the number of hours each character was used, so I can report that these four provided a total of exactly 1,842 hours and 20 minutes of participant observation inside this most impressive of virtual worlds.

I began my research in January 2007, the month in which the original two continents (Kalimdor and the Eastern Kingdoms) gained a third, Outland, in the Burning Crusade expansion. This was also when the Blood Elves and Draenei were added to the original eight races. I continued my research through the Lich King expansion in November 2008, when a fourth continent, Northrend, was added, along with the death knight class. Thus, Maxrohn the Human represented the original form of *World of Warcraft*, because the other three characters could not have been created before the expansions. Both he and Catullus thoroughly explored Outland, as did Annihila who came into being long after this continent had been added. Many other more detailed changes occurred during the two major expansions. Notably, the maximum experience level was originally 60, rose to 70 with the Burning Crusade expansion, and reached 80 with the Lich King [2].

Northrend and the two original continents are on the planet Azeroth. Outland is actually a fragment of a second planet, Draenor. As the names suggest, the Draenei came from Draenor. It was not their original world, and "Draenor" means *exile's refuge* in their language. They were native to the planet Argus. The guidebook for Burning Crusade describes the high civilization they had originally built there: "Masters of their world, they used intelligence and magical affinity to craft a society brighter than the stars themselves. Very little seemed beyond the reach of these people and Argus shone like a beacon across the cosmos" [3]. Evil forces conspired against them, and they fled from world to world.

On Draenor they re-established themselves, with fairly advanced science and technology, before being driven out by the native intelligent species, the Orcs, who were quite primitive and still living at the tribal stage [4]. The group of Draenei exiles who reached Azeroth did so in a spaceship called the Exodar, constructed by an even more advanced species about which we know little, the Naaru. Unfortunately, during the chaotic conflict Blood Elves apparently sabotaged the Exodar, and it broke up over Azuremyst Isle. Several main sections of the Exodar landed intact on the western coast of the island, and are now used as the Draenei city. Another section landed on an island immediately east of Azuremyst, where it now serves as the starting point for Draenei characters.

When my research needed a Draenei character, I asked my daughter, Constance May Bainbridge, to create one for me. She had originally given me *World of Warcraft* as a gift, thereby launching this scientific project, and she gave the character a scientific name, inspired by the star system Eta Carinae, which is luminous and turbulent. Etacarinae's first task when she recovered from the shock of the Exodar crash was to help fellow survivors who had been more seriously injured than she. After that, she helped the other Draenei deal with the dangerous creatures and humanoid enemies that infested the archipelago. Her third task, more interesting to her personally, was to learn the conceptual foundation and technical details of her chosen class. She was a shaman.

As the chief *World of Warcraft* wiki explains, "Shamans are spiritual visionaries of tribes and clans. These gifted healers can see into the world of spirits and communicate with creatures invisible to eyes of normal beings. They are beset by visions of the future and use their sight to guide their people through troubled times" [5]. The Orcs naturally had shamans, because theirs was a tribal, clan-based society, but the Draenei had long outgrown this primitive stage in the evolution of religion, and relied upon priests, which the Orcs have not yet developed. However, the trauma of their exodus had both caused them to doubt the effectiveness of their modern culture, and to revere the ancient traditions of the lost world. In addition, they quickly made friends with the indigenous Stillpine Furbolgs, intelligent bear-like creatures who were still in the tribal phase.

Etacarinae learned the Furbolg language, then paid homage to their sacred totems of Coo, Tikti, Yor, and Vark. The possibility that shamanism could become a significant source of technological power for the Draenei was immediately impressed upon her. The Coo totem tested her willingness to explore new ways of thinking by commanding her to leap off a high cliff. Draenei are humanoid creatures – different from Humans chiefly in having hooves, horns, and a tail – so jumping off a cliff would normally be fatal. But she suddenly acquired magical wings that allowed her to glide a long distance to her next shamanistic quest. Progressively over her first 30 levels of experience, she learned the ways of shamanism by direct encounter with personifications of the four primary elements: earth, fire, water, and air. Finally, she understood that the ancient shamanic beliefs of her people were not outdated superstitions, but accurate reflections of significant dimensions of reality that needed to be reincorporated in Draenei science and technology.

When the Draenei arrived on Azeroth, their long enmity toward the Orcs, and more recent unpleasantness with the Blood Elves, caused them to form an alliance with Humans, Dwarves, Gnomes, and with the Night Elves who were a faction of the once-great Elven race in direct competition with their kindred, the Blood Elves. Facing the Alliance was the Horde, consisting of Orcs, Blood Elves, Trolls, Tauren, and Undead. Etacarinae travelled extensively through Kalimdor and the Eastern Kingdoms, especially during the Midsummer festival, when she paid homage to many Alliance fire shrines, and desecrated many Horde fire shrines. At level 40 she gained the ability to wear mail armor and took training to ride an elephantine *elekk*. At level 50, she learned about the fifth element, spirit, that transcends the first four. Figure 9.1 is the last photograph of her, at level 50, returning on her elekk to the spot where she originally landed, at part of the wreckage of the Exodar, and where her remarkable intellectual adventure began.

The large structure in the background is a fragment of the Exodar which crashed miles away from the main portion that became the city, and which has been pressed into service as a first aid station for victims of the disaster. Between Etacarinae and the wreckage, a small team of scientists is working, Botanist Taerix on the left, and her two apprentices, Vishael and Tedon. The cage contains a volatile mutation of one of the local creatures. "The irradiated power cores from the Exodar have been wreaking havoc on the environment here," Taerix explains. "The nearby lake has been contaminated by one of the ship's power crystals. Many of the plants and

Fig. 9.1 Etacarinae at level 50 revisiting the crash site

animals of Ammen Vale have been mutated because of this." The Draenei seek to be good stewards of the advanced technology at their disposal, but same cannot be said of the Blood Elves.

It would be no exaggeration to say that Catullus, like all Blood Elves, is arrogant. He imagines himself to be a great scientist but also a man of letters, and alone of all my *World of Warcraft* characters, he has actually published a book chapter under his own name [6]. At level 80, he has seen it all, including having official certificates proving he has explored every tiny area of Outland and Northrend. Explorer that he is, he originally practiced two of the three gathering professions that require inter-acting with nature, herbalism and animal skinning, taking them to the maximum skill level of 450. Then, partly to provide metals so his guild-mate Annihila could advance in her engineering, he discarded skinning and learned mining up to level 450 as well. He liked to think that these achievements were comparable to having simultaneous doctorates in botany, zoology, and geology. When a character in the British television series, *Dr. Who*, asks the Doctor what he is doctor of, he gives the same answer as Catullus: "Practically everything."

When Catullus began at level 1 in Eversong Woods, he still had much to learn. In particular, of all ten races the Blood Elves were most desperately trying to advance their technological capabilities. The tragic tale of how the ancient civilization of Elves split apart into Blood Elves versus Night Elves is the history of catastrophic fragmentation of the natural world, as well. The continents of Azeroth had origi-nally been joined, then unwise experiments with a great well of forces split the continents apart and destroyed Elven unity [7]. Much more recently, the Third War that had consolidated the original Alliance and Horde factions had nearly destroyed

Silvermoon City, immediately south of Eversong Woods, and caused its inhabitants to join the Horde for mutual self-defense and to rebaptize themselves as Blood Elves, dedicated to the use of science-based technology to regain their lost dominance.

This does not mean they were unaware of the dangers of their technocratic strategy. In his very early training, Arcanist Helion warned, "Control your thirst for magic. It is a thirst unending, Catullus." Watcher Solanian echoed this concern, "You must master your insatiable hungering for magic before it masters you." A graphic novel, *Ghostlands*, explains, "Grieving for the loss of their homeland, most high elves have adopted a new name and a new mission. Calling themselves blood elves, they now seek out and siphon magic from any available source, including demons" [8].

Catullus is a priest, but priests are more like medical scientists than clergymen. The *World of Warcraft* wiki explains, "The priest is the master of healing and preservation, restoring his wounded allies, shielding them in battle and even resurrecting his fallen comrades from death. While he has a variety of protective and enhancement spells to bolster his allies, the priest can also wreak terrible vengeance on his enemies, using the grand powers of the Holy Light to smite and purge them or the devastating powers of the Shadow to decimate their minds" [9].

This is true for all priests, including my second-highest character, the Human priest, Maxrohn. The difference is in the ideology connected to the practice of priesthood. Among Humans, the religion of the Holy Light preaches three cardinal virtues: respect, tenacity and compassion [10]. Blood Elves never concern themselves with abstract ethical rules like these, but use the Light merely as a source of energy for their technologies, doing whatever they can to increase their power – in the sense both of the energies studied by physicists and in the sense of political influence.

Scientific and Philosophical Basis

World of Warcraft is explicitly the result of a decades-long tradition of science-fantasy games, which logically can be connected to general social-scientific theories of human history. A very large number of gameworlds, including this leading example, are often described as *medieval fantasies*, because they depict societies comparable in many ways to Medieval Europe, but with the difference that the superstitions of that era are literally true. Among the other notable examples are *EverQuest*, *Lord of the Rings Online*, *Lineage*, *Warhammer Online*, *Age of Conan*, *Dark Age of Camelot*, *Final Fantasy XI*, *Final Fantasy XIV*, and the originator of the genre, *Ultima Online*. These in turn were heavily influenced by the tabletop medieval fantasy role-playing game, *Dungeons and Dragons* (D&D) which also now exists in an online form.

When D&D co-founder Gary Gygax died, the *World of Warcraft* website said: "Many of us here at Blizzard got our start in gaming with Dungeons & Dragons or one of its computer adaptations and have fond memories of rolling dice, pouring over rulebooks, braving dark caverns and castle keeps, battling kobolds and hill giants. Gary Gygax's work on D&D was an inspiration to us and in many ways helped spark our passion for creating games of our own" [11]. About the same time, the new Isle of Quel'Danas north of Eversong Woods was dedicated to his memory. Gygax himself had paid homage to the influences that had helped inspire his own creative work, including Edgar Rice Burroughs [12].

Starting in 1911, Burroughs wrote a series of novels about a civilization on the planet Mars that had fallen from a more advanced state, and was in something like a medieval period, fragmented into competing city states and races [13]. Especially relevant here was his 1922 novel, *The Chessmen of Mars*, which actually includes the rules of a playable chess-like game called *jetan* that was supposedly popular among the Martians [14]. It uses a board of 100 squares, 10 by 10, and Burroughs explains it represents both the history and current social fragmentation of the planet:

> The game is played with twenty black pieces by one player and twenty orange by his opponent, and is presumed to have originally represented a battle between the Black race of the south and the Yellow race of the north. On Mars the board is usually arranged so that the Black pieces are played from the south and the Orange from the north [15].

The conception Burroughs had of Mars was greatly influenced by the theories of astronomer Percival Lowell that the red planet was dying, through progressive loss of atmosphere and desiccation. The straight lines that Lowell believed he saw through his telescope might be canals dug by the Martians to forestall the end of their civilization [16]. The first novel of the Martian series ends as the automatic atmosphere factory replenishing the air breaks down, and the hero must use telepathy to open the gate so that a technician could make repairs [17]. Mars, as described by Burroughs, is the same kind of mixture of advanced technology and medieval magic that marks *World of Warcraft*, but without powerful spells and using magic a bit more sparingly. Religions are often depicted in Burroughs novels as sinister conspiracies to hold power over people's minds, notably in *The Gods of Mars* and *The Master Mind of Mars*. Across all of his more than 60 books, cults provide much of the local color and motivation for action, just as they do in *World of Warcraft* [18].

Among the other influences Gygax acknowledged, three belonged to a later group of authors who collectively crafted a highly rational form of fantasy fiction: Fritz Leiber, L. Sprague de Camp and Fletcher Pratt. Especially important is the novel *Gather, Darkness!* by Leiber and the *Incompleat Enchanter* series by de Camp and Pratt. These are science-fantasy works that assume magic is based on principles every bit as rigorous as those of science, but applying to a different world from ours. These authors published originally in a pair of magazines edited by John W. Campbell, Jr., *Astounding Stories* and *Unknown Worlds*, who presided over what is often called the "golden age of science fiction" spanning roughly 1938–1953 [19].

Leiber imagines that Earth has just survived a devastating war, and scientists decide that further scientific discovery must be discouraged, until such time as they can devise a new form of society that can handle technology safely. They create a new Middle Ages, complete with serfdom and monks, but with secular and sacred power in their own hands. Confirmed atheists, the scientists pretend to to be priests of the one great god, using hidden technology to accomplish miracles. Among their secret tools of dictatorship are rays that control people's emotions. The avenging angels that fly over the heads of the astonished serfs are really airplanes.

De Camp and Pratt exemplify the *Unknown Worlds* assumption that magic is merely the rational technology that operates in a world with very different natural laws from our own. When the hero of their stories migrates from our world to a very different one, his accustomed technologies stop working and he must learn a new set. Like science, magic has fixed principles, rather than expressing human whims and serving to fulfill human wishes.

Characters in *World of Warcraft* experience this every day. A priest cannot cast spells after his supply of mana has run out, nor can a shaman operate her machine-like totems without sufficient mana. A death knight can use her death grip spell to draw an enemy into the reach of her swords, but only within a certain range and only with a well-defined frequency. The medieval quality of these fantasies suggests a radical model of the human future. Scientists and science fiction writers alike tend to think that technological progress can continue indefinitely, but this may not be correct. To a first approximation, we can indentify three related but distinguishable theories of human history: linear, episodic, and cyclical. Only the first of these can really be optimistic, and the second has extremely pessimistic variants.

The *linear* theory of human progress holds not only that knowledge and wealth grow steadily over time, but also that human beings can learn how to handle their increasing powers responsibly [20]. Prior to the politically radicalizing decade of the 1960s, this was the view widely held among social scientists. For example, in a pretentious and influential 1951 book titled *Toward a General Theory of Action* [21], Talcott Parsons and Edward A. Shils argued that society was inexorable modernizing along five dimensions they believed were the *pattern variables* that defined all cultures:

1. Affectivity – Affective Neutrality
2. Self-orientation – Collectivity-orientation
3. Particularism – Universalism
4. Ascription – Achievement
5. Diffuseness – Specificity

Traditional unscientific cultures of the world were emotional, selfish, tribal, clannish, and simple in structure. Modern scientific societies are rational, inclusive, follow universal norms of justice, value individual achievement, and possess highly specified roles and institutional structures. History, from the linear viewpoint, is a story of constant progress marked by the triumph of intellect over emotion. Episodes like the Second World War, which might seem to refute the theory that scientific advance entails ethical improvement, were anachronistic holdovers from ancient times of totem and taboo [22].

World of Warcraft directly contradicts this optimistic theory of constant progress. Technology is often used to gain power, by one person or group over others, leading to worse rather than reduced conflict. Especially in the aftermath of constant wars, there simply are not sufficient natural resources in the world to support everybody, so tribes battle to the death in pursuit of survival. Universalistic norms of justice sometimes express themselves ironically in philosophies like that of the Holy Light: It is moral to kill other people in order to gain their resources, so long as you do it with respect. The key value in post-industrial feudal societies will be group loyalty, what Parsons and Shils called *particularism*, in contrast to *universalism* who seeks to treat all people equally. If *World of Warcraft* is right, and the linear theory of historical progress is wrong, we face a grim but interesting future.

In contrast, episodic theories of history postulate no meaningful long-term trend, but sometimes suggest that a meaningful process can endure for a few centuries. These include theories of the rise and fall of civilizations, which are also played out on smaller scales in the rise and fall of local communities. The classic example is the fall of the Roman Empire, which was unavoidable but took centuries to complete [23]. In the aftermath of the First World War, many European intellectuals feared that the process of decay was happening all over again, to themselves [24]. A somewhat more optimistic episodic theory was that of Arnold Toynbee, who argued that civilizations face unpredictable challenges, and their fates depend upon how well they respond to them [25].

In *World of Warcraft*, several of the ten races are in decline that could be described as failure to respond adequately to challenges. Humans have lost great territories, including Lordaeron, their traditional capital city, and the wide areas east of Lordaeron devastated by biological warfare, the Plaguelands. Both the Gnomes and Trolls are refugees from fallen civilizations. As we already noted, the two races added in the Burning Crusade expansion, the Draenei and Blood Elves, have also recently suffered their own episodes of catastrophic defeat.

Perhaps the most interesting theories of civilization are cyclical. They are currently unfashionable, probably because they do not harmonize with the dominant political ideologies and do not offer government leaders much hope they can master the forces of history. Yet they involve clever social-scientific ideas, and might even be true, so they deserve to be dusted off and used as a lens through which to view our current situation. The best example is the theory of social and cultural dynamics proposed by Pitirim Sorokin [26]. For Sorokin, the most influential elements of culture are those that concern the inner experience of people, their images, ideas, volitions, feelings, and emotions. The essence of a culture is defined by the view people have of the nature of reality, the goals they value, and the means they emphasize in reaching these goals.

Out of a time of violent chaos, a social movement arises, based on a core set of ideas and values, leading to military and economic success and the establishment of a new culture. This young culture is *ideational*, meaning it considers reality to be essentially spiritual rather than material, and it seeks to achieve spiritual goals. This spirituality is likely to be very emotional, and depending upon the particular nature of the social movement it may not appear to be what modern people would like to call *spiritual*. It often is bloodthirsty, for example.

Over time, the leadership becomes entrenched and even bureaucratic, the passion and the ideas fade, and material success erodes the original principles on which the culture was founded. The society slowly loses its faith in spirituality, doubt sets in, and the culture begins to become *sensate*, a perspective on existence that is the opposite of ideational. A sensate culture believes that reality is whatever the sense organs perceive, and it does not believe in any supernatural world. Its aims are physical or sensual, and it seeks to achieve them through exploiting or changing the external world. This perfectly describes the Blood Elves, who combine extreme hedonism with aggressive scientific research aimed at controlling the powers of the universe.

Sorokin's theory postulates that civilizations may rise again after the collapse at the end of the sensate phase. Perhaps this is the meaning of the two factions in *World of Warcraft*, the Alliance and the Horde. Each faction is a combination of five diverse races that must find common principles to sustain their cooperation. Each faction is challenged by the other. The rules built into *World of Warcraft* inhibit communication and thus cooperation across the two factions, and discourage conflict within each faction. Each faction holds some territory, but much territory is contested between the two. Perhaps in a century we will learn whether the Horde and Alliance will evolve into two great civilizations, each stimulated by the challenge of the other, and each arising out of the ashes of the prior civilizations. Perhaps in a century we will learn whether any comparable greatness arises out of the wreckage of our own civilization.

Alchemy and Engineering in Outland

Players in *World of Warcraft* never remark upon the fact that their world is flat. Of course our own world seems flat to the people who dwell in it, and a great cultural revolution plus the Age of Exploration were required to teach us that the planet Earth is round. But that is not true in Azeroth or Outland, both of which are flat planets. Maps of Azeroth show two great landmasses on either side of a great ocean, and the only travel routes between them go over that ocean, whether by sailing ship or dirigible. Going west from Kalimdor, and east from the Eastern Kingdoms, leads nowhere.

Outland is not merely flat in principle, but observably flat, because travelers can go to the edge, look down, and see the void in which it floats. Indeed, as part of a fractured planet, it is crumbling, and at various places pieces of rock from the size of boulders up to mountains can be seem slowly tumbling just beyond the edge. This is especially the case in the Netherstorm zone, which consists of chunks of land floating in space, connected by bridges. Fragmentation of Draenor, which ripped Outland apart, was caused by misuse of magical technologies, and it may be a metaphor for the shattering effect of technological advance upon our own society. All this was well understood by one of the wisest of the wizards, Khadgar, who can be found in the center of Shattrath city. In the novel about the disaster that created Outland, he observed: "The damage has sundered reality as we know it. Gravity, space, perhaps even time itself no longer function properly here" [27].

A world cannot operate without strict rules. That principle applies equally well to the physical world we inhabit, as well as to any gameworld. For example, the physical world would evaporate quickly if energy were not conserved in physical processes. If the energy of a closed system could either increase or decrease, then the system would be unstable and fall apart. In our world, energy is conserved, and in *World of Warcraft* mana is conserved. At any given moment, a priest like Catullus or Maxrohn has a definite quantity of mana. When he uses it, the amount he has diminishes. It does replenish over time, but that can be conceptualized as the transmutation of time into mana. A mage can conjure up mana, but this takes time, and conjured mana returns to nothingness in time. The point is not that the conservation of mana in *World of Warcraft* follows rules identical to the conservation of energy in our physical world, but that it must follow some set of rules that prevent the world from being ruined either by accidental events or by the actions of its inhabitants.

The alchemy profession in *World of Warcraft* functions with some analogy to chemistry in our world. As an alchemist, Maxrohn needed to find raw materials from which to make the potions that restored mana or performed other useful functions. That is why his second profession is herbalism, which allows him to gather plant resources as he travels across the landscape. Prior to the Burning Crusade expansion, all professions were capped at skill levels of 300, so-called *artisan* level.

For example, an advanced artisan alchemist can make two very valuable potions a character can drink during a battle, superior mana potion and major healing potion, that replenish mana and health respectively. Each requires a crystal vial to contain the potion, and these can be purchased from alchemy supplier vendors. One unit of superior mana portion also requires two units of sungrass and two units of blindweed, herbs an herbalist can gather in fairly high level zones. One unit of major healing potion requires two units of golden sansam and one unit of mountain silversage, two other herbs. So work must be invested to get the materials from which to make these potions, just as in a "real" economy. And the alchemy requires manufacturing from the correct ingredients, just as in our world's chemistry.

With the Burning Crusade expansion came many new alchemical recipes, plus the possibility of training up to skill level 375 in the advanced *master* level. Some of these are simply more powerful versions of the potions available at lower levels. For the first time, transmutation of elements also became possible, again following very restrictive rules and requiring special training.

An alchemist needs a philosopher's stone to perform transmutations. The recipe to make one can be bought only from a goblin named Pestlezugg in the Capital of the Steamwheedle Cartel, Gadgetzan, in the Tanaris desert zone of southeastern Kalimdor. The required ingredients include four units each of purple lotus and firebloom, which an herbalist can gather, but also four iron bars which can be smelted only by a miner, and one unit of black vitriol which again only miners can obtain. Since one character cannot have three major professions – alchemy, herbalism and mining – some of these ingredients must be bought from other players, whether in person or through the impersonal auction houses in major towns.

Once he had a philosopher's stone, Maxrohn could gradually learn how to transmute elements, following strict rules on what could be transmuted into what, and requiring the philosopher's stone to cool down for the better part of a day after each action. The main cycle of transmutations is as follows: air-fire, fire-earth, earth-water, and water-air. Each transmutation path is bidirectional; for example, just as air can be turned into fire, fire can be turned into air. Air can be transmuted into earth, its opposite, but only going through two steps, first transmuting air into either fire or water, which similarly are opposites, and from there into earth. Another set of transmutations adds three elements to the periodic table of elements: fire-mana, earth-life, water-shadow. Any of the four primary elements plus mana can be transmuted into might, the eighth element, but only by a high-level master alchemist. Transmutation conserves the amount of material the alchemist has, merely changing its form, but costs time. All these elements have uses, chiefly as ingredients in making powerful items. For example, might is needed to make an improved version of the philosopher's stone called the *alchemist's stone*, the recipe for which can be obtained only in Shattrath city in Outland.

The major source of the four primary elements are non-player characters called elementals, beings that represent earth, air, fire and water and often can be looted for their elemental substances after killing them. These same four elements are fundamental to the practice of shamanism. To gain her four elemental totems and the power they conferred, Etacarinae had to complete quests that earned her the right to receive initiatory experiences from four friendly personifications of these elements, the last of them not until general experience level 30. At level 50, in order to earn her fifth totem, spirit, she was required to collect one unit of each of the four primary elements. Etacarinae did so by killing elementals at each of the four element-specific circles of binding in the Arathi Highlands zone, Stonehenge-like structures around which elementals of one particular type circle.

Each elemental totem allows a shaman to learn a particular set of associated powers, and it is unwise to specialize in just one. Etacarinae tended to rely upon her fire and earth totems. When fighting a water elemental or an air elemental, any of her powers functioned properly. However, earth elementals are immune to earth attacks, and fire elementals are immune to fire attacks. Other non-player characters, and indeed enemy players, may possess armor or spells that increase their immunity to one or another elemental attack. Thus, the four primary elements are not a mere mythology, but are part of the fundamental reality experienced in *World of Warcraft*.

All existing professions gained opportunities in the Burning Crusade expansion, not alchemy alone. It was Annihila's job to explore the new possibilities for engineers, getting the costly materials required from the high-level mining done by Catullus who sent her the metals through the mail. The most important engineering accomplishment made possible by the expansion was building a flying machine. Before she could operate it, Annihila needed to reach level 70 in general experience, skill 350 in engineering, and expert riding which cost fully 800 gold coins, while the instructions to make the machine cost an additional 12 gold coins, purchased from Jonathan Garrett in Outland's Shadowmoon Valley zone.

When Annihila made her flying machine, the ingredients required were 2 adamantine frames, 8 handsfull of fel iron bolts, 5 adamantite bars, 30 fel iron bars, 8 pieces of star wood, and four elemental seaforium charges. Each adamantine frame required four bars of adamantite metal plus one unit of primal earth. An elemental seaforium charge required a fel iron casing, a handful of fel iron bolts, and two units of elemental blasting powder. While all of this was difficult to obtain, except the star wood which she purchased from an enchanting supplier, the seaforium charges were especially challenging. These required a schematic that cost six gold and eight silver coins from Karaaz at the Stormspire in Netherstorm, but he would not sell one until the buyer had gained a revered reputation with his organization, the Consortium. About two full days of quests for the Consortium were required to accomplish this. She also needed to be at an anvil where she could shape the parts using a blacksmith hammer and an arclight spanner, but these were usual requirements for engineering work.

Etacarinae learned jewelcrafting, a new profession introduced in the Burning Crusade, which primarily allowed jewelcrafters to use materials collected through mining to manufacture wearable jewelry that conferred added abilities to the user. By the time she completed her assigned research tasks at level 50, she had a substantial jewelry collection in the bank, while wearing her three favorite items. Her engraved truesilver ring boosted five different capabilities by three points each: strength, agility, stamina, intellect, and spirit. To make it required only one bar of truesilver metal, but also two filigrees, each made from two bars of the mysterious mithril metal. Her golden ring of power added five points each to her intellect and spirit, boosted stamina by four points, and increased her spell casting power by six points. It was made from four gold bars and one gem of each of the following types: jade, citrine, and lesser moonstone. But her favorite was her barbaric iron collar, which increased her attack power by ten points. Making it required eight iron bars and two bronze settings, each of which was made with two bronze bars, each of which in turn was made by smelting together one tin bar and one copper bar. But the ingredient that made Etacarinae treasure the collar was a pair of large fangs she had hunted from raptor dinosaurs.

The Social Environment

The alternative science and technology of *World of Warcraft* take place within a well-organized social context. The main social division is between the Horde and Alliance factions, but within each faction its five races have somewhat different characteristics, including different mixes of classes. Any class or race can learn any profession, so the chief division of labor has two independent dimensions, class and profession. We can inspect the class significance of the two new races introduced in the Burning Crusade expansion, in Fig. 9.2. The data came from a census of all characters online at any point during Saturday, January 12, 2008 – a year after the expansion when the social system had stabilized – on two contrasting realms (computer servers), Emerald Dream and Scarlet Crusade. Both are *role playing* (RP) realms, with an officially expressed but unenforced preference for taking the mythology seriously, and staying in character at least much of the time. The difference is

Fig. 9.2 Classes of 22,851
World of Warcraft characters

Class	Blood Elves	Draenei	Other Races
Druid	0.0%	0.0%	13.4%
Hunter	14.8%	12.9%	15.7%
Mage	13.7%	10.4%	10.4%
Paladin	33.7%	13.8%	7.6%
Priest	10.8%	11.1%	8.7%
Rogue	12.8%	0.0%	13.3%
Shaman	0.0%	41.6%	4.8%
Warlock	14.2%	0.0%	11.0%
Warrior	0.0%	10.0%	15.1%
	100.0%	100.0%	100.0%
	3,301%	2,125%	17,425%

that Emerald Dream is a *player*-versus-*player* (PvP) realm, on which players outside the newbie starter areas attack each other at will, creating a much more violent climate than in normal realms where players cannot fight each other unless both agree to do so.

Repeatedly through the 24 hours of the sampling day, I ran the CensusPlus add-on program, which tallies a census of all characters online at the moment in a given faction [28]. I did so using two accounts and two computers, plus having two characters in each realm – one Horde, and the other in the competing Alliance faction – because the program can be run only while operating a character of the given faction and realm. The number of characters totaled fully 22,851, of which 12,051 were on Emerald Dream, and 10,800 on Scarlet Crusade, with the full range of experience levels from 1 to 70. The census does not include all characters that have been created in the two realms, but it is a reasonable selection of active characters. Many people create characters and then lose interest in them, and some subscribers are relatively inactive as well, and thus will not have logged in during the day of the census.

It is immediately apparent in Fig. 9.2 that no Blood Elves were druids, shamans, or warriors, and no Draenei were druids, rogues, or warlocks. Indeed, members of each race could belong to only six of the classes. The next most obvious facts are that Blood Elves are especially likely to be paladins, and Draenei are especially likely to be shamans. The reason is that prior to the expansion, none of the Horde races could be paladins, and none of the Alliance races could be shamans. Players tend to belong to guilds, guilds are limited to one of the two factions, and advanced players tend to have multiple characters in order to experience different aspects of the world and play different roles with their fellows. When a guild was preparing a raiding party, I have often seen players log off as one character and log back on as a different character whose abilities were better suited to the particular mission.

These are not trivial observations. In the real world, a cultural division of labor often guides members of particular ethnic groups into certain economic roles, and much of the past century of politics has concerned broadening opportunities for each group. In *World of Warcraft*, the races are "separate but equal," to use a

Variable	Blood Elves	Draenei	Other Races
Number of Characters	290	182	1,045
Percent of Races	19.1%	12.0%	68.9%
Percent Female	44.5%	54.4%	27.4%
Mean Experience Progress per Day	0.219	0.199	0.199
Mean Professional Skill Level	162.2	156.5	160.1
Percent Alchemists	11.4%	12.1%	15.8%
Percent Engineers	10.0%	12.1%	14.4%
Percent Jewelcrafters	14.8%	32.4%	4.2%
Percent Guilded at Time 1	74.5%	69.2%	72.2%
Percent Guilded at Time 2	72.8%	70.3%	73.0%
Percent Emerald Dream (PvP) Realm	57.6%	39.6%	54.4%

Fig. 9.3 1,517 characters initially levels 20–39

discredited phrase from the real history of race relations, but we can doubt whether this arrangement could preserve equality in the real world.

CensusPlus is an example of high-quality open source software, written in the Lua language that can be run inside *World of Warcraft*. Its chief limitation is that it gathers very few variables about each character: name, guild (if any), experience level, faction, class and race. To get data about gender, profession, reputation, and the aggressiveness reflected in PvP play, I had to employ an online database, the Armory, which generates web pages on the fly for each guild and each character level 10 or above [29]. I accessed them manually, and did so in random order to avoid biases from the inescapable work delays. Each character is represented by multiple pages, so data collection was limited to the first data page, which luckily includes the character's professions. The pages were saved in XML format, and then I wrote a parser program to convert the data for a spreadsheet.

Randomly, 1,517 characters were selected with experience levels 20–39, excluding a few who were involved in the subsidiary arena competitions, which are common at level 70 but tend to involve only very specialized "twink" characters at early levels. The range 20–39 was chosen because such players have left the newbie zones and selected their professions, but still have a long way to go before completing their climb up the latter of experience. Figure 9.3 shows some results, again comparing Blood Elves and Draenei with the other races.

Given that there are ten races, by chance one might expect each one to constitute 10% of the characters, but we see that the two Burning Crusade races are more popular than this, especially the Blood Elves. It should be kept in mind that the expansion was a year old at the time of this census, so this is not simply a reflection of the novelty of these races. It is interesting to see the higher fraction of female characters, especially among the Draenei, who also are especially likely to be jewelcrafters. As a matter of fact, Draenei have a very slight advantage in jewelcrafting, starting out at skill level 6 rather than 1, but I suspect that the somewhat pacifist culture of the Draenei may be more responsible. In their lore, the Blood Elves are more aggressive race, and we see that they are more common on the PvP realm, whereas Draenei are less common.

Playable characters are by no means the only ones who use technology, and in Outland both the Consortium and the Goblins do so. Goblins and Furbolgs were only two of the many races and factions of non-player characters, with the Goblins being high-tech capitalists, and the Furbolgs low-tech tribalists. NPCs are part of the social life of virtual worlds, and in future as artificial intelligence techniques improve, they may be even more significant. The Cataclysm expansion, that came long after I finished my research, added Goblins as a playable race in the Horde. In all gameworlds, NPCs carry much of the culture, precisely because they do not have the freedom to depart from their programming.

The Burning Crusade expansion introduced the Consortium, super-high-tech humanoids who compete with the Goblins. Their bodies are composed of shimmering energy, and their several outposts in Outland include zapping, lightning-filled devices reminiscent of old Frankenstein movies or the *Flash Gordon* serials. The Goblin town in Outland is named Area 52, clearly a reference to the military test station called Area 51 that has featured in flying saucer lore. It boasts an auction house, a hotel, various merchants, and a tall space rocket which unfortunately seems to be broken and never gets repaired despite all the best efforts of the Goblin engineers.

Of the eight original playable races, Gnomes were the most technological, and they also have a town in Outland, but of course limited to the Alliance to which they belong, staffed by Gnome NPCs who are constantly bustling around adjusting their comical machines. It is named Toshley's Station, a clear reference to Tosche Station from the *Star Wars* saga. Although we never see the place in the films, Luke Skywalker does comment he wanted to pick up some power converters there, and one of the quests associated with Toshley's Station involves getting power converters. Figure 9.4 shows Maxrohn launching into space using the electrostatic catapult at Toshley's Station, called the Zephyrium Capacitorium and operated on an experimental basis by two Gnome clones, Tally and Rally Zapnabber. In this particular run of the experiment, poor Maxrohn crashed not far away. Outland has many such references to popular science fiction. Another of the NPCs at Toshley's Station is named Razak Ironsides, a reference to a character named Rasczak played by an actor named Ironside in the movie *Starship Troopers*. Indeed, the town is under siege by huge insects, a reference to scenes in that movie.

The Goblins' broken rocket is an accurate metaphor for the real space program. Yes, chemical fuel rockets can take people to destinations in outer space, as the Apollo program proved, but only with the greatest difficulty and at unacceptable cost. New launch technologies, like the Gnomes' catapult, are uncertain at best and none has been developed to the point at which it can really be tested. The only way to travel between Outland and Azeroth is by teleport, a technology based on magic, relying upon natural laws that do not exist in our universe. *World of Warcraft* literally makes fun of advanced technology, but beneath the surface it offers severe criticisms. The Zangarmarsh zone of Outland is being ruined by pollution and water

Fig. 9.4 Maxrohn catapulting upward as a test subject for the Outland Gnomes

depletion, whereas the Hellfire Peninsula zone has been devastated by high-tech war. Thus, *World of Warcraft* presents a very bitter-sweet image of what science and technology may bring to us in the future.

Conclusion

After her nostalgic visit to the crash site on Azuremyst Isle, Etacarinae decided to dedicate her efforts toward the future. She rode her elekk back to the dock near the Exodar, rode a ship to Auberdeen, the Night Elf port on the west coast of Kalimdor, and there rented a hippogryph to fly to Ratchet, the Goblin port on the east coast. Another ship carried her from there to Booty Bay, and the southern end of the Stranglethorn, jungle, where she flew on a gryphon to Nethergard Keep in the Blasted Lands. There she rode southward, through desolate territory, toward the Dark Portal marked on the horizon by constant lightning flashes. At the edge of the crater that surrounds the portal, she was attacked by a level 55 Felguard sentry and his level 55 felhound, and only barely escaped with her life.

Knowing that no one could pass through the Dark Portal before reaching level 58, she prepared her mind to meditate on the meaning of barriers, limitations, and the finite span of her life. This portal was the place where Orcs invaded Azeroth from Draenor, launching the first of the three great wars, thus a symbol of doom and of danger from unexpected directions. She met three neutral NPCs, Warlord Dar'toon, Watch Commander Relthorn Netherwane, and Advisor Sevel, who were examining a large map of Outland. Beyond them was the Dark Portal itself, a huge stone arch flanked by colossal statues of hooded warriors and topped by a sculpted serpent coiled in the shape of an infinity symbol. The span of the arch was ringed with swirling green mists, around a seas of stars.

She stepped forward, knowing she could not enter but longing to do so. At any moment, she expected to be thrown backward and told by some unearthly voice that those at lowly level 50 were not allowed into Outland. Then, suddenly, she realized she had passed through! The traditional barrier was gone! Before her, on the Stair of Destiny, a violent battle was in progress, against attacking elementals and dragons. To the left she found a gryphon station, and – wonder of wonders – was able to buy a ride to Shattrath City. There she was further astonished to discover that the Aldor faction welcomed her as a member, and she was able to set her hearthstone in its hotel, so she could easily return by teleporting whenever she wanted. A portal in the very center of the city allowed her to teleport easily back to the Exodar. Now, two and a half years after the Burning Crusade expansion, Outland had become no longer a distant goal to strive for, but an integral part of the ordinary *World of Warcraft*.

References

1. Lummis M., Kern, E.: World of Warcraft Master Guide. BradyGAMES/DK Publishing, Indianapolis (2006); Sumner C. (ed.) World of Warcraft Atlas. BradyGAMES/Pearson Education, Indianapolis (2006); Corneliussen H.G., Rettberg J.W. (eds.) Digital Culture, Play and Identity: A World of Warcraft Reader. MIT Press, Cambridge (2008); Nardi, B.A.: My Life as a Night Elf Priest: An Anthropological Account of World of Warcraft. University of Michigan Press, Ann Arbor (2010); Bainbridge, W.S.: The Warcraft Civilization. MIT Press, Cambridge (2010)
2. Sims, J., Sims, K., Hall, D.: World of Warcraft: Wrath of the Lich King. BradyGames, Indianapolis (2008)
3. Davis, H.L. (ed.): World of Warcraft: The Burning Crusade, p. 64. BradyGAMES/DK Publishing, Indianapolis (2007)
4. Golden, C.: Rise of the Horde. Pocket Star Books, New York (2007); Lord of the Clans. Pocket Books, New York (2001)
5. http://www.wowwiki.com/Shaman
6. Catullus: Letter to a supernatural being. In: Miah, A. (ed.) Human Futures: Art in and Age of Uncertainty, pp. 247–255. Liverpool University Press, Liverpool (2008)
7. Knaak, R.A.: The Well of Eternity. Pocket Books, New York (2004); The Demon Soul. Pocket Star Books, New York (2004); The Sundering Pocket Star Books, New York (2005)
8. Knaak, R.A., Kim, Jae-Hwan: Ghostlands. Tokyopop, Tokyo (2007). Unpagenated but about page 5
9. http://www.wowwiki.com/Priest
10. http://www.wowwiki.com/Church_of_Light
11. http://www.worldofwarcraft.com/index.xml. Accessed 5 Mar 2008
12. http://www.geocities.com/rgfdfaq/sources.html
13. Lupoff, R.A.: Edgar Rice Burroughs and the Martian Vision. Mirage Press, Westminster (1976); Porges, I.: Edgar Rice Burroughs: The Man who Created Tarzan. Brigham Young University Press, Provo (1975)
14. Burroughs, E.R.: The Chessmen of Mars. A. C. McClurg, Chicago (1922)

15. http://www.gutenberg.org/dirs/etext98/cmars13.txt

16. Lowell, P.: Mars as the Abode of Life. The Macmillan Company, New York (1908)

17. Burroughs, E.R.: A Princess of Mars. A. C. McClurg, Chicago (1917)

18. Burroughs, E.R.: The Gods of Mars. A. C. McClurg, Chicago (1918); The Master Mind of Mars. A. C. McClurg, Chicago (1928)

19. Bainbridge, W.S.: Dimensions of Science Fiction. Harvard University Press, Cambridge (1986)

20. Gilman, N.: Mandarins of the Future: Modernization Theory in Cold War America. Johns Hopkins University Press, Baltimore (2003)

21. Parsons, T., Shils, E.A. (eds.): Toward a General Theory of Action. Harvard University Press, Cambridge (1951)

22. Viereck, P.: Metapolitics: From the Romantics to Hitler. A. A. Knopf, New York (1941)

23. Gibbon, E.: The History of the Decline and Fall of the Roman Empire. Macmillan, New York (1776) [1896]

24. Spengler, O.: The Decline of the West. A. A. Knopf, New York (1926–1928)

25. Toynbee, A.J.: A Study of History. Oxford University Press, London (1934–1939)

26. Sorokin, P.A.: Social and Cultural Dynamics. American Book Company, New York (1937)

27. Rosenberg, A., Golden, C.: Beyond the Dark Portal, p. 418. Pocket Star, New York (2008)

28. http://www.warcraftrealms.com/census.php. Retrieved Nov 14 2008

29. http://www.wowarmory.com/

Chapter 10
The Chronicles of Riddick

On April 1, 2009, I received a phone message on my office voicemail: "This is Vin Diesel. GameStop will have *The Chronicles of Riddick: Assault on Dark Athena* in stores by tomorrow afternoon. So stop into your local GameStop and pick up your copy – or else!" This was no April Fool joke, but a robot alert recorded by the actor, Vin Diesel, and sent to me because I had pre-ordered the game. Actually, there were two games on the DVD, the other being *Escape from Butcher Bay*, and I finished them both on May 9, taking 1,200 screenshots and many notes about ethnographically interesting observations. I did so playing the role of Riddick himself, because the series does not allow players to express their individuality by creating their own avatars.

This is a complex world, spanning a prison, a planet, and a spaceship, yet it is not what is generally considered a massively multiplayer gameworld, because most of the action is a solo-player game. Only at the end is there a possibility for playing small tournaments online against other players. Yet this futuristic game is relevant for this book, precisely because it makes the point that our future might be solo rather than collective, and we may become lone psychopaths rather than cooperative utopians. Many gameworlds involve crime, although murder is often defined as justified military action to render it moral. At the dawn of time, humans were hunters and gatherers, so killing opponents to loot their corpses is just the modern expression of our ancient hunting and gathering tradition. What will the future expressions be of murder, imprisonment, and escape from society?

A Dark World

Richard B. Riddick, the protagonist of a pair of computer games and a pair of popular movies, is the nastiest criminal in the universe. The series begins when he seems to have met his match, incarcerated in Butcher Bay, the worst penitentiary in the universe – the "triple-max slam." Yet he thrives in this depraved environment, easily exploiting the other inmates, who at best are psychopaths or psychotics. As he

W.S. Bainbridge, *The Virtual Future*, Springer Series in Immersive Environments,
DOI 10.1007/978-0-85729-904-8_10, © Springer-Verlag London Limited 2011

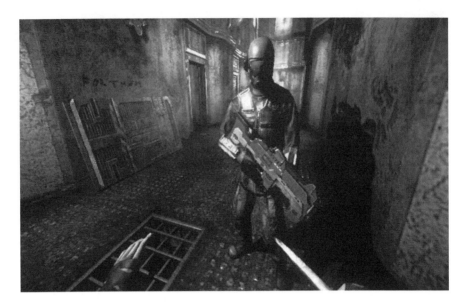

Fig. 10.1   A prison guard about to be killed by Riddick

explains at the outset, "They say hope begins in the dark, but most just flail around in the blackness, searching for their destiny. The darkness, for me, is where I shine." Riddick constantly strives to escape until the end of his adventures, when he falls into the one trap from which there is no escape, becoming emperor of the Necromonger galactic conquerors.

The two Riddick games, *Escape from Butcher Bay* and *Assault on Dark Athena*, are not MMORPGs, but solo player first person shooters (FPSs). In an FPS, the player sees through the eyes of the character, becoming Riddick, seeing his own hands, the weapon he holds, and perhaps his shadow on the wall. Figure 10.1 shows a Butcher Bay guard from Riddick's perspective, clutching a huge gun but no match for Riddick's simple knife, given who wields it. Except in cut scenes and brief animations of climbing an obstacle, the player does not see Riddick's whole body from a third person perspective.

The world in which Riddick dwells is depicted with greater visual realism than in most MMORPGs discussed in earlier chapters, but none of the other characters are avatars of players. Only at the end, through some special online game levels, does one player interact with others – if any survivors can be found. Thus the Riddick games, and solo first person shooters in general, are egocentric gameworlds in which everything revolves around the self. As a character, Riddick is the epitome of a sociopathic loner, who seemingly cares nothing for anybody else. We do not know what horrible crimes he may have committed, but he has no hesitation about killing repeatedly and no commitment to any higher goals than his own desire to be left alone. Seeing the world from his own perspective, it is a hostile place, lacking friendship, beauty, and much intelligence beyond animal cunning. Riddick is a nihilist, but in a world where extreme pessimism is realism.

Playing Riddick is not necessarily asocial, however. In *Escape from Butcher Bay*, I chose to be guided by prior players who wrote five competing sets of step-by-step instructions for getting through the levels successfully, what are called *walkthroughs* [1]. When a new popular videogame is released, several avid players race with each other to see who can post a good walkthrough online first. We do not see that for MMORPGs, because they are simply too complicated. The walkthroughs not only were very helpful getting through the many challenges, but also assisted me in understanding what was happening in the story, and reduced significantly the burden I faced in documenting my observations. Given how difficult it was simply to get Riddick past his many enemies, these different kinds of help were exceedingly valuable.

An illustration of how the walkthroughs helped, and of the general flavor of Riddick's grim world, is how he achieved his first major success, the ability to use guns. At first, Riddick kills guards with his hands, punching them to death or breaking their necks. Then he gains knuckledusters and shivs, crude prison-made metal fist enhancers and knives. When he reaches for a dead guard's weapon, however, he gets injured and cannot pick it up, because each rifle, revolver, and shotgun has a DNA reader. Only if Riddick's DNA is on file with the mainframe computer, can he use a gun. That requires him to escape from his cell block, by way of the infirmary, where he is able to upgrade his stamina by 25% in his first encounter with a Nanomed Health Station. Creeping along a catwalk, he drops on the single guard. By one quick murder and by placing his hand on a palm-print interface, his DNA goes in the system and he can pick up his first rifle. Several more kills, and he comes to the end of this stage of his escape.

An ambush awaits Riddick in a large room containing several crates and two catwalks, one on each side, with alcoves beneath them. Using the collection of guns he has been assembling from dead guards, it is not very difficult to kill the ambushing guards. However, a few seconds after the last one dies, a nearly invulnerable armored riot guard descends on an elevator and begins searching the room. Here is where things got especially difficult. It is possible to kill the guard, but only by shooting a sufficient number of times on a vulnerable spot on its back. My first 20 attempts failed miserably, and Riddick died an equal number of horrible deaths. Guidance from the five walkthroughs proved especially problematic.

Two of the five agreed that the way to kill the riot guard was to lure it into one of the alcoves, then run out and around and shoot it from behind. I found it hard not to stumble on the crates that littered the floor, and the guard always turned to face me. A half dozen times, I tried the very different tactic in a walkthrough written by somebody with the pseudonym Wasabi X: "If you have a lot of health, you can destroy it by getting behind it and shooting its back. But, I suggest the following, run to one side of the room, make sure he sees you. Then, when he is lured out, run into the elevator he came down and go up before he can do too much damage." Unfortunately, although I seemed to be able to activate the elevator switch, it never elevated me out of danger.

The remaining two walkthroughs suggested a third method. Here's how the 13th-Jedi explained it: "There are four guards in this room. One on your right, three on your left. Kill righty first, then shoot out the light in his general vicinity, and run over there for cover. Now, pick off two of the three remaining guards. Leave the one with just the gun alive. Now, climb up the crates and take out the last guy. Then immediately get onto the catwalk to your right." The reason for waiting to kill one guard only after climbing the crates is to get nearly to the catwalk before the robot enters, because he will attack immediately and climbing takes time. Indeed, I had to try several times before figuring out exactly where to climb. Some guards were carrying a powerful assault rifle or shotgun, capable of shooting me off the crate, so I needed to select the weakest guard to kill last. Once the guards were dead, I quickly climbed from the crates to the catwalk, where the heavily armored riot guard could not reach me. Several attempts with an assault rifle finally halted him, and it was then possible to loot the bodies of weapons and take the elevator to the next stage of the game.

Notice that I was playing a solo game, but five past players were in a sense playing with me, through the advice offered by their walkthroughs. Much of their advice coincided exactly. For example, one of the goals of Escape from Butcher Bay is to collect about 60 cigarette packs, the legal tender of a macho prison, called *smokes*. With great reliability, the walkthroughs explained where to find them. Action options were usually extremely limited. Riddick absolutely needed to find the Nanomed Health Station and the mainframe hand interface, because without increased stamina and the ability to use guns, his goose was cooked. The route to these intermediate goals was along narrow, twisting corridors, that offered no alternative paths. Only in the room with the riot guard was there much real choice, and two of the tactics suggested in the walkthroughs would not work for me.

The episode in Butcher Bay that most exemplified the whole Riddick experience for me was when he faced three riot guards, two of them simultaneously, within sight of a spaceship that offered escape. Perhaps what made it difficult was that I had failed to pick up a minigun from a Mech in an earlier challenge, a weapon that could take down riot guards. I was rattled, because the Mech was impervious to my weapons, and the only way to kill it was to shoot at fuel cells on a conveyor and make them explode next to him. To reach the hanger where the spaceship waited, I rushed past a riot guard, who then blocked the door so I could not retrace my steps to get a minigun, without depleting my health to a dangerous level.

Two riot guards blocked the way in the hanger. If I had a minigun, I could have handled, them, or I could have used grenades, if I had any. The official Prima guidebook to Butcher Bay confidently told me I could defeat the riot guards with shotgun blasts to their backs, and indeed a rack of shotguns stood on the left wall [2]. But I never could seem to stay behind one of them long enough, and they killed me several times. After about 20 failed attempts, I despaired of ever escaping from this supermax slam. Analyzing all five walkthroughs, I decided it might be possible if I could climb on a large box near where the riot guards stood. But they kept shooting me down when I tried to do so.

The solution to the problem was to use my own death to set up just the right conditions. I ran past the riot guards toward the ship. They ran after me and killed me. Now, when I came back to life, at the entrance to the hanger, I could climb the box because the riot guards were still over near the ship. I fired one shot with my assault rifle to draw them closer, and stepped to the back end of the box, where they could not reach me. Laboriously I fired again and again, whenever the opportunity presented itself to hit the very tops of their heads, as they milled around the front of the box. First one fell, and then the other, just as I ran low on ammunition. Picking up other weapons, I quickly killed the three ordinary guards at the ship, and entered, joyful that I neared my freedom.

Then a cut scene began, like many on the two games, a short movie using computer animation to advance the story. Riddick met an ally, Jagger Valence, and the two of them attempted to open the locked door to the cockpit. A bounty hunter named Johns ambushed them, the same man who had originally brought Riddick to Butcher Bay, and in the melee that followed both Johns and Riddick were severely wounded, Valence was killed, and the warden, Hoxie, ordered Riddick put into cryosleep. In this form of suspended animation, escape was believed to be impossible, even for Riddick.

Scientific and Philosophical Basis

Alan Dean Foster, the veteran novelizer of science fiction movies, begins his Riddick book by acknowledging the backward state of the social and behavioral sciences: "No matter how long or how hard they strive, no matter how extensive their education as a species, no matter what they experience of the small heavens and larger hells they create for themselves, it seems that humans are destined to see their technological accomplishments always exceed their ability to understand themselves" [3]. On a simplistic level, the specific form that ignorance takes in the Riddick universe is *criminology*: We do not fathom the mechanisms that churn the depths of human depravity. On a somewhat more enlightened level, ignorance arises from the fundamental ambiguity of morality in a society of predators.

Like military science and medical science, criminology has opponents, namely the criminals, which at various times it conceptualizes as enemies or a disease. Yet this sets criminology apart from other social and behavioral sciences, which tend to sympathize with their subjects of research. Indeed, within sociology there is a subdiscipline called *deviance* which studies criminals from a more sympathetic perspective. For 7 years, I taught the Introduction to Deviance course at the University of Washington, twice a year with about 300 students each time. Crime and delinquency were only two of the topics covered, and others included mental illness, religious radicalism, and sexual deviance which might or might not be included in criminology, depending on the local laws at the moment. Parallel with courses like mine, there was a flourishing criminal justice program, and I occasionally served on its committees or did research in collaboration with its faculty.

I was especially impressed by the senior criminologist, Clarence Schrag. If anybody could have interviewed Riddick to learn the truth about his criminal career, Clarence was the man. One of his hands was wooden, and covered with a black glove. Sociologist Dean MacCannell reported "his hand had been shot off in a prison break while he was doing research," but I never had the courage to ask Schrag himself for confirmation [4]. In any case, he had immense practical experience with the Washington state prison system, as well as being a thoughtful intellectual.

We actually had a low-security prison facility on campus, part of a rehabilitation program for non-violent prisoners who attended class by day and were locked up by night. Also, many former convicts were attracted to my deviance class; I supposed they figured they already knew the subject and could easily get good grades, although they were often mistaken about this. It was very gratifying, however, to see many of them work hard to build a life for themselves in conventional society.

My most memorable ex-con student claimed to have committed three murders, one of them while in prison, and began behaving in a way that suggested to me he might be contemplating a fourth. For example, he cursed judges and punched his fist through the wall. His mind was very unusual, and one time he came to my office hour to recite by memory a long poem he had written about me. Without wanting to get into the intimate details, I had solid evidence that many of the strangest things he said about himself were factually true. He was flunking my class, a fact he knew before I did because he was working in the office that did computer grading of the multiple choice tests. One day, when things got especially worrisome, I suggested he talk with Clarence Schrag. They had a nice chat, and the fellow was no trouble thereafter.

The focus of this book is the future, so what does criminology say about it? Despite occasional mass media hysteria over crime waves, and occasional reform movements that peter out after a few years, the criminological future seems to look like the past. Clarence himself was pessimistic about any major positive changes, given how constrained the criminal justice system is by other social factors. Forty years ago, he wrote:

> The prison is viewed as an element in the system of justice that operates under constraints imposed by the broader society. Many of the contradictions observed in the prison's goals and in its achievement strategies have their counterpart in community disorganization. Accordingly, any major improvement in the prison's efficiency will probably require a fundamental overhaul of both the system of justice and the community's normative structure. Such overhaul encounters strong resistance from the community and the agencies of justice. Most current efforts at prison reform are therefore regarded as stopgap measures [5].

Yet traditionally social scientists have held that the nature of crime changes as human society changes. Over a century ago, Italian criminologist Cesare Lombroso asserted that human beings were evolving from a brutish condition toward civilization, and crime was largely the result of "born criminals" who were atavistic throwbacks who accidentally had the genetic makeup of prehistoric savages in modern times [6]. He listed a number of Neanderthal-like physical traits that supposedly identified these cases, and he said there was no point trying to rehabilitate them since their criminality was innate. Pessimistic about the future of any given criminal, Lombroso's theory was optimistic about humanity, because it asserted that our species was constantly improving.

At the same time, other writers like the French sociologist Emile Durkheim were arguing that so-called primitive people were not immoral savages at all, and indeed many forms of deviance were increasing as a result of modern life, not decreasing. Durkheim's 1897 statistical study of suicide popularized the idea that a breakdown of social relationships (*egoism*) and a breakdown of cultural values (*anomie*) were results of the increasing complexity and chaos of society, magnifying social pathologies of many kinds [7]. A similar view dominated American sociology during the 1920s and 1930s, holding *social disorganization* responsible for much criminal behavior by individuals [8]. In the 1960s research in this tradition focused on the importance of *social control* in forcing people to obey the law, and argued that the people who violated societal norms simply lacked the social relationships that enforced normality in others [9].

Debates raged between so-called *control theorists* in criminology and those who blamed either *poverty* or *deviant subcultures*. Robert K. Merton said that people would turn to crime if poverty prevented them from achieving by legitimate means the values extolled by society, but the poorest groups in society tend to suffer from social disorganization, so it is hard to be sure which factor is more responsible [10]. Other writers, like Albert K. Cohen, argued that criminals are not norm-violators, but, rather follow the norms of subcultures that are opposed to the dominant culture in society [11]. However, subcultures tend to abound in disorganized societies, as we pointed out in the chapter on *The Matrix Online*.

Half a century ago, social science was like a banquet: an array of distinct, competing theories, each of which claimed to explain crime and other forms of human behavior. Today, it is as if the banquet has been put through a food processor and ground into mush. An optimist would say that each theory turned out to be true but applies only under special circumstances that usually cannot be specified. For a time statisticians thought that quantitative methods of analysis could tell us exactly how much each theory explains in a matrix of correlation coefficients, but it turned out that our data are never nearly good enough to complete the analysis. A pessimist would say that we understand crime less well than we did 50 years ago, but the optimist would reply that we were mistaken about how well we understood it back then. Perhaps Alan Dean Foster would say that criminology has always been a rather sober form of science fiction.

The history of recent decades in criminology has tended to confirm the prediction made by Clarence Schrag. Greater clarity has not emerged, nor have we found better methods to prevent or to respond to crime than we practiced decades ago. To the extent that society is disorganized, or that subcultures are common, or that poverty is prevalent, there will be more crime. To the extent that people, as individuals and groups, compete for scarce resources, many of them will take what they want or lash out in rage. And perhaps to the extent that individuals biologically differ in aggressiveness or the capacity to form lasting bonds with each other, some will always be criminals. Add to that the possibility that corrupt governments will themselves be run by thieves and murderers, then you have a prescription for a society in which there is so much crime that it can be called a *criminal society*. I cannot judge whether that is the kind of world we live in today. It certainly is Riddick's world.

Science and Technology in the New Media

There are, of course, two levels of technology in the Riddick series, the future technologies depicted inside the games and movies, and the contemporary multi-media technologies that make them possible. This latter is an excellent example of how electronic games, movies, and online websites can be integrated to produce something that transcends any one of them. Indeed, the websites have little games on them, and the games include movies. In a very real sense, each of the two games is a movie, consisting of a series of short computer-animated scenes that can be unlocked only by performing certain tasks in the game. A very large fraction of them must be performed in a set order, making the whole experience highly linear as a movie is, running from beginning to end without major side-branches, let alone fundamental choices. This contrasts with all the non-linear gameworlds described in the other chapters, which offer the user a nearly endless diversity of routes to explore.

All the Riddick media incorporate technology that could be described as dehumanizing, sadistic, and gamelike. In the typical fantasy game, a character can restore health by drinking innocuous potions, sitting on a chair, or being healed by another character. In both Riddick games, health is regained by sticking one's head into a grimy machine that pierces one's neck with huge needles. Both movies involve chase sequences in which the characters must run for their lives, with little incentive to help each other, as the inexorable laws of celestial mechanics move their planet into a position lethal for human life.

The series began as a science-fiction horror movie, *Pitch Black*. Produced in 2000, it came first in production chronology, but the two games – Butcher Bay in 2004 and Dark Athena in 2009 – are prequels, explaining how Riddick came to the point a few months before the action of the movie began. *Chronicles of Riddick* is a 2004 science fiction adventure film that brings the story to an apparent conclusion. Extra material on the movie DVDs, and the websites for the various products, provide tiny fragments of history, like the cement between the bricks that are the products themselves.

Pitch Black begins as a spaceship encounters a meteor storm or rogue comet while the crew and passengers are in cryosleep suspended animation. The pilot is immediately killed, and co-pilot Carolyn Fry suddenly finds herself struggling to control the vessel as it falls through the atmosphere toward a barren planet. At one point, she tries unsuccessfully to jettison the passenger cabin, in hopes of gaining control at least over her command module. When she and 11 passengers survive the crash, she realizes that she would have been a murderer if she had succeeded in sacrificing them all to give herself a better chance. Among the survivors are Abu "Imam" al-Walid and three boys accompanying him on a religious pilgrimage to New Mecca, a girl pretending to be a boy named Jack, and a drug addict bounty hunter named William J. Johns with Riddick in his custody. The human drama revolves chiefly around Fry, Johns and Riddick, concerning whether there is any hope at all that they can trust each other.

None can survive without cooperating – except possibly Riddick who escapes soon after the crash. The planet is desolate and dry, but the group locates a small settlement, where they gradually discover that the previous inhabitants were all killed 22 years earlier by nocturnal monsters. Thankfully, there is no night on the planet, because it orbits in a system with three suns, but they learn than an eclipse is coming soon, when the title of the film will be fulfilled. In pitch black, swarms of horrible monsters attack. In addition to his strength and courage, Riddick has the advantage of eyeshine, an ability to see in the dark, which he gained while a prisoner in Butcher Bay.

There are actually three theories about how Riddick gained eyeshine. In *Pitch Black*, he says he paid a doctor some cigarettes to operate on his eyes, using some undefined technology to make them more sensitive to light. But in the Butcher Bay game, he performs a mission for a mysterious character named Pope Joe, retrieving Joe's voicebox from dark caverns under the prison. It seems to be an ordinary radio but may have supernatural significance. As soon as he gives Joe the voicebox, he hears a mysterious woman's voice, and his eyes are transformed. So, was it a doctor paid for his services, some technical feat by Pope Joe, or the magic of this invisible woman?

Eyeshine gives Riddick the power to see in dark caverns, the ability to overwhelm prison guards once he has shot out the lights, and the talent to find his way through pitch blackness. Yet eyeshine may also be a kind of philosophical enlightenment, letting Riddick understand the reality of human existence, unblinded by ideology. The cost of this gift is trust, because he is under no illusion that anyone is trustworthy. While cowards cling to each other in self-deluded dependency, he is aware that the best he can do is be brave and deal individually with whatever fate brings him. This is not the same thing as freedom, because his attempts to escape always fail in the moment of their success, each exit merely leading to another trap. This is the linear quality of a movie, in which the outcome is preordained, equivalent to saying that Riddick cannot escape his fate. It is said that the truth sets us free, but Riddick would say that was merely another illusion.

As *Pitch Black* nears its climax, and the monsters are eating the survivors one by one, Johns suggests to Riddick that they sacrifice the others as decoys, and run to an escape ship with the power cells needed to operate it. Instead they fight, and Johns becomes the decoy. Riddick reaches the ship with the power cells, leaving Fry, Jack and the Imam hiding in a cave. As Riddick is about to escape alone, Fry also reaches the ship. He comments, "Strong survival instinct, I admire that in a woman," and suggests they escape together. But she insists on going back for the others, her survival instinct overpowered by her guilt at nearly killing the passengers earlier.

After helping Fry, Riddick lies wounded some distance from the ship, while the others have reached its safety. Fry returns to rescue him, too, and just as she does, she is dragged away by the monsters. Knowing she has already died, he shouts, "Not for me!" A blogger using the name wcooley, speculated about his words: "It is noble for the stronger to sacrifice for the weaker, not the other way around. His cry of 'Not for me! Not for me!' after the creature yanks her away is one of shame at having her die for him." If so, this is the shame of a man proud of his strength, not one who feels sympathy for other people [12].

The story has much of the feel of a computer game, in which violence is unleashed or constrained by a series of technical, *if-then* propositions. The monsters are extremely dangerous, but they attack *only if* it is dark. With suns at opposite sides of the sky, darkness comes *only if* there is an eclipse. The escape ship can fly away, but *only if* power cells are dragged to it from the crashed ship through dangerous territory. The survivors can escape *only if* one of them knows how to fly the ship, and only Fry, Johns and Riddick have that skill. People cooperate, but *only if* they need to, or in the case of Fry, only because her trauma has programmed her to do so. The opening credits introduce the planet's solar system, in the form of an orrery – a mechanical toy model of a solar system that shows how the planets move over time – a perfect expression of the theory that events are predetermined. Fry repeatedly plays with this orrery, and eventually learns from it that the fatal eclipse is coming.

A short animated movie, *Dark Fury*, tells what happens to Riddick, Jack, and Imam immediately after escaping the planet. They are captured by a huge *merc* (mercenary) ship, captained by a bizarre middle-aged woman named Chillingsworth, whose great passion is collecting extreme criminals, freezing them in cryosleep, then putting them on display as greenish statues in her private museum. Their minds are fully conscious, and they suffer horribly, imprisoned in paralyzed bodies that take a day even just to close an eyelid. Yet again Riddick must escape, and he delivers his two passengers to New Mecca on the planet Helion Prime, then disappears into the wastes of space. On the *Dark Fury* DVD, director David Twohy suggests that Riddick chooses self-exile as a strange act of nobility, knowing that bad things happen to anyone who cooperates with him.

In a brief clip on the *Pitch Black* DVD, Twohy states the fundamental principle of the final movie, *Chronicles of Riddick*: "It is not a story about good guys versus bad guys. It is a story about bad guys versus evil guys." Aereon, emissary of the Elementals, puts it differently in her introductory narration: "If we are to survive, a new balance must be found. In normal times, evil would be fought by good. But in times like these – well, it should be fought by another kind of evil." Later, she explains that the natural balance has been upset by the Necromongers, a religious-military crusade that sought either to convert or kill all peoples. As quoted in Foster's novelization, she explains, "Balance is everything to Elementals. Water to fire, earth to air. We have 33 different words for this balance, but today, here, now, we have time to speak only of the Balance of Opposites" [13].

Led by an absolute monarch, called the Lord Marshall, these death-dealers seem to represent collective unity, whereas Riddick represents individual autonomy. Restoring the balance, therefore, might mean returning to a middle ground between these extremes. The Lord Marshall is the sixth in his series of dictators, and he gained power by assassinating his predecessor, following the Necromonger maxim, "You keep what you kill." To hold office, however, it was not enough to be the supreme killer. The Lord Marshall was also required to make a pilgrimage to the edge of the UnderVerse, and gain super-human powers. The faith of Necroism holds that life in this "verse" is a corrupting influence and must be destroyed. Thus the Necromongers destroy planet after planet, converting some inhabitants of each to their army, through a technological as well as ideological process that seems to work by inducing pain that in time counteracts all other kinds of pain. The ultimate goal of this crusade, is to cross over to the UnderVerse, via death, to dwell in that perfect realm forever.

There are faint hints that the Necromongers may represent Christianity, although naturally no Christian would recognize any resemblance. Their movement evolved from an earlier monotheistic religion, demands total adherence to a uniform creed, and has undertaken a crusade to eradicate all other religions on its way to Heaven. The command ship of their fleet is the Basilica, a term used by Christians to describe an important church. When they come to New Mecca on Helion Prime, they find an explicitly Islamic society that is tolerant of other religions, not unlike the cosmopolitan Islamic society dominant in the Middle East when the European crusaders invaded. When first presented with this situation, and asked to help resist the crusaders, Riddick replies, "Not my fight." He does not share Imam's faith, and is not committed to the preservation of any large-scale social system.

Colm Fiore, the actor who played the Lord Marshall, was asked by an interviewer how the parable of Riddick related to today's real world: "It's to take from our past and our communal understanding as human beings, what is it we recognize about this kind of fascistic, overwhelming power – what I call the tyranny of the majority? How do we resist that? And, where do we see it in our daily life? And do we see it? Yeah, we see it everywhere. And that's part of why the movie will be interesting, because you'll recognize places along this journey, and say: How do I, as one individual, stand up against it? Well, Riddick stood up! Riddick defied them!" [14].

As the story unfolds, we learn something about Riddick's origins. He was born on the warrior planet Furya, whose inhabitants may have unusual powers and personalities. Thirty years before the action of the movie, a soothsayer told the Lord Marshall that his downfall would come at the hands of a Furyan male, so he ordered his army to kill everybody on the planet, rather dramatically strangling boy babies with their umbilical chords. Apparently Riddick was a small child at the time of the massacre, and may have been roaming the universe alone since then. Given that everybody he may have known or loved was murdered, it is not surprising he feels alienated from the living. He does not seem fully aware of the Lord Marshall's genocide until near the end, but when they face each other at the climax, each is fully committed to killing.

Key to the drama in *Chronicles* is the issue of whether Riddick feels any bond of friendship or kinship with the two people he unintentionally rescued from Pitch Black, Imam and Jack. Imam has settled on Helion Prime and started a family. Jack has tried to become like Riddick, killed people on her way, and wound up in the slam on a hellish planet aptly named Crematoria. Even in *Pitch Black* and only 12 years old, she had shaved her head and donned goggles, like those Riddick wears to protect his sensitive eyeshine eyes. Now, 5 years later, she has grown into an adult woman, changed her name to Kyra to express transformation, and is playing Riddick's game: "Who's the better killer."

When bounty hunters come to the ice-bound planet where Riddick lives in self-imposed exile, he quickly defeats them, but wonders who could have hired them for such a difficult and expensive job. Checking the computer on their ship, he discovers that the price on his head was set by Imam: "You don't expect these mercs to have any honor, any code. But this new bounty from a holy man – a guy whose neck I saved – a lesson learned. There is no such word as 'friend.' It can only end badly to let someone get too close – bad for them."

When he confronts Imam, he learns that the bounty was a way of calling him back to help resist the Necromongers. Imam invokes Kyra, to goad Riddick's conscience, saying she worshipped him and considered him a brother. When Imam asserts that Riddick left when Kyra needed him most, Riddick replies, "She needs to stay away from me. You all do." Yet when Riddick is again captured by bounty hunters, he manipulates them into taking him to the slam on Creamatoria, perhaps to rescue Kyra.

The escape from Crematoria is like a level in a computer game. In *Pitch Black*, darkness was lethal, during the long chase sequence. In *Chronicles*, day is substituted for night as the time of danger. The planet is so close to its blazing sun, that dawn suddenly brings rock-melting heat that no one could survive more than a few seconds. Riddick, Kyra and other prisoners race across the volcanic surface ahead of the dawn, hoping to reach an escape ship before the guards, who are racing underground through tunnels. Whether Riddick will risk his own life to save Kyra, and whether she herself prefers to live or to kill, remain in doubt.

In the final scene, in the throne room of the enemy, Kyra has been transformed into a Necromonger, and Riddick faces the supernatural power of the Lord Marshall. When he asks her, "Are you with me, Kyra," she walks past him into the crowd. At a crucial moment in the duel, when Riddick faces certain death, Kyra stabs the Lord Marshall, but then is fatally wounded herself. In despair, Riddick sits on the throne, as the camera pans back and shows that all the Necromongers are bowing in homage to him. This, of course, is the ultimate penitentiary, from which there is no hope of escape. Only by killing Riddick can someone else become Lord Marshall, so only by remaining on that throne can he continue to live.

Society of Darkness

Created last, but coming early in development of the story, the game *Assault on Dark Athena* offers a mature version of Riddick's philosophies and of his social world, prior to the existential challenge posed by the Necromongers. We do not know what crimes Riddick committed before the first game begins. As he says, "It's not where I'm from, but where I am that matters." When Riddick finally confronts Hoxie, the warden of Butcher Bay, this coward tries to bargain for his life, offering Riddick whatever he wants. "I wanted to be left alone," Riddick comments. He ties Hoxie in his chair, gags him, and turns the chair so the guards who enter a moment later cannot see his face. Assuming the seated figure is Riddick, they blast away at it. In a sense, Hoxie dies because Riddick gave him what he himself wanted, to be left alone.

Riddick is absolutely fearless, as if all his fear is directed outward into the people around him. At one point, when entering an area, he says, "Now the monsters have something to fear." Another time he says, "I'm going to show these monsters the true meaning of fear." He does not believe in half-measures, once saying,

"I don't rile people, I kill them." He calls himself "Hell's messenger," yet he has a prayer: "Where there's hatred, sow justice. Where there's injury, pardon. Where there's doubt, hope. And may a swift and certain death befall anyone who stands in my way." Thus, there are hints that Riddick follows some set of ethical principles, that may exist in tension with the self-interest that seems to guide his every action.

Clearly, Riddick is shrewd, rather than being a dumb predator. Surveying the misery and corruption around him, he observes, "Where there's desperation, there's opportunity." Another time he verbalizes his own personal view of free will: "I play the hand I'm dealt, and then I cheat." In Butcher Bay, Riddick briefly disguises himself in a guard's suit, and comments, "The wolf moves amongst the sheep." In *Assault on Dark Athena*, we get to see more varieties of sheep.

Athena is a military-class spaceship that was purchased by a mercenary named Irvin Senate, who thought of himself as a businessman, not a pirate [15]. Among his entrepreneurial plans was finding value in death-row prisoners, whom he turned into cyborg drones that could be sold for use in wars and cut-throat commercial enterprises on the periphery of civilization. Since these prisoners had no morals anyway, it seemed an improvement to replace the part of their brains that had free will with electronic components that would allow their owners to control them at a distance. Note that when a merc is operating a drone, he is behaving just like the player of an electronic game controlling a character. When the drone is killed, the merc can easily switch to another one.

Senate's mistake was in hiring Gale Rivas. Her parents had been executed for piracy when she was a child, and she continued this family tradition, first by becoming the leader of a street gang, then by brutal war service in the marines, then by staging a mutiny on the Athena and seizing command. From the moment Riddick's ship is seized by the Athena, and he eludes capture, a strange relationship rages between him and Rivas. She frequently sends him messages, urging him to surrender. One even gets the sense she might want him as a sexual partner – the euphemism "lover" would imply either of them was capable of love – but only if she were in absolute control over him. Naturally, he ignores her messages.

Soon after boarding the Athena, Riddick meets Lynn Silverman, a brave little girl hiding in the ventilation ducts of the spaceship. Her father was killed by Rivas's mercs, and her mother, Ellen, is locked in the same cellblock as Senate. Lynn is extremely intelligent, constantly exploring the bowels of the ship and trying to figure out how everything works. In this, she plays a role like that of a game player, because the rules of electronic games are often implicit, and learning what they are is part of the challenge. Naturally the question arises whether Riddick might rescue Lynn. But he assumes that any relationship with another person is ultimately futile: "When I help people, they end up dead."

The third noteworthy character is Max Dacher, a prisoner in the same cellblock as Ellen Silverman and Irvin Senate. For 30 years, he had done industrial espionage, acting as a double-agent for two competing corporations who finally discovered his dual treachery. With his beloved wife, he escaped on a transport to the Newland Colony, hoping to start life afresh. When disease ravaged the transport, and his wife died, he befriended little Lynn Silverman and helped her find her parents. He is extremely competent, especially with the communications technology on the ship, and he offers to help Riddick, in hopes that Riddick will help him and the Silvermans in return.

Another character worth mentioning, ironically named Jaylor, is locked in the cell nest to Ellen Silverman. He confides in Riddick that his fondest hope is to rape her, but only after first killing her. Riddick needs this madman, because he can provide a tool necessary for opening passageways on the ship, but not until Riddick kills Jaylor's worst enemy and brings the corpse's gold tooth as a trophy. Again and again, in both games, Riddick murders people who do not threaten him in any way, only to get a resource needed for his escape.

Jaylor's head is wreathed in tattoos, suggesting that his humanity has been engulfed by swirling nightmares. The same is true for Spinner, chief assistant of Gale Rivas. However, while watching Spinner die, Riddick observes, "In the end, everybody bleeds the same." Perhaps they are not so different, after all. At one point in *Pitch Black*, Johns and Fry are talking about Riddick, unaware that Riddick himself is hiding in the darkness of a monster skeleton right behind them. Coolly, Riddick reaches forward with his knife and cuts off a lock of Fry's hair, without her even realizing. He sniffs it, then tosses it away.

After many struggles, Riddick brings a datapad to Max Dacher, who uses it to control some of the ship's machines, for example shutting down a huge fan so Riddick can climb through it, and sending codes that open the cells. At one point, Riddick takes control over a drone, using it as his disposable agent. At another, he encounters a prisoner named Miles who is in the midst of the surgical process to transform him into a drone. At this point Riddick had the choice of taking on one of the only two significant optional missions in the game, and I decided to do it – for scientific research, naturally, not out of sympathy for Miles. I made Riddick shoot him to put him out of his misery, and went to a communications station to deliver his last, sentimental message to his family.

Riddick returns to the cellblock, just in time to watch Jaylor kill Ellen, then kills him before he can rape her corpse. Note that by opening all the cells, Dacher and Riddick have liberated the inmates to do whatever their individual desires demand, whether it is to murder or to escape, and in most cases to die. Riddick reaches Dacher near an escape pod, but finds that Rivas has killed him. As he blasts away from the Athena in the pod, Riddick sees little Lynn gazing out a window. He made no attempt to save her.

Riddick lands on the seashore of a planet named Aguerra, where a colony is in the last stages of disintegration. Nearly deserted, except for drones and mercs, the city of New Venice is a maze of dangerous alleyways and corridors. A former concentration camp inmate and mine foreman, Pavlo, asks Riddick to get him a gas mask from the supply depot, in return for a marvelous weapon called the SCAR gun. As one might by now expect, Pavlo is already dead when Riddick brings him the mask, but the gun is indeed marvelous. It can fire explosive shells into a target, and detonate them only when the user wishes, as many as five at one clip. This is useful for moving objects, demolishing barriers, and killing enemies in very interesting ways.

A stranger named Gabril asks who Riddick is, when a communication device accidentally connects them. He replies, "When Death calls, don't be in a hurry to answer." In the second of the two major optional missions of the game, Gabril asks

Fig. 10.2 Looking from Riddick's viewpoint inside a riot guard suit at an opponent

Riddick to destroy five enemy signal jammers, and offers him a sniper rifle as reward. On his way, Riddick enters Old Town, commenting: "This will be the ghost town, built on fear and empty promises – my kind of place." When he completes this mission and meets Gabril in person, the man is already dead, but has left the sniper rifle for him. It is worth noting both that people who promise to help Riddick actually do so, and he is not directly responsible for their deaths, although the partnership ends badly for them, while benefiting him.

These principles come into question when Riddick reboards the Athena, as his only route off the planet, and contacts little Lynn. She had sabotaged the ship's engines, keeping it on Aguerra in hopes he would return, and now she has used her engineering genius to take control of drones, which she sets against their former merc masters. Riddick enters a nearly invulnerable riot guard suit, and for a while Lynn rides on his shoulders, telling him which way to go through the complex passageways of the Athena. Figure 10.2 shows his view from this suit, as he faces an opponent, a nice metaphor of mutual dehumanization. After the final encounter between Riddick and Rivas, he and Lynn are in complete control of the ship, and the game is over. It remains completely unclear whether Riddick would have lifted a finger to help this brilliant little girl, had she not been useful to him.

Conclusion

I tried several times to experience Riddick's virtual world through multiplayer interaction, but every time I logged into the Internet server, there was no one there. Checking Internet blogs, I discovered that other people had been disappointed in the same way. Finally, on the evening of Sunday, May 17, it was do or die. I repeatedly searched for an online group, and repeatedly tried to start one, always ending in failure. I entered five of the virtual environments set aside for multiplayer combat, and always found them empty. The one I especially wanted to experience was called Pitch Black. In a ruined city, boxes of weapons lay on the ground near holes that led to dark passageways beneath. The first player to enter would become Riddick, with the eyeshine ability to see in this darkness, and the other players would try to kill him, hoping their flashlights would last until he was dead. Whoever killed Riddick would become Riddick, and the game would continue.

Despite my disappointment, I recognized that the failure of the multiplayer system was appropriate. Only in the alienated, solo game could I ever become Riddick, and then I had no choice who to be. If the future is dominated by crime, then the world may be a very lonely place.

References

1. David "Ryan_Dunn" Donaldson http://www.gamefaqs.com/console/xbox/file/919755/31857; Evert "From Earth" van Aart and Bob3739; http://www.gamefaqs.com/console/xbox/file/919755/49189; Robert Allen Rusk http://www.gamefaqs.com/console/xbox/file/919755/31042; Wasabi X http://www.gamefaqs.com/console/xbox/file/919755/38375; the13thJedi http://www.gamefaqs.com/console/xbox/file/919755/30628
2. Knight, D.: The Chronicles of Riddick: Escape from Butcher Bay – Prima's Official Strategy Guide, p. 126. Prima, Roseville (2004)
3. Foster, A.D.: The Chronicles of Riddick, p. 1. Balantine, New York (2004)
4. MacCannell, D.: Working in other fields. In: Berger, B. (ed.) Authors of Their Own Lives: Intellectual Autobiographies by Twenty American Sociologists, p. 70. University of California Press, Berkeley (1990)
5. Schrag, C.: The correctional system: problems and prospects. Ann. Am. Acad. Polit. SS. **38**(1), 11 (1969)
6. Lombroso, C., Lombroso-Ferrero, G.: Criminal Man. G. P. Putnam, New York (1911)
7. Durkheim, E.: Suicide. Free Press, Glencoe (1951 [1897])
8. Anderson, N.: The Hobo: The Sociology of the Homeless Man. University of Chicago Press, Chicago (1923); Thrasher, F.M.: The Gang: A Study of 1,313 Gangs in Chicago. University of Chicago Press, Chicago (1927); Faris, R.E.L., Dunham, H.W.: Mental Disorders in Urban Areas. University of Chicago Press, Chicago (1939)
9. Hirschi, T.: Causes of Delinquency. University of California Press, Berkeley (1969)
10. Merton, R.K.: Social structure and anomie. In: Social Theory and Social Structure, pp. 185–214. Free Press, New York (1968) [original publication of chapter in 1938], cf. Cloward, R.A., Ohlin, L.E.: Delinquency and Opportunity: A Theory of Delinquent Gangs. Free Press, Glencoe (1960)
11. Cohen, A.K.: Delinquent Boys: The Culture of the Gang. Free Press, Glencoe (1955)
12. http://www.rottentomatoes.com/vine/showthread.php?t=135682
13. Foster, A.D.: The Chronicles of Riddick, p. 56. Balantine, New York (2004)
14. http://www.youtube.com/watch?v=iYJAk8WwWmQ
15. Knight, M.: The Chronicles of Riddick: Assault on Dark Athena – Prima Official Game Guide, pp. 21–25. Prima, Roseville (2009)

Chapter 11
The Skylark and the Shuttle

This book has applied the methods of sociology and anthropology, drawing upon concepts from science and technology studies plus futurology, to understand our era's distinctive new artform: prophetic gameworlds. Virtual worlds depicting possible futures may, in time, teach us to know what has hitherto been unknown, through directly experiencing radical alternative to conventional life. Of course, this is not to say that current virtual worlds are realistic. But as the years pass, and the number and diversity of online role playing games increase, we can use them to prototype the real futures we may create for ourselves. This book describes the first decade of online science fiction gameworlds. What will the tenth decade be like, or the hundredth?

Stanley Kubrick's much praised 1968 movie, *2001: A Space Odyssey*, based on ideas by Arthur C. Clarke, assumed that by the beginning of the first decade of the twenty-first century, humans would not only have a permanent base on the moon, but be ready to send an expedition to the planet Jupiter. However, the most historic flights of the real year 2001 were the suicide attacks on the World Trade Center and the Pentagon. That also was the year when *Anarchy Online*, the first of these interplanetary gameworlds, was launched.

The worlds covered here span a decade, 2001–2010, but are only dim harbingers of what may come during this century. As the first wave in this new field, they deserve very special study, and their creators deserve tremendous respect. The criticism that they are unrealistic loses force when we realize that conventional institutions of society have lost their grip on the future – both in the sense that these institutions fail to understand the transformative forces in the world today, and that they appear unable to control central social, economic, and political trends. Recognizing that prophetic gameworlds are an imperfect lens by which to view the future, we can at least see through them some of the shapes of things to come.

W.S. Bainbridge, *The Virtual Future*, Springer Series in Immersive Environments, 183
DOI 10.1007/978-0-85729-904-8_11, © Springer-Verlag London Limited 2011

Optimism Versus Pessimism

Except for the claustrophobic *Bioshock* and *Matrix Online*, all the games featured in this book take place in outer space. Although science fiction has many themes, time travel and nanotechnology among them, the fundamental assumption has been that humanity could experience great adventures if it voyaged beyond the Earth. Ever since Sputnik I and the Apollo Program demonstrated the feasibility of space travel, it has been a symbol of exploration in general, *the final frontier*. If further advances into the solar system proved impossible or unprofitable, the very notion of scientific and technology progress would be shaken to its core. Fantasy may die under the withering blast of reality.

There is wide agreement that the first really influential science fiction novel about interstellar flight was *The Skylark of Space* by E. E. "Doc" Smith and Lee Hawkins Garby. Reportedly written between 1915 and 1921, its first installment appeared in the August 1928 issue of *Amazing Stories*, the first science fiction magazine, coincidentally the same issue that contained the first Buck Rogers story. Smith went on to become a leading writer of space opera, including his hugely popular Lensman series that depicts rapid-fire galactic adventures by a corps of nearly superhuman soldiers, which would make an excellent online game. It is hard to imagine a more optimistic story than *Skylark*. In the very first breathless paragraph, a scientist discovers the means to propel spaceships at high velocity with little fuel:

> Petrified with astonishment, Richard Seaton stared after the copper steam-bath upon which he had been electrolyzing his solution of "X," the unknown metal. For as soon as he had removed the beaker the heavy bath had jumped endwise from under his hand as though it were alive. It had flown with terrific speed over the table, smashing apparatus and bottles of chemicals on its way, and was even now disappearing through the open window. He seized his prism binoculars and focused them upon the flying vessel, a speck in the distance. Through the glass he saw that it did not fall to the ground, but continued on in a straight line, only its rapidly diminishing size showing the enormous velocity with which it was moving. It grew smaller and smaller, and in a few moments disappeared utterly [1].

Seaton had discovered the "intra-atomic energy of copper," and soon he and a friend were zooming across the galaxy in a spaceship propelled by it, named the Skylark. What is a skylark? Or, more precisely, what does the skylark metaphor mean? In his 1820 poem, "To a Skylark," Percy Bysshe Shelley admitted that his skylark was not really a bird, and offered this hint:

> Higher still and higher
> From the earth thou springest,
> Like a cloud of fire;
> The blue deep thou wingest,
> And singing still dost soar, and soaring ever singest [2].

Perhaps *skylark* refers to the human imagination. How does this square with actual space travel as we experience it today? The first Earth satellites were launched by ballistic missiles, and the Apollo project employed hugely expensive multi-stage rockets that were destroyed each time they were used. The space shuttle was supposed to open space to extensive exploitation, by carrying a variety of payloads to

Fig. 11.1 A space shuttle on Mars in *Active Worlds*

low Earth orbit at low cost. Unfortunately, it failed. Indeed, it was the worst kind of failure, because it seemingly worked, so it was not quickly abandoned in favor of something better. But the costs were "astronomically high," two fatal disasters destroyed half the fleet, and it proved too difficult to develop a better replacement given the funds and technology available. Most scientific payloads were moved off the shuttle after the 1986 Challenger explosion, and the scientific payoff to date from the expensive International Space Station is approximately nil. One US administration launched an expensive effort to return to the Moon, using old technology and lacking clear scientific aims, then its successor cancelled it. Despite impressive accomplishments by robot exploration missions throughout the solar system, the symbol for the post-Apollo period remains the space shuttle.

What is a shuttle? It is the little wooden piece moved back and forth to draw the weft strings between the warp stings in a loom. Or it is the runt subway train that shuttles endlessly between Times Square and Grand Central in Manhattan, an easily walkable distance. A shuttle is definitely not a skylark.

It is a sad fact that the only space shuttle that ever reached another planet did so in a virtual world, the Mars area of *Active Worlds* which is widely regarded as the first of its kind, having been launched in 1995 [3]. Figure 11.1 shows this vehicle for leaving Earth incongruously poised at a Martian space base. *Active Worlds* is a non-game virtual environment in which users own territory and create content, in a hierarchy of universes and worlds. Its Alphaworld section is maintained by the AW Historical Society which cultivates the past of this future, including reconstructions of some of the original buildings dating to 1995 and 1996. Its COFMeta is a gloomy futuristic city, based on Neal Stephenson's novel *Snow Crash* which provided much inspiration for virtual worlds [4]. Currently, one named *Blue Mars* is under development, using advanced graphics to represent the possible human future on the red planet [5].

There is good reason for pessimism about space travel in the physical universe. Perhaps humanity was simply unlucky. Across this wide cosmos, somewhere there may be a civilization that arose on one planet of a solar system that had a second habitable planet, easily colonized at low cost and with great advantage. To support a two-world civilization, many kinds of space technology would be developed, making it much easier to move on to other less friendly worlds.

However, the conditions necessary for the evolution of intelligent life may preclude interstellar flight in our cosmos. If the stars were close together, they would frequently pass near each other or even collide. This would constantly disrupt the orbits of planets, whereas a billion years of stability is required for biological evolution to the level of intelligence. In addition, nearby supernovas would periodically fry the surfaces of the planets. Intelligent life will evolve only in a universe in which the stars are too distant to visit. Thus, if interplanetary civilizations are very rare, interstellar ones may be nonexistent.

Is there reason for optimism? Again, yes. Given that this book is about how the future is depicted in gamelike virtual worlds, we should focus on the sources of optimism that connect to these new environments. Four distinct levels of optimism can be discerned, admittedly debatable each in its own way, but worth considering.

First, the experience of virtual interstellar travel in the games may encourage people's faith in the future of real space travel. The diversity of stories in the games will build a culture in which much continues to be expected from interplanetary exploration, and people have the variety of viewpoints on it conducive to creative thinking. Over time, a sophisticated pro-space movement may gradually develop forms of real-world science and technology, plus the motivations required, that will lead to the colonization of Mars.

Second, virtual worlds may become a legitimate substitute for other planets, giving people the sense of exploration, discovery, and adventure. Planets are big lumps of matter, but people may come to feel that information is what "matters," and thus that an information-technology world is just as real as a physical one. In a *New York Times* op-ed piece titled "The End of the Space Age," Ross Douthat compared the mild public reaction to the cancellation of NASA's effort to return to the Moon with the popularity of the most spectacular sci-fi movie: "'Avatar,' not NASA, probably represents the future of the American relationship to distant planets. In the real world, we'll be permanently earthbound – but inside the carapace of virtual reality, we'll be kings of infinite space" [6]. To see this as optimism, we must believe with *Star Trek* that people are interested primarily in people, and the lifeless objects strewn for 15 billion light years in all directions cannot be significant to us except as symbols of human possibility.

Third, the first two kinds of optimism may merge, to produce a totally fresh approach to space travel. It is impossible today to predict the details of that new vision, but here is a semi-plausible idea that can serve as a placeholder for it. At the time I am writing this, the Spirit rover is stuck in one place on Mars yet still communicating, while its twin, Opportunity, continues to explore – fully 6 years after landing in an environment that would kill an unprotected human in a minute. Perhaps we shall travel to the stars as robots – physically encased avatars using advanced artificial intelligence techniques to emulate our personalities – that transmit their experiences back home.

Fourth, whatever may be achieved in space, science-fiction virtual worlds may benefit terrestrial society in ways similar to physical colonization of the solar system. Only an infinitesimal fraction of humanity actually went to the Moon in Apollo, and only a slightly less tiny fraction would ever actually go to Mars. The majority of us can gain only vicariously and through spin-off benefits to terrestrial society and culture. Already, gameworlds give people pleasure and offer fresh ways of thinking about life.

Gameworlds as Social Commentaries

There has existed a different kind of virtual world before, first appearing as early as the ancient Greeks, and prominent during some decades of American history. I refer to the utopian communities established by volunteers, who dedicated their lives to exploring radical social and cultural alternatives, such as Oneida.

John Humphrey Noyes, the Yale graduate who founded the Oneida commune in upstate New York in 1848, was a perfectionist. In religious terms, this meant that he sought to transcend all sin, and in scientific terms, that he sought to breed perfect human beings. At Oneida, several dozen adults were in a sense married to each other, and children were raised collectively. They practiced a disciplined form of sexual intercourse that did not produce children, except when Noyes decreed that two of them should complete the act, because he judged they would engender a spiritually advanced child. Logically enough, he himself fathered many of the children with several of the women. The Oneida experiment lasted more than a generation, but it depended upon a shared utopian ideology and a strong charismatic leader. Whether group marriages of various types could be viable under modern, secular conditions is an open question that can be answered only after many people have tried to create group-marriage alternatives, at some risk to themselves and their children [7].

The Process Church of the Final Judgement, which I studied in the same manner as I did the virtual worlds reported here, also had a group marriage system for its 100 most dedicated members. But it was secondary to their primary purpose, which was using a variety of psychoanalytic and mystical techniques to develop their own personalities. Founded by Robert de Grimston and Mary Anne MacLean, who had met in the London branch of Scientology, it drew upon the spiritual technologies of this new religious movement, which had been founded by science fiction writer L. Ron Hubbard. It also drew upon Alfred Adler's power-oriented version of psychoanalysis. Established as a hierarchical secret society living in communes, the group wore flamboyant uniforms and harangued the public with apocalyptic visions of the Union of Jehovah and Lucifer, and the Unity of Christ and Satan. For the inner members, these deities were actually personality types not unlike those measured by psychologists. Among the technologies Processeans used to try to uncover their hidden natures were an electronic, lie-detector device derived from Scientology called the P-Scope, and past lives regression trances [8]. Frankly my 2 years of adventurous participant observation inside the Process were very much like the similar amount of time I invested in *World of Warcraft*, just happening in the physical world.

Clearly, few people would be willing to leave conventional society to create one of these high-demand utopian communes, whether or not it went so far as to practice group marriage. But many people are ready to experience low-demand online game-worlds that give them a more distant experience of radical alternatives. In a special issue of *netWorker* magazine, published by the Association for Computing Machinery, which focused on the new opportunities offered by broadband communication networks, I have called these virtual worlds *etopias*:

> Utopia means noplace. Eutopia means an ideal place. We could define "Etopia" to mean an electronic place, perhaps nowhere, perhaps ideal, broadband in the sense of broadening human possibilities. Given the growing economic and social turmoil in the world today, society at large may indeed be ready to adopt innovations developed in virtual worlds by Etopians [9].

Edward Castronova has already suggested that online games like *World of Warcraft* may give people a more egalitarian or achievement-oriented economic ideology [10]. Unlike in real life where children inherit the social class of their parents, in *World of Warcraft* each person starts with exactly the same opportunities, then receives benefits in proportion to the effort he or she invests. In essentially all of the virtual worlds, people can create things – whether by starting a guild or by assembling material and components to make something. Annihila (and I) gained a great sense of accomplishment by gaining the skills and reputation required to construct her autogyro, for example. In *Anarchy Online*, *Star Wars Galaxies*, and *Entropia*, a person may buy a house and fill it with virtual objects, achieving a sense of status comparable to that of owners of real houses without wasting natural resources on ostentatious conspicuous consumption.

Like much fiction – soap operas as much as space operas – gameworlds thrive on conflict. Thus they may depict unrealistically violent futures. Yet everybody understands that the relative peace in the real world that has prevailed since 1945 is precarious. The spread of free markets has not led to much political reform in China or many Islamic societies, and the dream of world government seems ludicrous today. The fact that players of many gameworlds are divided into factions, that are often in direct conflict, may be an entirely realistic portrayal of our real world, today and tomorrow.

In terms of factions, *Tabula Rasa* and *Riddick* represent the extremes, all players belonging to a single group in the former, and no players belonging to groups in the latter. *World of Warcraft* and *Star Trek Online* each have two opposing factions – Horde versus Alliance and Federation versus Klingons. *Star Wars Galaxies* and *Anarchy Online* have two main factions – Empire versus Rebel Alliance and Omni-Tek versus Clans, but with the option for a player to remain neutral. *The Matrix*

Online has three factions – Machines, Zion, and the minions of the Merovingian – with only a theoretical possibility of remaining neutral. *EVE Online* starts out with four factions – Amarr, Minmatar, Caldari and Gallente – but advanced players tend to withdraw from the particular fictional group in which they began and to devote their loyalties to their player-created corporations. *Entropia* lacks the explicit quest missions that make a faction salient, and any groups that exist will be player-created and may reflect existing real-world friendship circles.

In most cases, the ideologies of the factions are well-developed but may not matter much to players. Especially interesting is the status of religion in gameworlds. Previous research has shown that computer game players tend to be less religious than the average person, and that the religions in games tend to be non-standard ones that provide the cultural setting for fantasy stories [11]. Social science has not arrived at a consensus about the nature of religion, but one widely respected theory holds that it offers psychological compensation for things that people lack in their lives, notably social status, health, and indeed life itself when death approaches [12]. Arguably all forms of art and entertainment provide similar compensators, and gamelike virtual worlds seem to provide many of them. To some real extent, therefore, gameworlds substitute for religion in people's lives, not through belief but through suspension of disbelief.

From the standpoint of the social sciences, three things are missing from these gameworlds: family, democracy, and usury. Players tend to be young males, somewhat less so in *World of Warcraft* than the others, so there is not a solid demographic basis for family life. I know of some real-world families that use virtual worlds as venues for family activities, especially when relatives are geographically dispersed, but people do not act out family relations in these environments. In the abstract, people play parent and child roles, as when mentors in *Entropia* teach newcomers, and guild masters in *World of Warcraft* lead junior members. But, as yet gameworlds do not cast new players explicitly in the role of children, and assign specific experienced members to be their parents.

The political systems in these gameworlds are highly authoritarian on two levels. First, most of the rules are set by the game designers and enforced by the game's programming. Second, the player who starts a formal group in one of these environments can function as a dictator, deciding what rights all the others will have by setting the rules in the software module that governs the group. To be sure, dissatisfied members can leave a group, so a very selfish dictator will lose power. Players could set up their own democratic institutions outside the rules of the game, but I have very seldom seen them try to do so, and my avatars have not belonged to long-lasting democracies. *EVE Online* is distinctive for having an advisory council of players, and its many separate corporations of players require greater initiative than *World of Warcraft* guilds, so gameworlds may become laboratories for experimentation with democracy, but they are not fundamentally democratic.

The lack of usury means that none of these gameworlds have systems to facilitate lending, borrowing, and the payment of interest, key dimensions of capitalist economies in the real world. *World of Warcraft* has the most complete system of economic distribution, centered on a flourishing auction system, but no mortgages, bonds, and financial derivatives. Some property is held jointly by guilds, and they may set up rules for sharing among members, but generally ownership is in the hands of individual players, and cannot be compromised by debts within the established system.

Thus, the socio-economic systems in these gameworlds are different from those experienced by most people in the real world. For our purposes, this is a not a flaw but an insight. Today's world system represents either a transitory stage in the development of our species, or an historical accident, and in neither case will it be permanent. The social organization of *Tabula Rasa* and *Star Trek Online* is military. *World of Warcraft*, *The Matrix Online*, and *Star Wars Galaxies* are explicitly feudal in structure. Perhaps the real world will return to feudalism, after historically brief experiments with capitalism, socialism, and communism. The Queen of England and the Emperor of Japan may not regain power, but stable oligarchies may become the dominant forces in society. It is worth remembering that the fundamental source of human social organization is the biological family, and the family was the basis for all early large-scale structures: clans, kingdoms, and empires [13]. Perhaps the gameworlds are telling us that the future will involve as much regression as progress.

These worlds embody progress, to be sure, in the area of information technology. They may even be training grounds and prototypes for information technology of the future. Today, a player joins a *World of Warcraft* guild after enjoying good quests with some of its founding members, then engages in social and economic exchanges with fellow members, and undertakes a series of difficult projects such as multi-hour missions into subworld instances. All the while, the game's software allows members to communicate where ever they are, and to assemble task-oriented groups of 40 members in realtime but on the basis of planning and preparation. Already, technology-supported teams like this exist in the real world, most obviously in the military and in civilian emergency response. A tremendous amount of research is being conducted today in computer-supported cooperative work, and in ubiquitous and mobile computing. In a few years, many ordinary human activities may be carried out in a manner similar to raiding parties in today's online gameworlds.

The Future of Virtual Worlds

To imagine the future of virtual worlds, we can consider one that does not yet exist, based on the amazingly popular and technically innovative movie, *Avatar*, directed by James Cameron [14]. *Avatar* takes place in a mining expedition to Pandora, a moon of a planet in the Alpha Centauri system, over 4 light years from Earth, in the year 2154. In a very real sense, this movie was filmed inside a computer-generated virtual world. It focuses on combat between two societies, comparable in some ways to the Alliance and the Horde in *World of Warcraft*, and thus it has elements of a player-versus-player game. A videogame was released along with the film; although not ambitious in storyline, it does a nice job of depicting the natural environment.

The computer technology used by humans in *Avatar* is not very far advanced over what we have today. For example, there is little evidence of artificial intelligence, which would have added a distracting superfluous theme to the story. The striking improvement of computer technology in the year 2154 is that it is ubiquitous, mobile, and integrated fully into all human activities. It is noteworthy that the people are fully comfortable with the technology and handle it without difficulty.

The ten-foot-tall blue humanoid natives of Pandora, the Na'vi, have little apparent technology, beyond spears, bows, and poison-tipped arrows. The human invaders differ in their feelings about the natives, but they all consider Na'vi society to be primitive. This is a big mistake and reveals the first level of *Avatar's* philosophy of the relationship of people to technology. Earth civilization is based on *machinery*, the convergence of mechanical engineering with computers, and the structure of the society is fully adapted to such systems. Indeed, the principles for building human social systems are precisely *mechanical*, in which commercial and military bureaucracies mirror the design of machines.

The Na'vi in contrast, are an advanced society based on *biology*, even possessing the biological equivalent of Internet, as the trees communicate through their roots. The Na'vi appear to be a simple tribal society with primitive kinship structures, but only gradually do we realize that this is only a superficial impression, because they are integrated into the ecosystem in ways that the mechanistic human civilization can hardly imagine. Figure 11.2 shows my avatar in the computer game, Dejah, in conversation with Beyda'amo, a dominant warrior of the Tipani clan who gave her much grief until finally according her begrudging respect.

The central character of the movie is a marine named Jake Sully who falls in love with Neytiri, a native Pandoran woman who teaches Jake the ways of her people. She is the daughter of the shaman matriarch of the Omaticaya clan. She may someday inherit her mother's responsibility to interpret the will of Eywa, the Great Mother who represents the totality of living creatures on Pandora. When Neytiri first meets Jake, she calls him an ignorant child, and says his "skypeople" can never learn to *See*. The standard greeting in the Na'vi language, "I See you," implies something more than mere vision, something even more than empathy, but a form of connection between two creatures. A Na'vi proverb says, "When you see nothing, you will See everything."

Neytiri teaches Jake to ride a horselike *pa'li*, not by tugging on reins but by forming a neural interface with the mind of the beast. Later she challenges him to form a personal relationship with a flying dragon called an *ikran*, forming a direct link between their brains. Thus the Na'vi connect biologically to the other species with which they live symbiotically. My avatar, Dejah, spent most of her time killing humans, and like most Na'vi would be perfectly happy to see them leave Pandora forever.

There are five main human characters in the movie, each of whom significantly affects the outcome and has a different relationship to science and technology. Grace Augustine is a botanist who seeks knowledge for its own sake but who has become combative in her difficult struggles to gain support for her research and who needs to regain her compassion. She respects the Na'vi and wants knowledge about them

Fig. 11.2 Dejah and Beyda'amo at the Iknimaya village of the Na'vi

for its own sake, yet she has been hired by the mining company to try to find a cheap way of convincing the natives to give up sacred land that happens to be a deposit of *unobtanium*, the extraterrestrial mineral the company wants. Augustine represents pure science, and she faces the dilemma that funding sources may require her to provide information they will use for inhumane purposes.

Parker Selfridge is the administrator of the mining operations on Pandora. He cares only about the corporate bottom line and represents the way capitalism exploits both people and technology for financial gain. He is scornful of humane values but capable of rethinking strategies for attaining his goals. Analyzing everything in terms of rational calculation of costs and benefits for the corporation, he conceptualizes harm to the Na'vi merely as potential damage to the company's reputation in the marketplace.

Colonel Miles Quaritch expresses militarist values, using technology as an amoral instrument of power, exuding macho aggression and skilled in *wushu* martial arts. Intelligent and reflective, he is aware that he is only being used by the corporation. Two key scenes in *Avatar* show him using an electromechanical exoskeleton called an *ampsuit*, the huge metal fists of which inflict great damage as he shadowboxes while wearing computer control gloves. Quaritch harbors doubts about his own worth, and enhances his physical power by means of technology so he can feel pride.

Trudy Chacón is a technically proficient combat pilot who is sympathetic to the Na'vi. She represents people of good will who are competent with technology but not dominated by it, capable of fitting well within the machine that is advanced technical society, but also capable of distancing herself from it. More important to her are personal loyalty and principles of justice, for which ultimately she is willing to risk her life.

Jake Sully was paralyzed in combat in Venezuela, and is now confined to a wheelchair because his military medical benefits will not cover the cost of repairing his severed spine. He sees technology as a way not only of overcoming disability, but ultimately of achieving transcendence. His identical twin brother was a scientist in training for the program, but died, and Jake has the right DNA structure to take over his brother's avatar which allows him to survive on Pandora. This avatar is not a phantom on a computer display, but a biologically cultured duplicate of the Na'vi operated remotely through a brain-computer interface. One of the amazing scenes of *Avatar* is when Jake first awakens inside his avatar and experiences again the ability to walk, first haltingly then gaining his sense of balance until running becomes ecstasy.

What is an avatar? People interested in computers tend to define the word as a graphic representation of a person, inside a virtual world or similar kind of software. Yet in Hindu religion, the word originally referred to one of the forms a deity used when entering our world, far simpler than the deity itself, yet transcendent. Combining these connotations produces a third definition: An avatar is a representation of a human being in the form of an archetype, conceptually simplified and allowing the user to experience his or her identity in a novel manner. In that sense, the five key characters of the movie are all avatars representing the viewer vicariously, related to each other within an overarching conceptualization.

What is a world? The challenge in transforming *Avatar* into an online gamelike world is similar to the which faced *Star Wars Galaxies*: The story focused on a closed system of a small number of characters, whereas a world must be open to millions of inhabitants all possessing unique stories. If I were translating *Avatar* into a world, I would first remove the humans and the avatar technology, given that the player's character already provides a sufficient connection from our world to that of the Na'vi. A user could enter the world through any of a set of characters born as children under different Pandoran conditions, mature through a set of initiation rituals such as those required to ride an *ikran*, and undertake exploration quests and missions that respond to natural disasters and that defuse inter-tribal conflict.

While *Avatar* focuses on the forest-dwelling Omaticaya clan, and Dejah's Tipani clan lives under identical conditions, the movie does briefly reveal that other peoples live in the treeless plains and near the seacoast. Thus, it would be necessary to flesh out the world of the Na'vi, imagining a variety of cultures adapted to different ecologies, and the best source of material for that is the anthropology of hunter-gatherers in our world, and of people for whom agriculture has not yet entirely transformed the conditions of life.

The big watershed in human history was the Neolithic Revolution in which the development of agriculture led to population explosion, development of cities unleashing many technologies, and the organization of armies to seize and defend agricultural land [15]. A Na'vi gamelike virtual world could depict one society that was on the verge of developing agriculture, and use it to raise the key issues introduced by the Neolithic Revolution, including kingship authority structures, mass warfare including genocide, and a host of customs that combine small tribes into nations. Thus, each of the five relationships between humans and technology depicted in the movie could be the basis of decision points in quests that Na'vi characters in a gamelike virtual world would face.

The anthropological literature on simple agricultural societies includes many interesting facts that could enhance a gameworld, such as the belief among the people of Dobu that their neighbors used sorcery to induce vegetables to walk from one farm to another [16]. But most of the Na'vi gameworld would need to avoid agriculture and build its cultural diversity on ecological diversity and on accidents of history. The forest-dwelling Omaticaya clan reminded me of the people of the Ituri Forest in Zaire, studied by anthropologist Colin Turnbull [17]. Colin's books include many anecdotes that could be transformed into episodes of the game, including the poignant time he tried unsuccessfully to make crutches for a disabled girl who could not run through the forest as life there required.

I could imagine translating the work of Bronislaw Malinowski to Pandora, setting his Trobriand Islands just off shore and letting their inhabitants live off bountiful nature without needing to develop agriculture. In *Argonauts of the Western Pacific*, Malinowski described how they undertook dangerous voyages across the open sea in dugout canoes, in order to exchange stories and ritual goods with inhabitants of other islands [18].

Many other anthropologists have studied conflict between technologically simple groups, providing insights that could be the basis of quests in games. Jules Henry reported that bands of Kaingáng in Brazil had been displaced from their traditional homeland, which had the effect of disrupting ties between previously-adjacent bands and causing them to lapse into extreme conflict whenever they met [19]. Napoleon Chagnon studied how tribes of Yanomamö struggled to minimize fatalities through ritualistic expression of hostility that might fall short of killing each other [20].

The deep interest in dreams among many pre-literate peoples, reflected even in the bible, suggests that some side missions could require the player to enter dreamworlds, essentially fantasies within a fantasy, completing quests that advanced the avatar's spiritual abilities but affected no material possessions [21]. My plan to translate *Avatar* into a gamelike virtual world may or may not be the right one from the standpoints of James Cameron or the paying public, but it makes an important point about the subject of this book.

The best real future may be a fulfillment of original human nature, as experienced by people tens of thousands of years ago, merely enhanced by greater health, security, and the ability to explore diverse cultures. By imagining Eden on a different planet, we project it into the future, suggesting we could achieve it by hard work and right choices, rather than locating it in the past we have forever lost. In the coming years, a diversity of gameworlds will allow us to play with possible futures before we decide which one to make real. Of course that is what playing games has always done for children, helping them grow, explore, gain new skills, and define themselves [22]. We are still children, after all.

References

1. http://www.gutenberg.org/etext/20869
2. http://classiclit.about.com/library/bl-etexts/pshelley/bl-pshel-sky.htm
3. Damer, B.: Avatars!: Exploring and Building Virtual Worlds on the Internet. Peachpit Press, Berkeley (1998)
4. Stephenson, N.: Snow Crash. Bantam Books, New York (1992)
5. Childers, R.: A new mars. In: Bainbridge, W.S. (ed.) Online Worlds: Convergence of the Real and the Virtual, pp. 101–109. Springer, London (2010)
6. Douthat, R.: The end of the space age. New York Times, 11 Feb 2010. http://douthat.blogs.nytimes.com/2010/02/11/the-age-of-space/
7. Noyes, J.H.: History of American Socialisms. Lippincott, Philadelphia (1870); Noyes, P.: My Father's House: An Oneida Boyhood. Farrar and Reinhart, New York (1937); Carden, M.L.: Oneida. Johns Hopkins Press, Baltimore (1969); Foster, L.: Religion and Sexuality. Oxford University Press, New York (1981)
8. Bainbridge, W.S.: Satan's Power: A Deviant Psychotherapy Cult. University of California Press, Berkeley (1978); Social Construction from Within. In: Richardson, J.T., Best, J., Bromley, D. (eds.) The Satanism Scare, pp. 297–310. Aldine de Gruyter, New York (1991); The colorful dark age. TheBlowUp Magazine **3**(Spring/Summer), 50–55 (2005)
9. Bainbridge, W.S.: Etopia. Networker **13**(1), 35–36 (2009)
10. Castronova, E.: Exodus to the Virtual World: How Online Fun is Changing Reality. Palgrave Macmillan, New York (2007)
11. Bainbridge, W.S., Bainbridge, W.A.: Electronic game research methodologies: studying religious implications. Rev. Religious Res. **49**(1), 35–53 (2007)
12. Stark, R., Bainbridge, W.S.: The Future of Religion. University of California Press, Berkeley (1985); A Theory of Religion. Toronto/Lang, New York (1987)
13. Lévi-Strauss, C.: The Elementary Structures of Kinship. Beacon Press, Boston (1969)
14. http://www.foxscreenings.com/media/pdf/JamesCameronAVATAR.pdf
15. Childe, V.G.: Man Makes Himself. New American Library, New York (1951)
16. Fortune, R.: Sorcerers of Dobu. Routledge, London (1932)
17. Turnbull, C.M.: The Forest People. Simon and Schuster, New York (1961); Wayward Servants: The Two Worlds of the African Pygmies. Natural History Press, Garden City (1965)
18. Malinowski, B.: Argonauts of the Western Pacific. Routledge, London (1922)
19. Henry, J.: Jungle People: A Kaingáng Tribe of the Highlands of Brazil. J. J. Augustin, New York (1941)
20. Chagnon, N.A.: Ya̧nomamö, The Fierce People. Holt, Rinehart and Winston, New York (1968)
21. Wallace, A.F.C.: Dreams and the wishes of the soul. In: Middleton, J. (ed.) Magic, Witchcraft, and Curing, pp. 171–190. Natural History Press, Garden City (1967)
22. Winnicott, D.W.: Playing and Reality. Basic Books, New York (1971)

Index

W.S. Bainbridge, *The Virtual Future*, Springer Series in Immersive Environments, 197
DOI 10.1007/978-0-85729-904-8, © Springer-Verlag London Limited 2011